THE
PURPLE DIARIES

Mary Astor and the Most Sensational
Hollywood Scandal of the 1930s

JOSEPH EGAN

DIVERSIONBOOKS

Diversion Books
A Division of Diversion Publishing Corp.
443 Park Avenue South, Suite 1008
New York, New York 10016
www.DiversionBooks.com

Front cover image by A.L. Schafer.
Back cover image, courtesy of Gabrielle Roh and the Roh/Thorpe/Astor Family
Collection: Mary Astor as Fritzi and Marylyn on the set of *Desert Fury*.

For more information, email info@diversionbooks.com

First Diversion Books edition November 2016.
Print ISBN: 978-1-68230-299-6
eBook ISBN: 978-1-68230-298-9

"What is life all about? Maybe I'll be able to figure it out some day."
—Mary Astor, October, 1934

M.A.
M.R.

Set of *Red Dust*. L to R: Director Fleming, Astor, Clark Gable, and Jean Harlow.

FOREWORD

Because my mother, Frances Roh Yang, is Mary Astor's first grandchild, every year while I was growing up, for the holidays, the family would gather around the television to watch a VHS of *Meet Me In St. Louis.* In the film, when Mama March sits at the piano and sings with Papa March, my mother would announce:

"That is your great-grand-mommy. Your grammy's mama."

Mary Astor's role was small, but rooted the film in the way an idyllic mother roots any household—constant, ever present. Somehow, the woman in that Technicolor picture connected me, as a kid in Utah, to this glittering, glamorous, thrillingly happy world of celluloid dreams. This "saint of motherhood" loomed over my childhood—a protective, soothing, caramel-voiced ghost.

Thus, it seemed like some sort of duty to destiny that in school I was always involved in theatre. In a small twist of fate, I ended up designing costumes for a show and soared down a path of costume design—and somehow, in 2003, I ended up attending the Fashion Institute of Technology in New York City.

As a college student, struggling to find my identity and inspiration for countless student collections, I returned to the stories and pictures of my great-grandmother. I discovered an old movie picture store where I would stop between fabric pickups and purchase photos of my great-grandmother doing costume tests, glamour shots, or between takes with Clark Gable and Jean Harlow.

She was my protector, my reminder to return to the core of my artistic strength whenever I was lost. I binged on every film of hers I could find. In New York, I could even catch screenings of her films in big screen theatres, where I could drag my friends and convince them of her talent. She proved a muse, a glittering star from whom I drew inspiration.

Eventually, I stumbled upon a *Los Angeles Times* Web page that profiled a wild and scandalous court case in which Mary Astor was involved, fighting over custody of my Grammy Marylyn. Since I kept a blog, I wrote about my discovery. This wasn't a custody case; this was a sensation—and it was in a language that many of my friends and peers could understand: the language of tabloid media and scandalous thrills. During that trial Mary Astor went from being a saint to being a star.

Through the Internet, I found myself being contacted for interviews about my great-grandmother from movie buffs around the world. And then, from the family grapevine, I found out that my grandmother was talking to a writer who was interested in writing a book about that scandal; the biggest Hollywood scandal of the 1930s.

My grandmother kept up a lively exchange with this writer and, every so often, forwarded me some of their notes before finally connecting us directly. When Joe and I started corresponding I was thrilled to have discovered, at the heart of it, another Mary Astor fan—but one who was deeply connected to the era in which she lived—in short, a film historian. He was attempting to chronicle one of Mary Astor's greatest starring roles, a role that dominated the front-page headlines of every national newspaper for weeks. It wasn't a film, but it would have made a great one. It was a high-octane courtroom drama with a stunning lead actress and handsome male lead—my great-grandfather, Franklyn Thorpe. It had sex, booze, and a cast of gossiping nannies, combative attorneys, flimsy flings and, at the center of it all, a radiant four-year-old girl—my wide-eyed baby grammy.

When I traveled to upstate New York to visit Joe and his wife, to share with him some pictures and scanned memorabilia, I was surprised to discover that he had embarked on his endeavor to chronicle this courtroom saga over ten years earlier. He shared a stack of four-inch-thick binders carefully archiving almost every newspaper article written about the case as well as scores of paparazzi and studio photos from the period. Here was someone who knew more about my great-grandmother than I did.

Mary Astor may not have been the greatest actress of all time—but her story is the fullest breath of every actress. She lived her archetype as an artist through and through. She was discovered as a teenager in a beauty contest, shimmered in silent films, and survived into the talkies. Her first husband died tragically in a plane crash in 1930, and her second embroiled her in a tabloid custody battle that set the stage for how every star today lives under the media microscope. Her second act in films was her artistic peak; she won her Oscar and finally got parts where she could dazzle. And then she prematurely aged out of her glamorous roles and, in countless MGM films, became the mother on film that she could never be in real life. She left Hollywood, returning to her craft in theatre and the early years of television before finally discovering writing. She was a tempestuous woman who was torn between her work, her family, and her life—a life that no one could say was not fully lived. In this book, we get a glimpse into the starring role she never got to play on screen, and that ride, from beginning to end, is thrilling.

Andrew Yang

THE BACKSTORY

1

FEBRUARY 1935

Mary Astor walked into the Beverly Wilshire Hotel. The actress had a lot on her mind and was anxious to speak with George Kaufman. The two had been seeing each other almost daily since early January, when the Broadway playwright had arrived in LA to do a rewrite of a Marx Brothers picture. Their on-again, off-again affair began two years earlier in New York, and had become, with the exception of Astor's three-year-old daughter, Marylyn, the single most important thing in the actress's life.

Although Astor was building up the courage to leave her husband, she also knew that Kaufman would never marry her. When she had pressed him the answer she got was, "I wish I were madly in love with you, but those things just can't be arranged. I haven't been in love for many years and I doubt very much if I can again." In other words, no matter how much she might love George Kaufman, George Kaufman saw their relationship as purely physical.

For a woman who, just five months earlier, had believed that marriage and children were possible with the famous playwright, this painful reality hadn't come easily. But it was now February and Astor's objectives with Kaufman had simplified. All she wanted was to be with him as much as possible. What she liked to term their "spiritual communication," as well as the sense of completeness that the sex, laughter, and hours of talk gave the actress, had now become her only rationale for being with him.

On that Monday evening she and Kaufman had dinner reservations at the Trocadero. They would be seen at the nightclub and, later, the hotel. Since both were married, there would be talk. There had been talk when Astor had been with Kaufman in New York and the gossip continued when he had traveled to Hollywood a year later to write a play. But Mary Astor didn't care anymore. Kaufman was not only Broadway's most successful playwright but also an intellectual and world-class wit. He carried with him an aura that made his companionship coveted. That Kaufman wanted to spend his time with Mary Astor was something the actress had no desire to hide. On the contrary, she rejoiced in it.

This night was different. In his hotel suite, and on the way to the car, Astor sensed that something was troubling the writer. He was on edge. Since Kaufman—the quintessential New Yorker—couldn't drive, Astor took the wheel as they headed for the Trocadero. In the privacy of the car Astor asked what was bothering him.

"Feeling lowish?"

"M-m-yeah… I'll tell you all about it."

Kaufman did want to talk about it, but not now and not while Astor was driving. He wanted her relaxed after a drink or two.

Astor had her suspicions. Earlier in the day she had been shopping with her friend Marian Spitzer. Spitzer, a story editor at Paramount, had once worked on the *New York Globe* when Kaufman was still a drama critic for the *New York Times*. The two had a brief affair and now Kaufman was a close friend. In fact, it was Spitzer who had arranged for Astor to meet Kaufman in May 1933.

That morning, locked in a fitting room at Magnin Department Store, Spitzer made a confession. The previous October Astor's husband, Dr. Franklyn Thorpe, had asked Marian to speak to Kaufman. Thorpe had heard talk about the Astor-Kaufman affair and, in September, his wife had told him everything. Astor calmly informed her husband that she would continue to see Kaufman and told Thorpe to mind his own business. It was about that time—October 1934—that Spitzer was planning to visit New York and, without his wife's knowledge, Thorpe asked Spitzer to plead with Kaufman to end the affair.

Spitzer refused the request. She knew if she were stupid enough to relay any such message, Kaufman would tell her to mind her own business. In any case, Spitzer didn't want to put herself in the middle of a sticky entanglement. So she assured Thorpe that, no matter what his wife might feel, women were an addiction to Kaufman. All Thorpe needed to do was sit tight and wait until it blew over. Taking Spitzer's advice, Thorpe swore her to secrecy. Thus, the reason why Spitzer hadn't told Astor about the meeting. Recent developments had changed that.

"Like what?"

"Well, I saw George yesterday and we had quite a talk."

"About what?"

"Let George tell you if he wants to."

Hours later, noticing how jittery Kaufman was in the car, this only made the actress more apprehensive. Arriving at the Trocadero they headed downstairs to the bar and, at a table, she ordered drinks. When the waiter disappeared, Kaufman finally spoke.

"Should I wait until you have a drink or should I plunge right in?"

"Plunge in. I'm dying of curiosity."

"I had a visit from your husband."

Astor's mouth dropped. As she would write in her private diary—a diary she had been keeping since 1928, "I practically went through the floor." She couldn't believe that Thorpe had attempted to come between her and Kaufman. Mary Astor was both angry and outraged.

As Kaufman described it, the morning before, Dr. Thorpe had arrived unannounced at Kaufman's hotel suite for what Kaufman would later call "that scene with the leading lady's husband." The doctor wanted to "straighten" things out between them "man-to-man." Thorpe was agitated and Kaufman—well aware of the doctor's reputation as crack shot, his hot temper, and skill at fisticuffs—feared things might turn physical. Noticing Kaufman's reaction, Thorpe assured him that all he wanted was to talk. Kaufman had one question.

"Does Mary know you've come here?"

"No, and I don't believe we ought to tell her."

Thorpe told Kaufman that he knew Astor had almost insatiable physical and emotional needs, needs that he could never fully satisfy. But he didn't believe that a high-profile affair was the answer. Finally, there was their little girl. Marylyn was just two-and-a-half years old, and the destruction of this little girl's family would cause irreparable emotional damage. The doctor made it clear that he was an old-fashioned man who loved his wife and daughter and believed marriage was both sacred and a lifetime commitment.

If the affair continued Thorpe was worried that his life and everything that he had struggled for years to build might fall apart. Tears welled up in the man's eyes as he begged Kaufman to stop seeing his wife. If not, Kaufman could expect Thorpe to "fight to protect" his wife, his child, and his home.

This scene was uncomfortable for Kaufman, who found sentimentality of any kind embarrassing. Astor had been writing and talking to him for months about leaving Thorpe. In fact, she had first wanted to divorce her husband two years earlier—six months before she and Kaufman met—but Thorpe pleaded with her to stay. Kaufman knew that there was a basic flaw in that marriage that had nothing to do with him. With or without Kaufman, the Thorpe-Astor marriage would soon be over. Nevertheless, the playwright could see that behind Thorpe's tears there was a very real threat.

"Fight to protect" meant that Thorpe would contest a divorce suit. With the world watching, he could name the playwright as co-respondent. Since Kaufman was extremely discrete about his affairs—even close friends didn't know—the threat of public exposure was something he dreaded.

So Kaufman lied. He told Thorpe that he hadn't known all the facts, apologized for the affair, and promised Thorpe that he would immediately extricate himself from it. Kaufman added, carefully wording what he said, "I'm sorry, and I hope I won't be brought into your personal affairs." Pressed, the playwright pledged not to see Astor until after the doctor spoke with her about their conversation. This was another lie. Kaufman had dinner plans with the actress the following evening and needed to know what she might do.

Now, in the nightclub, hearing what her husband had done, Mary Astor was outraged. She couldn't believe that her husband had made such a "Mid-Victorian" fool of himself in front of a sophisticate like George Kaufman. Kaufman's open marriage with his wife, Beatrice, was common knowledge on Broadway. If anything, this only strengthened Astor's resolve to leave Thorpe, and that was exactly what she told the nervous playwright.

Because Mary Astor didn't want to hurt Kaufman or harm his career she told him that, if he wanted to get out of their relationship, she would understand. Kaufman smiled, assured her that he had no intention of ending their affair. He just asked one favor. So that it might appear he had kept his promise to Thorpe, he asked Astor not to discuss what had transpired between Thorpe and himself until Thorpe brought it up to her.

Astor made a mental note to call Marian Spitzer, as she was anxious to hear what her friend had to say. Mary Astor then pushed everything to the back of her mind. She was with George Kaufman and they'd be alone together for the rest of the night. She had no intention of allowing Franklyn Thorpe to spoil one more second of what promised to be a wonderful evening.

2

In a business satiated with beautiful women, Mary Astor was one of Hollywood's great beauties. It had been that way since she was fourteen, when her "Madonna-child" face had earned her a string of movie roles. Controlled by a greedy, money-mad father, Astor quickly gained stardom in the mid-1920s as an ingénue playing opposite Hollywood's most popular leading men. By 1936, at age twenty-nine, the Madonna-child had transformed into a stunning patrician beauty, whose cool sophistication lifted her above the mediocre films to which her lucrative studio contracts had relegated her. Yet beneath this cool, seemingly untouched and untouchable exterior existed a complex, troubled woman whose inner needs far outstripped her limited emotional resources.

More in love with being in love than actually able to love, Mary Astor was obsessed by an uncontrollable need for over-the-top neurotically romantic as well as intensely erotic relationships. Insecure and emotionally immature, she had never been able to develop or maintain a single mature relationship with a man. In spite of this, or perhaps because of it, as each relationship failed—as each romance inevitably drifted into indifference and boredom—she found herself searching for another man and another romance to rescue her from an almost crippling lack of both an emotional center and a true sense of self-worth.

Complicating these almost insurmountable emotional problems was Astor's distorted view of the bedroom. In the arms of her first famous (and much older) lover, iconic actor John Barrymore, she had been taught to approach it as a schoolroom and him as a teacher of not only sex but of art, literature, music—all the things that an extremely bright woman with a limited education might think held the keys to both happiness and inner fulfillment.

In 1923 Mary Astor was seventeen and John Barrymore was forty. Considered one of this century's great connoisseurs of women, Barrymore had seen Astor's photograph in a magazine and requested that she appear opposite him in the film version of Clyde Fitch's play, *Beau Brummell*. Meeting her for the first time during a costume test, Barrymore whispered into Astor's ear, "You're so goddamned beautiful that you make me want to faint."

Bewitched by both his charm and animal magnetism, Mary Astor found herself attracted to this outrageously handsome, charming, intensely alive man.

Peers and public alike considered John Barrymore the greatest actor of his day; a reputation earned not by his screen work but by years on the stage. In his day Barrymore was to acting what Marlon Brando would be a half-century later. He single-handedly transformed his craft. Since movies were considered a poor relation to the theatre, Barrymore looked down on the "flickers." He performed in what he called the "mooo-vies" because they made him world famous and provided the exorbitant income necessary to support his extravagant and hedonistic lifestyle.

By the 1920s, Barrymore's boozing and womanizing was legend. At forty years old the actor prided himself that there was nothing on the stage he couldn't play, and no woman he couldn't bed. In 1923 he wanted to bed Mary Astor. He had rivals. They weren't lovers. Mary Astor had never had any. They were two avaricious and possessive parents who controlled every part of their daughter's life.

• • •

Otto Ludwig Wilhelm Langhanke—Astor's real name was Lucile Langhanke—was an ambitious man whose grandiose dreams

Helen and Otto Langhanke.

of success were impossible to realize due to his neurotic temperament and cock-eyed thinking. What Langhanke did have was a beautiful daughter, and the minute he realized her potential, he turned her into a money-making machine and then pocketed 100 percent of her income. After meeting Langhanke, director D. W. Griffith confided to Lillian Gish that Astor's father "was a walking cash register." Barrymore saw something more. In the process of turning Lucile Langhanke into Mary Astor, her father had destroyed his daughter's ability to trust a man in a mature fashion or see herself as anything other than a docile victim.

By the end of the 1920s Astor was making close to $4,000 a week, every cent of which her father was spending on a lavish lifestyle that included a mansion, three servants, and a chauffeur-driven limousine. The most his daughter ever saw of the nearly half million dollars she earned while under his roof was the $5 a week in pin money her father grudgingly doled out.

During these years Mary Astor rarely received a word of encouragement or praise from her tyrannical father. Instead, every effort was met with a barrage of negative criticism, as Langhanke browbeat and bullied his daughter into believing it was best to do exactly what he told her to do. Robbed of her self-confidence, Mary Astor learned to always defer to the choices made by others.

In addition, living with her father was both emotionally and spiritually exhausting. She and her mother were forced to sit through nightly pontifications and lectures about anything and everything that popped into his uninformed head. These mindless lectures went on for hours, and Astor and her mother were not allowed to interject a single opinion or complaint.

By her late teens, Mary Astor had been turned into an unquestioning victim who felt safe from potential attack only when following orders. Not permitted friends her own age—or anything resembling the life of a normal teenager—her world became home, work at the studio, and the chauffeured drive between. In short, Mary Astor lived in an ivory tower filled with gilded drudgery.

John Barrymore—himself a product of emotional deprivation—could relate to Astor's need to break away from the suffocating dominance of her father. So with incredible skill, and using all his formidable charm, Barrymore "cultivated and awed" Astor's parents. He made them feel they were his equals and manipulated Astor's father into believing that he was genuinely interested in the old man's crackpot ideas and opinions. Secretly, Barrymore despised Langhanke, and told Astor that the only profession to which her father was suited was a butler. Having earned Langhanke's trust, when the actor suggested that he help Astor with her acting, which, as Langhanke saw it, would increase her earning potential, the old man jumped at it.

At first this instruction took place in the Langhanke living room with Astor's parents looking on. Then, Barrymore persuaded them that Astor was "too self-conscious"—afraid what her parents might think. He needed to work with her alone. So, every Sunday, while Mrs. Langhanke knitted on the hotel veranda, Barrymore gave Astor "instruction" in his Beverly Hills Hotel suite.

This was when the affair began in earnest. Because Astor's parents were not physically demonstrative—no hugs, no kisses, no touching or being touched by a comforting parent—she was deathly frightened of any form of physical contact. Here Barrymore was both patient and understanding. "Much like a young boy in love, courting his sweetheart—not bashfully but gently." Barrymore waited for Astor's growing sexual desires to overcome her physical hesitancy. Only when she herself was ready; as years of physical restraint gave way to unbridled passion, did they finally make love. But

Astor and Barrymore in a
Charles Albin photograph.

it was not he who ravished her; it was she who ravished him. Sex had become more than merely physical pleasure; it had become Mary Astor's first emotional and intellectual contact with another human being.

Barrymore made her read books on philosophy, art, music, drama, and poetry as well as sexually explicit material that opened up a world of erotic experience completely unknown to her. And, more importantly, he talked to her about what she read. He didn't want her mimicking the ideas of others but to finally think for herself. "Most important," she recalled, "he taught me that there was a world other than that which was run by Otto Langhanke." While her father had taught her to accept authority without questioning it, Barrymore taught her to value her own thoughts and ideas. Thus, for the first time in her life, Mary Astor began to sense her worth as a human being.

Barrymore soon became her father, her lover, her teacher, her god. "He gave me a love," she remembered, "wholehearted and undemanding such as I had never known before. I grasped at that love with unthinking and unquestioning violence. I didn't ponder over it; I didn't analyze it. I just gathered it to me greedily and thankfully."

Acting was what Barrymore knew best and acting became their strongest bond. "I could make you a truly great actress," he told her. "I could teach you things that will make an audience want to wrap you in their arms." Over and over he would tell her, "You can never develop your potential as an actress until you develop as an individual." He told her that her parents had turned her into a meal ticket and were stifling her as a person and as an actress. He told her that she had to build up the courage to break away. He told her things that she was afraid to hear but knew to be true.

• • •

The affair went on during the summer *Beau Brummel* was filmed and continued that fall in New York, when Barrymore appeared on Broadway in a return engagement of *Hamlet*. The greatest *Hamlet* of its day, Orson Welles thought it "tender, verbal, witty, dangerous" and Barrymore "a man of genius." Enraptured by that genius, Mary Astor sat in the wings watching performance after performance. By now her parents had become suspicious, forcing the lovers to become even more devious.

For over two years Barrymore had been legally separated from his second wife, poetess Michael Strange, and when a divorce finally became possible, he asked Astor to marry him. He didn't ask her once. He asked her a hundred times, and whenever he did she always sidestepped, saying that she didn't feel capable of giving him what he needed in a wife. The truth was that marriage would displease her father. More profoundly, marriage meant assuming responsibility for herself and breaking away from her father's dominance. Astor may have hated that dominance, but felt secure within its constancy. This was a condition of which Barrymore was painfully aware.

"You don't have the guts," he told her, "the vitality, to be an individual, do you? It would be an impossible thing for you to say, 'I want to be with my beloved—I want to go with him and the hell with you.'"

"Not just now" was always her answer: the answer of someone who didn't know how to fight for herself.

When *Hamlet* completed its New York run, and Barrymore took the production on limited tour, they parted. In the letters and telegrams he sent he called her Rusty—referring to her red hair—or his little Goopher, and sighed them Pop Hamlet. The two planned to be apart for only a few months, but because Astor was obligated to return to work in Hollywood and Barrymore had to take the play to London, it was almost seventeen months before they saw each other again.

Barrymore was exhausted from too much drinking but exhilarated with triumph. He had taken an American production of *Hamlet* to England and it was acclaimed as the greatest *Hamlet* ever performed. Now Barrymore had important plans for Astor. While away he had made arrangements for Astor to work with his vocal teacher, Margaret Huston Carrington. He wanted Astor to improve her vocal range so she could project on stage. Barrymore intended to recreate his much-praised *Richard III* in London and he wanted her to play Lady Anne. It would be a short engagement—only a few weeks—but for Astor it would be an audacious career move. Appearing on the English stage opposite the greatest actor in the English language would instantly catapult her beyond the "moo-vies" to the forefront of her profession. Although it was the opportunity of a lifetime, Astor had trepidations. Barrymore waved them away. He would help her create a performance filled with fire and brilliance. All she had to do was want it enough to fight for it, and he would do the rest.

When Barrymore proposed his plan to Astor's parents at dinner, it didn't go over well. In fact, it didn't go over at all. "We couldn't afford it. It wouldn't be practical." Langhanke's chief concern—his only concern—was the disparity between theatre money and movie money and his daughter not earning the income necessary to keep her father living like a millionaire. Barrymore hadn't expected anything different.

The person whose response he had hoped would be different was Mary Astor. He hoped that during the time they had been apart she had grown up and finally developed the courage to stand up to her parents. But throughout dinner, as Barrymore fought for her future, Mary Astor remained silent.

"You haven't changed a bit," he told her later. "Nothing has changed."

She didn't know it then, but it was over between them.

Astor had hoped to star opposite Barrymore in a screen version of *Moby Dick*. Committed to other projects, she was forced to withdraw, and twenty-one-year-old Dolores Costello stepped into the part. Barrymore thought Costello "preposterously beautiful" and it wasn't long before Astor heard from friends that Barrymore and Costello were involved in a passionate affair. Exactly how passionate Astor learned on the set of *Don Juan*. Starring opposite Barrymore, on a day Astor wasn't scheduled to work, Astor visited the set. Off to the side—as he had done with her during the filming of *Beau Brummel*—Barrymore had set up two camp chairs. Now the person Astor found sitting next to Barrymore was Costello. Astor's reaction was instantaneous: "All my hopes and dreams died and I wanted to die with them."

Things grew worse during the production. Barrymore did his best to ignore Astor or admonish her for the slightest mistake. He had written Mary Astor off and, by humiliating her, hoped she would turn her back on him as he was doing to her. Although Astor was crushed and humiliated, try as she may, she could not put the affair behind her. Once she even sneaked into Dolorous Costello's empty dressing room and, seeing photographs of Barrymore everywhere, wept for hours.

What made this doubly painful was Astor's realization that it was her own inability to break away from her domineering parents that lost her Barrymore's respect and finally his love. Eventually, her pain and anger focused where it should have been focused. For the first time in her life, Mary Astor began to fight her parents.

• • •

It started the day she first saw Barrymore with Costello. Mary Astor was so despondent that she had skipped her singing lesson. Arriving home early, she was confronted by an irate father.

"Lucile, I want you to explain why you are not on schedule with your vocalizing."

Heading for the stairs, she walked right past him. "I don't feel like singing. I have nothing to sing about. I hate singing."

Grabbing her by the shoulders, her father began shaking her.

"You are going to do as you are told!"

To her father's utter astonishment, Mary Astor yanked herself free and, in a display of temper, slapped Langhanke's hands away.

"You keep your hands off me—forever. I'm nineteen years old and I won't take anymore of this shoving around and being slapped when you're mad. And when I feel like singing again I'll sing!"

Her father was so shocked he wasn't able to speak. It had taken Astor a long time but it finally dawned on her that, as the bread-winner, she wielded the real power in that house. It wasn't long before she announced that she no longer wanted her mother to accompany her on set. Since she had never been allowed any money of her own, she demanded and received an allowance.

Finally, several months later, after an interminable lecture by her father on all her faults, Mary Astor looked at her face in a mirror and told herself that she had had enough. That night, while her parents were asleep, she packed a small bag walked out onto her bedroom balcony and, tying a sash to a tree, swung to the ground. She then walked to a hotel, booked a room and, not knowing what she would do next but happy to be out of her father's house, fell soundly asleep.

Mary Astor, internationally famous movie star—one of Hollywood's most emulated and written about women—had just run away from home.

3

When Astor returned home a week later things had changed dramatically. She had given her parents quite a scare. The two had suddenly realized that Astor's sizable checks, and their whole way of life, might walk out the door with her.

So they began treating their daughter more like an adult and, for the first time, Mary Astor was allowed to have friends. Never having learned to be accepted for herself, she quickly became part of the crowd. She smoked cigarettes, barbed her hair, drank "cocktails," learned to drive, and partied all night. Although her father frowned, there wasn't much he could do. For the first time in her life Mary Astor was doing exactly as she pleased, and began enjoying herself.

To prove, if only to herself, that she was over John Barrymore, Astor started seeing men and, within a few months, was engaged to assistant director, Irving Asher. As she had expected, her father didn't like this, and Astor enjoyed hearing him say that Asher was a nobody, and then laughing when the anti-Semitic Otto Langhanke railed against the man because he was Jewish.

Soon after her engagement, Astor began an affair with film writer John Monk Saunders. She would later write, "I had experienced the shattering upheaval of physical attraction but I did not know love, and therefore I could not love. The moment that the fire of desire ceased to burn brightly, the moment it flickered and began to die, I became restless, thinking that love itself was dying." It wasn't long before her engagement to Asher was off, her affair with Saunders over, and Mary Astor was seeing other men.

The pattern might have continued if not for Kenneth Hawks. Hawks was unlike any man Mary Astor had ever met. Sincere and

The Astor-Hawks wedding.

gentle, as well as supportive and understanding, Hawks made Mary Astor feel both cherished and important. He gave her the warmth, acceptance, and the deep felt tenderness that she had craved all her life. Unlike other men, Hawks never pressed Astor for sex and so sex never became an issue. It didn't need to be. Astor had always used sex to elicit tenderness from men. Now that she had the real thing she no longer needed a substitute.

Hawks was twenty-six and a producer at Fox who planned on becoming a director. His family had money; he was a Yale graduate and champion tennis player. Although Hawks may have lacked the worldliness of Jack Barrymore, he had a superb education. He knew books, music, and the theatre, and shared them all with Astor. Unlike her time with Barrymore, where she had felt tutored and guided, Hawks treated Mary Astor as an equal. Since Hawks was demonstrative and affectionate, Astor would often "curl up in his lap" as they read the same book together. It was an American "apple pie" courtship. After her parents, after John Barrymore, after all the men she had known, Mary Astor had finally found someone who could make her feel loved for herself. They were soon engaged. Eighteen months later, they had the perfect Hollywood wedding.

The same could not be said about their honeymoon. Since she and Ken had refrained from sex, Astor was surprised and then disappointed on their wedding night when all she received was a good night kiss. This bedtime scene was repeated for months afterward. "We often slept together in Ken's big double bed," she recalled. "I loved him and loved the feeling of closeness but it wasn't enough."

Astor found the occasional sex they did have maddeningly inadequate. In all other respects Kenneth Hawks was an ideal husband, who gave her a marriage with "rainbows around it." After growing up in a home where, one moment to the next, she feared for her emotional safety, Mary Astor was now living with a man who saw it as his job to make her feel happy and secure. For the first time since she was fourteen, Mary Astor was living in a home in which she wasn't paying the bills.

She and Ken played tennis together, golfed together, and went everywhere together. In their circle of friends, which included MGM production chief Irving Thalberg, his wife Norma Shearer, Ken's brother Howard and wife Athole—Norma Shearer's sister—as well as Florence and Frederic March, they were thought to be the perfect "couple." If Astor were the naive innocent brides were expected to be in those days, she might have been satisfied. But she wasn't.

The affair was with a film executive. She rationalized that it would save the marriage but that didn't eliminate the guilt; Astor was racked with it. Bad turned to worse when she became pregnant and convinced Hawks that having a child right then would damage her career. So he reluctantly agreed to an abortion, and it was this abortion that finally forced Astor to confront the damage she had caused her marriage. What Astor didn't know was that Hawks knew the truth—her mother had told him—and blamed himself. Previously only a social drinker, he now drank until he passed out. When Astor finally ended the affair she felt lucky. Her husband's health and attitude improved and, learning to adjust her sexual needs to what her husband could provide, life once again became simple.

• • •

By the fall of 1929, Hawks had directed his first film. It opened to good reviews and equally good box office numbers, and his career was off to a healthy start. By the end of the year Hawks had already finished his second film when, in January 1930, he went up to Point Vincent, California, and personally reshot a parachute jump. Two camera planes interlocked—Hawks was on one—and exploded in mid-air, killing everyone on both planes.

Astor was devastated. In an instant, her secure and happy world was gone. Fearing a breakdown, Astor kept her "grief under tight control." She refused to return home, staying instead with friends Florence and Fredric March. She later rented a small, furnished apartment at the La Layenda in Whitley Heights. She took nothing from the house, not even her clothing, and cut herself off from the Hawks family and their mutual friends. Since there was no money left from her husband's estate—Hawks lost heavily in the '29 crash—Mary Astor went back to work. One film followed another and, as long as she kept busy, she didn't have to think. The depth of her grief wouldn't become evident for months.

Eventually, Astor took up with actor Lee Tracy. Offscreen the actor was as outrageous and funny as he was on-screen. But he drank heavily—often into an alcoholic stupor. Dates were broken, and one night Tracy drank himself so sick that a doctor was called in. The doctor, gynecologist Franklyn Thorpe, was a friend. So, after giving the actor a sedative, Thorpe called Astor to let her know what was happening.

The two spoke, and Astor would write, "His soft soothing voice thrills me to the core." The next day, Astor phoned. She wanted Thorpe's medical opinion about the red splotches covering her abdomen. He examined her and the diagnosis was physical exhaustion. Suppressing her grief over Hawks' death, Astor had lost almost fifteen pounds and was suffering from malnutrition. Thorpe ran tests and the x-rays turned up a tubercular patch. Fortunately, the disease was at an early stage and still treatable.

In the early 1930s, tuberculosis had the same aura that AIDS had in the 1980s. If the press or a studio found out, Mary Astor could kiss her movie career goodbye. So Thorpe proposed that, if she put herself under his care and followed instructions, her cure and recuperation could be undertaken at home. To prevent gossip, it was announced that she was suffering from exhaustion, and during her convalescence Astor saw only two people; her maid and Dr.

Franklyn Thorpe. For two months Astor remained secluded, and within weeks her health began to improve.

During those months Astor poured out her feelings to Thorpe, who was both sympathetic and understanding. As Thorpe would later recall, "She was in a temporary Hollywood ellipse and very much worried about her future," and so he became "her physician as well as her counselor." It wasn't long before Mary Astor found herself in love and wrote in her private diary, "I'll get that man. I get any man I go after." Attracted to Thorpe since their first meeting, her need to be involved with someone—anyone—robbed her of clear thinking. "There he was leaning over me," she thought during that first examination, "the very air was tinged with romance."

Because Thorpe was not part of Astor's Hollywood clique, she found him interesting. Because he seemed to understand her needs and longings, she thought him different. In short order Thorpe not only became her physical savior but, in Mary Astor's mind, at least, the solution to all her emotional problems. It was the same pattern— begun with John Barrymore—repeating itself. Blinded by loneliness, unhappiness, and an overwhelming need to be loved and be in love, she clung to Thorpe as a drowning person might cling to a lifeline. For him, finding a woman in great difficulty elicited a need to help and their relationship developed into "a magnificent friendship."

• • •

Franklyn Thorpe was thirty-nine when he met Mary Astor, and two people couldn't have had less in common. Born to an entrepreneurial father, when business was good Thorpe attended military school. When business was not so good he and his two sisters lived on their grandfather's farm in Maine, where Thorpe found himself behind a horse-drawn plow. Financially strapped, he was forced to work his way through college—one summer on the construction of the Panama Canal—and then Columbia and Tufts Medical School as well as additional training in Vienna and London.

What Thorpe did have that interested Mary Astor was looks

and charm. The ladies liked him and he liked them—not one, but usually several at the same time. When he married young his parents forced the couple to divorce so Thorpe could complete medical school. Undaunted, Thorpe then did the next best thing. While at Columbia Medical School, he lived with a woman and both claimed they were married. Later, he failed to mention these relationships to anyone, especially Mary Astor. He didn't mention other things as well. In order to do what he wanted, Thorpe had learned at an early age that it was easier to hide things when lies of omission weren't possible.

In 1925, living in Tampa, Florida, with an attractive widow and her young son, Thorpe let people believe they were man and wife. When Thorpe moved to Los Angeles the widow followed, and they continued living together for a while. Although Thorpe saw other women, the widow accepted this arrangement, leaving Thorpe to live as he liked. That is, until he met Mary Astor. The doctor had never met a woman like Mary Astor. With women Thorpe had always been the aggressor, and so Mary Astor was an anomaly. By candidly exposing her physical and emotional needs, and then pleading for help, this incredibly beautiful—and sexually experienced—woman created immediate intimacy. Thorpe could not understand what she saw in him. She was one of the most beautiful and celebrated women in the world. None of it made any sense, and he told her as much. Her answer:

"You're the only man I've ever really loved; the only one I will ever love."

Finally, in spite of his deep reservations, Thorpe found Astor's determination so compelling, and her sexual appetite so alluring, that his emotions eventually overrode his good sense. Within six months they were talking marriage and by the end of 1931 were husband and wife.

As Astor would confide to her private diary, "I looked in the mirror and laughed like hell because I had to beg him to marry me. I made him marry me, made him love me."

The following year, while on a yachting trip to Hawaii their

TOP: Franklyn Thorpe and Mary Astor shortly after their marriage.

MIDDLE: Newborn Marylyn Thorpe Hauoli with her parents.

BOTTOM: Astor with her car in front of the Toluca Lake house.

daughter, Marylyn was born prematurely in a Honolulu hospital. Soon after they built a comfortable North Hollywood home right on Toluca Lake. Mary Astor now had everything she believed would make her happy. So she hoped.

• • •

From the first Astor mistakenly saw in Thorpe a means to escape Hollywood, her parents, her work, the pressures; everything she blamed for her unhappiness. But her marriage failed to provide Astor with what she wanted. She would eventually write in her private diary, "now that I have everything the way I worked and grieved to get, it's so much ashes."

Because she wanted to get away from the movie industry and live the normal life of wife and mother, she and Thorpe devised a plan. Thorpe—who at the time was employed in a Los Angeles hospital clinic—would open a medical practice in the prestigious Hollywood First National Building. Then, during the time needed to establish a thriving practice, Astor would continue to work. When the practice was able to provide them with a comfortable lifestyle, Astor would retire from movies.

Unfortunately the practice never did become the success they had planned, and Astor continued to pay the bills. In addition to supporting her own household, she was still paying for the upkeep on her parents' mansion and their three servants. When Thorpe learned about this he was so outraged that, at age twenty-seven, Mary Astor finally took possession of her weekly paycheck. A highly publicized legal battle ensued with her parents suing for a share of their daughter's income. Instead, the court ordered them to sell their $200,000 mansion, and rent a small house. Put up for auction, the house eventually sold for $21,000.

During her ten years in Hollywood Mary Astor had earned over half a million dollars, and her father had squandered every cent of it. Astor now put her parents on a strict $100-a-month allowance, and the two were finally forced to live within their means.

THE PURPLE DIARIES   33

Consequently, as the sole supporter of herself, her daughter, her husband, her mother, and her father, Mary Astor's dream of giving up her film career became a practical impossibility. A year and a half into her second marriage, she felt even more trapped in her unhappy life than she had felt following Ken Hawks' death.

Only six months after the birth of her daughter the basic problems in Mary Astor's marriage were apparent. What had first intrigued her about Thorpe now became a bone of contention. Franklyn Thorpe knew nothing about Hollywood, art, music, or anything except medicine. He didn't enjoy Hollywood social life nor did he know how to mix with people. All she and her husband ever talked about were "patients that won't pay a bill, the servants, the gardener, the baby, money matters, and the trouble with her family." Astor often called him "a bump on a log with no sense of humor" and concluded that "while beautifully educated in one line he knows absolutely nothing of what is going on in the world outside his own profession."

What Thorpe did enjoy was hunting and, since Astor hated it, she never accompanied him on his hunting trips no matter who went along. One example was Clark Gable. Thorpe and the rising MGM star had become hunting buddies. On one of these hunting trips Gable suffered a severe attack of appendicitis and, after diagnosing the problem, Thorpe immediately drove Gable to a hospital and removed his appendix, most likely saving the actor's life. In appreciation Gable gave Thorpe an expensive Hamilton watch with the inscription "To My Pal," and the two remained good friends for many years. This was the sort of male camaraderie that Mary Astor had a difficult time understanding, much less appreciating.

Astor wasn't alone in her dissatisfaction. Thorpe considered his wife's friends "pseudo intellectuals" and told Astor that her life lacked purpose. Eventually, this disparity grew so wide that two years after her marriage, Astor would write in her private diary: "he is a fine man but we are simply worlds apart. We don't think alike and are not interested in any of the same things. I'm not myself with him."

Thorpe knew his marriage wasn't working. But, because his pride and self-respect were tied to a strict code of responsibility, he was committed to keeping it afloat. Yet as his own unhappiness increased, Thorpe became less and less tolerant of his wife.

Mary Astor was not, by nature, a nurturing person. Brought up to be hard on herself, she was equally hard on those around her. Thorpe on the other had been raised by a caring and devoted mother, who doted on her only son. Hence, beneath his man's-man veneer, he was an extremely sensitive individual. It was these qualities that Thorpe required a woman to support, and this was something Mary Astor was utterly incapable of providing.

So Thorpe soon took up again with Lillian Miles, the widow from Tampa. Miles was everything Mary Astor wasn't. She accepted Thorpe for who he was as well as who he wasn't. When Astor eventually found out, she came to hate Lillian Miles with an unbridled passion because the woman forced Astor to recognize her limitations as a wife. As the marriage disintegrated the fights began. Thorpe would argue with Astor over the least little thing, especially money. Money was a sore point with Franklyn Thorpe because his wife earned twenty times her husband's income—a detail she never failed to mention in their arguments. This ate at Thorpe's pride and transformed petty arguments into battles. The fights were so awful because, in spite of knowing better, when freed of inhibitions by alcohol, Astor allowed herself to be drawn into them even though she immediately regretted the cruel things she often said to her husband. So it wasn't long until Astor ceased expressing her real feelings. Instead, trying to make their times together less troublesome, she began acting the part of the wife Franklyn Thorpe wanted. Unfortunately it was a short-term solution to a long term problem, and only worsened matters. Unable to express her unhappiness, this dissatisfaction soon spread to almost every aspect of her life.

It wasn't until the winter of 1932 that Mary Astor finally asked Thorpe for a divorce. For Thorpe divorce was simply out of the question. It would tell the world he wasn't "man enough" to hold on to his wife. So, Thorpe pleaded with her for another chance. He promised to change and become a better husband. He promised to stop seeing other women. He also talked about their six-month-old daughter, crying when he told Astor how much he needed his wife. These pleadings went on for days, until Astor caved in, saying she'd give it another try. So, finding "the little bit of me that is middle class," she would write "that's the part of me I stretch and expand in order to be on some common ground with him; and that's just what it is—common." Mary Astor had—as she had living with her parents—become comfortable in the situation as it was. Fear of change, not Franklyn Thorpe, was her reason for staying.

Astor no longer felt any passion for Thorpe. Without the obsessive intoxication of passion she felt empty and incomplete. So, as any sexually liberated woman today might do—and what her husband functioning in his "double standard" world was already doing—Mary Astor decided to look elsewhere to fulfill those needs. She found men, found many of them. By default, as the two had already stopped sleeping together, Mary Astor and Franklyn Thorpe now had a de facto open marriage.

4

Astor had three weeks off in May 1933 and decided to vacation in New York. Since it would be the first time that Astor would be in the city by herself, Marian Spitzer wrote two of her oldest friends and asked them to show Astor the town. One was publisher Bennett Cerf, and the other was playwright George S. Kaufman.

Astor arrived in New York on Monday, May 24, checked in at the Ambassador Hotel, and immediately telephoned Cerf and Kaufman. Kaufman was out of town, but Cerf wasn't. In fact, when she mentioned that she was Mary Astor, Cerf actually thought someone was playing a joke. Saying he would call her back, he telephoned the hotel, found out that she was who she claimed to be, and then asked what he could do for her.

"I'm dying to see New York and meet people."

Cerf obliged, and that first week the two enjoyed dinners together and attended the theatre. New York publisher Cerf was fascinated by Hollywood, while Astor was nurturing literary aspirations, so the two had a lot to talk about. But because she wasn't his type, Cerf never made a pass and the relationship remained platonic.

Friday morning Kaufman was back in town and called Astor to set up a Saturday luncheon date at the Park Casino. Spitzer had told Astor that she would probably "like George but fall for Bennett." She thought Kaufman very amusing but too old for Astor. The woman couldn't have been more off the mark.

From the moment Mary Astor met George Kaufman she was entranced. A few years earlier, Kaufman's writing partner, Moss Hart, had met Astor while writing for the movies and thought her the "smartest gal in California." Now George Kaufman was about to see for himself, and in the process introduced Mary Astor to a world that she had only heard about. In his hands, New York circles of theatre, literature, and music sprang open for her. Kaufman made her laugh and he made her think. As her infatuation grew, her New York vacation transformed into an intoxicating romantic adventure.

She would confess to her diary, "I met George and it made me feel exactly as if I had been in a foreign country for the past four years and suddenly came home and found someone who spoke English."

Bennett Cerf spotted the two at a cocktail party given by Kay Swift, and remembered "they just disappeared together. It was absolute chemistry. When I looked around to find Astor, she was gone. So was Kaufman. It was instant combustion. George was like that. Theirs was such a great, great love affair."

• • •

In May 1933 George S. Kaufman was one of Broadway's brightest lights. A Pulitzer Prize and one hit play after another had already established Kaufman as the most successful playwright in America. He was a disciplined, prodigious writer who thrived on work and an ardent perfectionist who was never completely satisfied with anything he did. When Mary Astor met him, Kaufman had two plays running simultaneously on Broadway and was finishing up a new play for the fall.

Successful as he was as a playwright, Kaufman was equally successful with women. Thirty years after the fact, many women would shiver when they spoke of their times with the playwright. "Kaufman was a man," friend and biographer Howard Teichmann wrote, "who could never satisfy himself in work or in sex. Frequently he employed one as a substitute for the other. It is of no small importance that he was compulsive in both." Groucho Marx's assessment was brief and to the point. "Kaufman was only interested in two things: playing bridge and screwing." For

George S. Kaufman and Beatrice Kaufman.

producer Max Gordon, George S. Kaufman was nothing less than a "male nymphomaniac."

These formidable skills came late to Kaufman. At age twenty-eight, he was still a virgin on his wedding night. So was his wife Beatrice, who was twenty-two and would later remark, "We were *both* virgins, which shouldn't happen to anybody." A year later, after the birth of a stillborn baby, the Kaufmans ceased having sex. At first it was Beatrice who "could no longer accept him in that role," and then it became Kaufman's choice as well.

Friend Howard Teichmann concluded that Beatrice had become a mother figure and, since Kaufman thought of women in terms of "Madonna or whore," he could no longer bed his wife. He was probably the only person in New York who felt that way. To everyone else Beatrice Kaufman was a brilliant, magnetic woman who was the equal of her husband in any conversation. Within three years of their marriage she had transformed herself from an overweight, "hickey" Rochester Jewish-American princess into one of New York's most brilliant hostesses. Her clothing, hairstyles, even how she smoked using a cigarette holder were imitated and emulated. She was a woman who "set the styles" and the only honor greater than attending a Kaufman gathering was the Kaufmans attending one of yours.

Before Beatrice, George Kaufman was a *New York Times* drama critic with aspirations of being a playwright. He was a shy, withdrawn man whose preferred form of socializing was a game of bridge. Now, with her encouragement, management, counsel, and nurtured contacts, Beatrice enabled her husband to become the hottest playwright in town as she managed both his life and career. Beatrice soon transformed their home into a glittering salon, where George S. Kaufman's formidable wit shined the brightest. A week didn't go by without a Kaufman quip quoted in a syndicated column or New York newspaper.

With enough chutzpah for ten, Beatrice forged her own career as a successful literary editor and managed to shine in a spotlight quite separate from that of her husband. Having learned that there were more important things about the Kaufman union than sex, she took lovers; men she considered her equals. Her husband eventually found out but instead of being hurt, George Kaufman was relieved. It freed him from guilt over his own sexual exploits.

Once George S. Kaufman moved into the world of theatre as a playwright/director, and became aware of the limitless availability of women this position afforded him, he was like a child with a sweet tooth in a pastry shop. He simply couldn't get enough.

Kaufman learned love-making in the same manner he had learned playwriting—as a perfectionist who strived to be the best at whatever he did. His education began with the highest priced and most skilled prostitutes. They taught him what women enjoyed in bed and exactly how to give it to them. Graduating to chorus girls, he learned what woman liked to hear and then, moving on to actresses, what they needed to hear. He became as professional and skilled a lover as he was a playwright. Sex, not love, was the goal.

Kaufman quickly learned that women, starved for male sympathy, would easily fall into the arms of any man who was patient enough to listen to their problems and show them the least amount of sympathy. He also learned never to deceive a woman or lie about his feelings. He also never sought out women who were his equals. He only sought out those easily dazzled by his intellectual brilliance.

What Kaufman lacked in looks he more than made up for with his quick and beguiling tongue. Kaufman could make anything seem funny, and when women laughed they were the most susceptible. And it wasn't just his words; it was his delivery that gave his humor a rakish edge. Groucho Marx's stage and film portrayals, although extreme exaggerations, were imitations of the Kaufman delivery style, which Kaufman conveyed with a light touch women found irresistible.

Most importantly, George Kaufman learned how to feed into a woman's innate need for the romantic—moonlit nights, thoughtful notes, flowers, candy, compliments, opening doors and lighting cigarettes. He learned how to make any woman feel as if she were the most important person in the world. This was the George Kaufman Mary Astor met in May 1933.

She met George on Friday. He called for her on Saturday. They did not kiss until Tuesday and by Tuesday night they were making "thrilling and beautiful" love in an apartment Kaufman kept on East Seventy-Third Street for his trysts.

During their time together George Kaufman listened to Mary Astor rattle on about her dreams, her disappointments, and her aspirations. He told her the things she wanted to hear and showed her the New York she had always wanted to see. Plays, dinners at 21, luncheons at the Park Casino, teas with the New York literati, the Algonquin Roundtable, brunches where George Gershwin played his latest hits, and, most of all the nights and morning afters. "It was just getting daylight," she wrote in her private diary, "so we drove through the park in an open cab and the street lights went out and the birds started singing and it was cool and dewy and pretty heavenly."

When Astor returned to California she did not allow herself to become "sensible" about her time in New York, but rhapsodized about it for months. Because the affair had meant so much to her,

Astor couldn't permit herself to see that, to George Kaufman, "she was only one among dozens" of conquests.

Since Kaufman was also skilled at keeping the heat under an affair, during the next six months he wrote Astor twice a month and would occasionally telephone her long distance. When he came to California in February of 1934 to collaborate with writing partner Moss Hart on a play, the affair resumed. They spent an evening together in LA. Then Astor drove down to Palm Springs, where Kaufman was working, and they became inseparable.

The weekend before Kaufman left California Astor again flew down to be with him. On Sunday evening he read her the completed draft of his new play, and when America's most successful playwright asked Mary Astor—a woman who dreamed of being a writer—what she thought, Astor's ego soared.

When they met again in May a new dream began to materialize. There was a part in the play that was perfect for her, and she would give her "eyes to play." It gave possibility to starring on Broadway and living in New York "in a comfortable apartment with the baby and a good nurse." Her dream of leaving Hollywood and the drudgery of movie work finally seemed within her grasp.

Kaufman returned to New York and, later that month, offered her a chance at the part if she could make it to New York for an audition. Astor was beside herself. So when she requested a leave of absence, and Warner Brothers refused, she was crushed. Her disappointment soon spread beyond the professional sphere.

"I don't like to be alone," she concluded. "I have to lean on someone… I'm scared to death of the independence and the result is that I'm always tying myself up. If I had the courage to break loose, have a good house cleaning—if I could first bring myself to manage my own life, my money, etc., I'd be a step further toward achieving some sort of happiness."

By now her relationship with Franklyn Thorpe had disintegrated into "a series of explosions, usually over minor things," and the strongest feeling that she could muster for her husband was fondness. Sometimes it was only pity. "He's very happy in this home with me," she reflected about the doctor, "and he adores Marylyn. I'd have to bust that up and break his heart."

By September 1934 she was writing, "I'm fond of Franklyn—would hate hurting him because he loves and needs me." In December it was, "I like to be with him sometimes, because of a certain niceness and warmth and 'used-to-ness.'" By January 1935 all pretense had fallen away. "I may as well be honest about it... I don't love him anymore."

Talk of divorce began. But whenever Astor brought it up Thorpe would cry and tell her—as he had done two years earlier—how much he needed her and the baby and promise to change. The times he didn't cry he shouted instead. "I will not have that child alienated from me—she is as much mine as yours. I will not see her raised as another man's child any more than you would like to see her with me and another woman." When this happened Astor would back down and agonize until she had again built up her resolve.

During this time, Astor and Kaufman grew closer. The previous September, she had been to New York and spent ten days with him. "Only ten days," she would confide to her private diary, "but enough for me to remember the rest of my life." Kaufman was immersed in the final days of rehearsing *Merrily We Roll Along*, the play in which she had wanted to star, but he still managed to take her to the theatre, dinners at "our" 21, rides through the park, and spend "lovely" nights with Astor in her hotel suite, where they experienced "glorious ecstasy in a few beautiful hours."

"It's beautiful, glorious," Astor would remember, "and I hope it's my last love. I can't top it with anything in my experience."

After such romantic intoxication, returning home to Dr. Franklyn Thorpe and shifting "back into low gear" couldn't be anything less than an enormous let down. On top of that, Thorpe was still seeing Lillian Miles, the thirty-three-year-old Tampa widow. Miles had become pregnant and, that September, Franklyn confessed to his wife that he had given Miles an abortion in his medical office, all of which Astor noted in her diary.

Surmising that the aborted child was Thorpe's, Astor felt it would be a good time to tell her husband about Kaufman. She was right. "It's a wonder," he told her, "you haven't turned to someone else long before because of the way I've treated you. I haven't kept my word to you. I've given you a raw deal. I have been expecting something like this and I wouldn't be much of a physician if I didn't understand it." Astor was surprised at how "big" he was about the whole thing. "It's a remarkable thing the way Franklyn took it when I told him about George—with a great deal of sympathy and understanding."

By the year's end she would conclude, "The only real happiness I've had has been with George. Everything else is forced." She would say of Kaufman, "A piece of mercury—a completely fascinating, illusive person who has the power to make me so happy that I want to laugh from sheer joy."

George Kaufman was about to travel to Hollywood. The new Marx Brothers' movie had script problems. Since Kaufman had worked with the brothers, and was the best play doctor in New York, Groucho Marx had suggested Kaufman to one-time MGM production head and now unit producer Irving Thalberg. At first the playwright had resisted. For a writer of Kaufman's stature, it would be a comedown writing for the movies. What changed Kaufman's mind was Thalberg's offer of a $100,000 paycheck for ten weeks' work. At $10,000 a week, this would make George Kaufman the highest-paid writer in history.

When Kaufman arrived in California in early January of 1935, Astor was overjoyed. They would have two—possibly three—months together. Kaufman would be staying at the Beverly Wilshire. No longer concerned about what people might think, Astor saw Kaufman whenever she could. Their brashness made it obvious to anyone who cared to know that Mary Astor and George S. Kaufman were very much more than "just friends." They were an "item."

5

The morning following her dinner with Kaufman at the Trocadero, Mary Astor called Marian Spitzer and told her everything. Marian persuaded Astor to consult with an attorney, and they went to see divorce lawyer Ralph Blum. Since Astor's main concern was custody of Marylyn, Blum assured her that custody wouldn't be a problem. Courts nearly always awarded a child to its mother. What she should be concerned about was the divorce itself. On the positive side, after telling Thorpe about Kaufman the previous September, by his continuing to live with her, Thorpe had—legally speaking—condoned the relationship. Nevertheless, if Thorpe decided to fight—if he named Kaufman as co-respondent—things could get messy.

During the meeting Astor kept repeating that she didn't want "George dragged into this." Both Spitzer and Blum told her this wasn't the time to be worrying about Kaufman. She needed to protect herself. "Kaufman is a man," Spitzer told her, "let him protect himself. In the eyes of the world he's been playing around with a married woman and he should be ready to take the consequences."

Astor was in a quandary. She had become so obsessed and protective of the playwright that the thought of losing him was unthinkable. She soon convinced herself that, much against Spitzer's and Blum's advice, she needed to protect Kaufman from the scandal of a messy divorce. When Astor left for a few days of location shooting Thorpe still hadn't brought up his meeting with Kaufman.

He just moped around the house "very wretched with hurt eyes and shaking hands." Then, after Astor returned, they went out to dinner at the Trocadero, and what began as a discussion turned into an argument. Once they got home it became a full-scale battle with shouting that continued until three o'clock in the morning.

Astor told her husband that she no longer loved him and wanted a divorce. At first he pleaded with her. Astor had heard it all before but, this time, she told him what she really thought. She couldn't understand why he would want to hold onto someone who no longer loved him and who, in fact, was in love with someone else.

Thorpe wanted to know if she intended to continue seeing Kaufman while he was in California. Given an unqualified yes, Thorpe told her that people were talking and it was becoming a scandal. Thorpe wanted his wife to understand what she was doing, if not for herself then for the baby.

When she brought up Lillian Miles, Thorpe's temper flared. So did hers. She told him that he still lived in the nineteenth century where it was okay for a man to have a lover but not a woman. Mary Astor thought this the height of hypocrisy.

"Is it that mid-Victorian thinking of yours that made you take it upon yourself to go and speak to George? Why do you interfere? Was it to frighten George to break off with me?"

Thorpe was surprised. "How do you know about that? Did he tell you? Why didn't Kaufman come and speak to me about it himself?"

"I practically went through the floor."

"Because I went to him man-to-man and told him there was talk, and he was breaking up my home, and asked him if he was man enough to withdraw?"

"How *dare* you. What did you expect to gain? What do you mean speaking to him like that? By what right did you see my lover? Do you think that you can come between me and George? It's none of your business what I do with George Kaufman. He's my lover, not yours. You're a big mid-Victorian fat fool."

"If I was a mid-Victorian fool about your affair with Kaufman

I wouldn't have taken it out in conversation. I'd have shot Kaufman's guts out after the approved manner of mid-Victorian fools. I talked to him to try and bring him to his senses, if you lost yours."

It went on for hours. Thorpe attacked Kaufman, accusing him of dangling promises of theatre parts to keep her interested and how Thorpe had thought that "a man with his reputation as a playwright would have some fortitude," but instead was the kind of man "who would hide out when the time came to defend" Astor's name.

"I can't talk to him," Astor wrote in her diary. "He will never answer a question directly and hasn't even heard it" with the issue of his talking with Kaufman, "completely justified."

So, finally Thorpe played his trump card. He told Astor that he would fight for custody and bring Kaufman's name into the divorce, creating a big fat scandal.

"Why would you want to do that? You know George Kaufman has nothing to do with our divorce. Now that this divorce matter has come up; now because we are miserable together you throw up George Kaufman to me so you can get control of Marylyn. I wanted to divorce you two years ago—before I even met him. Why would you want to drag in people who have nothing to do with our troubles? Anyway you couldn't do that. You've known about George since last October and since we have continued to live together you have condoned it."

"I don't care. I'll use any means I wish to get custody of that child. I'll let it be known that you've been living with Kaufman."

"No I haven't!"

"Yes you have. You told me you did. You lived with him in Palm Springs and you lived with him when you went to New York."

"No I didn't! That's not true!"

The bickering finally ended in the small hours of the morning when a tentative agreement brought a truce. If they shared custody, Thorpe wouldn't bring Kaufman's name into it.

Astor decided to keep her real plans to herself. She'd wait a few years after the divorce, go back to court, and gain full custody of Marylyn when a years' old affair couldn't be used against her.

The next day Thorpe was all apology, tearfully begging her to forgive him, repeating over and over "I need you." Astor told him that she would hold off on the divorce to give it some more thought. The truth was, Kaufman would be in town for another month and Astor wanted to see him without a divorce brouhaha getting in the way.

"I want to have a last few times of completely enjoying him," she wrote. "Then when he has left town I can start in again."

When Kaufman left California on March 13, Astor promised him that she would vacation in New York sometime in October after her Warner Brothers contract terminated. Breathing a sigh of relief, once safely back in New York, Kaufman told Beatrice everything. Beatrice counseled him not to worry, that "it will all blow over." For the moment at least, she guessed right.

Of her time with Kaufman, Astor mused, "It is a thoroughly satisfying relationship; no ties, no promises, no vows, nothing holds us together except our own desires. And that seems to be the way it should be." She no longer imagined or, for that matter, even wanted to marry George Kaufman. Astor had already begun looking for a small, furnished house. As soon as she found one she was going to tell Thorpe that it was over and, taking the baby with her, finally move out.

• • •

Then something happened that Mary Astor would regret for years to come. Just before she was ready to leave, Thorpe found Astor's private diaries kept locked in her writing desk. They were contained in two two-hundred-page, blue-bound, red-edged ledger books. She had been keeping them since her time with Kenneth Hawks and they contained all her most intimate and personal thoughts.

For all her reserve, Mary Astor was basically an emotion-based woman whose emotions could override clear thinking if she didn't keep them in check. Thus, Astor used these diaries as a sort of "safety valve" in which she felt free to express these emotions a fantastic story and I am keeping a record of the whole thing in the press clippings.

Well after about three days that died down and I could breathe again – the court action comes up April 5th so it will all break out again I suppose.

Saturday March 24th I got a wire from George saying they were leaving the following Wednesday and would not be coming back to Hollywood. By the grace of God I got a break, didn't have to work Saturday afternoon or Monday – so I caught the plane at 3.45. and had dinner at the Dunes with him Sunday we had a lot of fun – Harlan Thompson was there (Marion's husband) and he took pictures with his Leica of Moss & George and me on the kiddie slide and swings –

About 6:50 George called me into the bungalow and read the play to me – I was pretty puffed

A page from Mary Astor's diary.

without fear of criticism. She wrote candidly about Kaufman and Thorpe, about her affairs and those of her friends. She would later recall, "I wanted to talk about my own activities and my opinions of other people and the things they did. I wanted the assurance of individuality and reality and substance that the diary gave me."

When Thorpe finished reading these two volumes, he was beside himself. He now knew "exactly what his wife thought of him." He was so "astounded reading through the pages of her diaries" that reading them he saw himself as nothing less than a "sucker." "I felt," he would later write, "the whole structure of my life, career, all that I had struggled and fought for years to build crumbling around me. My wife was like a harp in the wind on which every breeze strummed its own tune and left overtures behind. So that finally, instead of one sweet, pleasant harmony, there was a jangling and horrid discord."

Mary Astor had gone to bed with "anyone else who even happened to catch her fancy" and Thorpe learned that he had been cuckolded not just by George Kaufman but by scores of men. He learned that while she pitied her husband, Mary Astor-Hawks-Thorpe had carelessly and often joyously given herself, and her love, to any man whom she thought "terribly attractive." A hatred welled up that transformed a perfectly reasonable, caring man into an avenging angel who wanted his pound of flesh and then some.

If Mary Astor thought she had seen Franklyn Thorpe's temper before, she was not prepared for what she now saw. He would grant her a divorce but he wanted the final say on all the property, all the money, and he wanted complete custody of the baby. He told her that she was morally unfit to control the upbringing of their daughter and he was prepared to do whatever needed to be done to protect their daughter from such a woman while conveniently ignoring his own indiscretions. If she didn't give him what he wanted he would make the diaries public and ruin her, ruin her career, and ruin the lives of every friend whose confidences she had written down in those two ledger books.

Astor realized that her the diary "was suddenly transformed

into a monster that threatened to devour me, my friends and, worst of all, Marylyn." Astor was beside herself. She demanded her dairies back. Thorpe refused. At first she couldn't believe that he would really do such "a horrible thing." Her first thoughts were about her baby and she asked him how, if he wrecked her career, could she earn the money to support the child—something he couldn't or wouldn't do.

He didn't care. If she didn't agree to give him what he wanted, Franklyn Thorpe would publicly destroy her. He'd blacken her name and the names of her friends on the front pages of every newspaper in America. He would wreck her career and ruin her life. The more she refused, the more he hammered. It went on for a week.

When Astor came down with the flu, Thorpe continued his threats until she became near hysterical with fear and trepidation. To avoid exposing the baby to her illness, she had set up a bed in the library. While she lied on this makeshift sickbed suffering from a fever, Thorpe hovered over her shouting that unless she gave him everything, he would plaster her own words on the front pages of newspapers so that every man and woman in America would see for themselves exactly what kind of woman she was. Astor was too weak to argue. All she could do was cry and plead with him to stop.

On March 28 they were in the bedroom. Astor was so sick that she couldn't think straight. The baby was there with the maid and, because Thorpe was shouting and shaking his fist, Astor asked him to let her send the baby back up to her room. The doctor turned to the frightened child and shouted at Marylyn to stay exactly where she was. He wanted her to remember what she was seeing. Watching Thorpe taking out his anger on a defenseless baby finally brought a rise out of Astor. Mustering all her strength, she lashed out at him.

"You can't do this dreadful thing to me, you just can't. You can't take my baby away because you feel I've wronged you. You can't do this horrible thing because I love George Kaufman instead of you."

This hit close to home. Thorpe shoved the sick woman into a chair and shouted that she had better get it into her head that he could do exactly as he pleased to her and to her friends, including

George Kaufman. He screamed that he would "do anything" he needed to do in order to see to it that they were destroyed along with his wife.

This proved to be Astor's breaking point. Pushed onto that chair, forced to listen to Thorpe rail at her—just as she had been forced to listen to her father—Astor realized that she no longer had the will to fight. Illness and fear convinced her that Franklyn Thorpe had no shame and was not only capable of making the diaries public but also of doing her physical harm.

A short time later Astor was on her sickbed in the library, preparing to sign an agreement that Thorpe and his lawyer, Ethel Pepin, had just handed her. The agreement gave her husband sole custody of the baby, half interest in the house that Astor had paid for, and control of all the money she had in the world. Mary Astor was heartsick and felt completely defeated.

The property settlement, and especially the trust agreement—forbidding Astor from taking the child out of the state without Thorpe's consent as well as establishing a fund to be used by Thorpe if Astor tried to regain custody—were so outrageously one-sided that even Thorpe's lawyer had ethical qualms about letting Astor sign it.

"You should understand," Pepin told the sick woman, "that Franklyn is going to go through with this divorce suit and I don't think it would be a fair deal for you to sign this unless you get an attorney to look them over first."

Turning on Pepin, Thorpe glared. "Ethel, you're going over to Mary's side. You're to stop that immediately. This thing is going to be the way I want it. I'm running this show and I'm going to have the say as far as the baby is concerned."

Having read, and taken seriously, the portions of Astor's diary where she momentarily contemplated moving to New York with the baby, Thorpe feared that Astor might actually do this after the divorce. If she did, he felt it would destroy any possibility of him ever enjoying a normal relationship with his daughter. The trust agreement was his assurance that this would never happen.

The only concession Thorpe had given his wife was to let little Marylyn live on with her mother under his supervision for six months each year. Astor, on the other hand, was to pay for the baby's up-keep twelve months each year. The next day, Astor and her three-year-old daughter moved to a small house on Tower Road in Beverly Hills with the understanding that, if Astor did or said anything concerning the divorce which Thorpe didn't approve of, he would take the baby away from her permanently.

Ten days later Franklyn Thorpe filed for and was granted an uncontested divorce on charges of mental cruelty and incompatibility. On April 18, 1935, he was named Marylyn Thorpe's sole legal guardian. A mother giving up custody of her child raised some eyebrows and forced Thorpe to comment publicly that Astor "thought it better I keep my daughter. Her work takes her away from home so much that she didn't think it would be good for Marylyn."

Since Astor made no public comment to the contrary, no further questions were asked. By verbal agreement the baby was to remain, for the time being at least, in the care of her mother.

6

Marylyn stayed with her mother at the Tower Road house from the time of the separation until October 12, 1935, when, as part of their verbal agreement, Thorpe demanded the child back. Astor had hoped to keep Marylyn longer, but Thorpe threatened to take the child away permanently if she didn't comply. So the baby returned to Toluca Lake, and would remain with her father until May 1, 1936. As this coincided with the end of Astor's Warner Brothers contract, she had three months off until a five-picture deal with Columbia Pictures commenced and decided to travel east to see Kaufman. She had tentatively planned the trip before the divorce but now that Thorpe had the baby she went ahead.

During the six months Astor had been living on Tower Road, Kaufman had returned to Hollywood for onset rewrites during the shooting of the Marx Brothers' movie. Astor and Kaufman's relationship continued, more discreetly now, although she did visit him on the set. In fact, while her father was busy at the studio, Kaufman's nine-year-old daughter, Ann, spent a few days playing with little Marylyn.

Now, in New York, things had cooled and, with Kaufman increasingly unavailable, by November the affair was officially over. The two would remain friends, and with Kaufman's encouragement, Astor coauthored a short story for the *Saturday Evening Post*. In fact, Beatrice Kaufman had even invited Astor to one of her cocktail parties and the two were extremely cordial. It was Beatrice at her social and political best.

Since Bennett Cerf's marriage to actress Sylvia Sidney was on the rocks, he and Astor tried consoling each other during a weekend together at the Princeton-Dartmouth football game. Unfortunately, the game was played during a blinding blizzard, which pretty much summed up their time together—"too busy moaning their own misfortunes to console anybody else's."

During the rest of her trip to New York and her Christmas and New Year's in Miami and Havana, Astor spent her time with a variety of men. One of them was Daniel Silberberg, a New York stock broker. Following the Havana trip she was often at Silberberg's Park Avenue penthouse.

So, affair with Kaufman now officially ended, Astor spent her time with the kinds of sophisticates, literary and theatre, whose company she had always craved. For good or bad, Mary Astor was now ready to move on with her life.

• • •

The following May, when Astor had the baby back, Thorpe moved to an apartment in town. Wanting to keep the baby's home life stable, Astor purchased Thorpe's half of the Toluca Lake house, and on May 1, 1936, she moved in.

As for Mary Astor's movie career, things couldn't be better. Earning one of the highest salaries paid a featured player, monetarily she was at the top of her profession. In contrast, Astor's personal life was at its nadir, entirely due to Franklyn Thorpe. During that whole year Thorpe constantly dangled his custody of Marylyn over Astor's head. Whenever he disapproved of something that his ex-wife said or did, Thorpe would threaten to take away the baby. This intimidation not only served to make Astor insecure in her relationship with her daughter but also undermined it, because she felt that at any moment her baby might be snatched away from her.

The intimidation began soon after the divorce, when Astor saw Thorpe giving Marylyn a severe spanking over some minor infraction. Astor tried to stop him, but instead of listening, Thorpe told Astor to mind her own business. If she interfered, he would

ABOVE: Mary Astor and "Little" Marylyn.

RIGHT: Photograph taken at Toluca Lake house when Marylyn turned four.

BELOW: Marylyn out with her father.

take the child away. She was also told not to criticize his treatment of his daughter either to his face or behind his back to the servants.

Unhindered, Thorpe grew more severe and felt free to take out his anger on the baby. He now said and did things he would never have done if Astor had retained custody. "He would take hold of her," Astor related, "and jerk and spank her during a fit of temper just because he was angry at her for some little thing she did or couldn't do." Whenever this occurred Astor was forced to keep her mouth shut.

Thorpe's restrictions on Astor soon went beyond his punishing the baby. If Astor didn't implement a particular diet Thorpe had prescribed for the child, Astor would be threatened with the loss of her daughter. If Thorpe felt Astor was spoiling the baby, she would be threatened. As the year progressed, and Thorpe continually used Marylyn as pawn both for revenge and to remain connected, Astor felt herself being stripped of her parental authority.

Not long after moving back to Toluca Lake in May 1936, Astor spent an afternoon at the home of her friend, popular film actress Ann Harding. Astor talked candidly about her situation—the diaries, the divorce, and especially Thorpe's treatment of the baby. Harding was outraged. She herself had recently won a much-publicized court battle to regain full custody of her little girl. Hearing what Astor was experiencing, she was incensed. Harding was a strong-willed, independent woman who, when she believed herself in the right, did not hesitate to battle not only her ex-husband but also her Hollywood studio. So, after listening to Astor, she told her friend exactly what she thought; Thorpe was exerting the worst sort of blackmail, and Astor shouldn't sit down for it.

Understanding her friend's fear of the diaries' potential for scandal, Harding suggested that she speak to a good lawyer and recommended Roland Rich Woolley. He had handled her custody case brilliantly and was a gifted attorney who could help Astor.

A consultation was arranged. Woolley listened to what Astor had to say. Woolley told Astor that since Marylyn had been with her for a year, and was physically and emotionally fit, he didn't see why the court wouldn't grant her custody. He also told her that the diaries could make things sticky but he felt sure he could keep them out as evidence. As he would need time to put the case together, he asked Astor be patient a little while longer.

For the first time in over a year Mary Astor felt that there might be a chance to regain custody and end Franklyn Thorpe's tyranny. Astor also realized that, whether the diaries came into the case or not, there would be an enormous scandal and a good chance her career in films would be over. So, she devised a backup plan. "I prepared myself to take up some other line of work. I talked to the head buyer at Magnin Department Store and he assured me that with my knowledge of clothes they could use me as their head buyer in Paris."

Then, just about the time Woolley informed her that they were ready to go to court, things reached a head. On Sunday July 5, 1936, the doctor spent the day with Marylyn in Encino. Later that evening, while Astor was at home entertaining her friend, the English actress Evelyn Laye, Thorpe phoned to say that he couldn't make it back in time and planned to have dinner with the baby.

This was becoming a pattern. Whenever Thorpe took Marylyn out he would upset the baby's regular schedule. Mary Astor was an absolute stickler about consistency regarding the child's upbringing. She would carefully note the baby's daily schedule in the diary she kept in which she judiciously logged Marylyn's development. Having been raised by the whims of her overbearing father, Astor knew how crucial stability and consistency were in the development of an emotionally secure child. Therefore, Astor found what Thorpe was doing upsetting because it wrecked havoc on all her efforts to keep the baby's life regulated and stable.

In the past Thorpe's threats had made Astor keep her mouth shut. Tonight was different. She told him to bring the baby home immediately as she didn't want the child to miss her bedtime.

Thorpe didn't see the harm. Anyway, who was Astor to talk; she had kept the baby up the previous night watching Fourth of July fireworks. Astor told Thorpe that was exactly what the problem was.

The baby had been up late the night before. Staying up late a second night might be a problem as the strong-willed child would use this as an opportunity to test the rules.

Thorpe insisted that it wouldn't and told his ex-wife that he was going to bring the baby home late and was ready to get off the phone.

Astor was extremely upset but instead of concealing it—fortified by a pre-dinner cocktail—she told him in strong words that it wasn't right for him to interfere with the baby's regular schedule.

"I want her home before her bedtime. You've already caused her to miss her lunch and nap a few times already."

Thorpe's temper flared. He didn't like being given orders.

"I'll do exactly as I please."

"You're being so selfish. You only have your own interests at heart while I'm thinking of the baby's welfare."

"Don't interfere or there will be trouble."

The phone conversation ended and, true to his word, Thorpe brought the baby home a full hour past Marylyn's bedtime. Astor was livid.

"I'm getting tired of this. Whenever you take the baby out you bring her back late."

"You're the selfish person, Mary. All you're interested in is yourself."

"That's not true. I'm thinking of the child and you're not."

"She's my child as much as she's yours and I won't have you telling me what to do with her. You're not to interfere."

With actress Evelyn Laye looking on, Thorpe started harping on his paranoid-sounding idea that Astor was turning Marylyn against him. When Astor complained that there was absolutely no truth to this, Thorpe brought up Ardys Clark. Clark had been the baby's nurse from June 1934 until Thorpe had ordered her fired because he believed she had been influencing the baby against him. A year earlier Clark had voiced her concerns about his harsh punishments of Marylyn. This precipitated a gargantuan fight between Astor and

Thorpe. Shouting, pounding his fists on the table, and calling Astor names, Thorpe demanded that the woman be dismissed immediately.

"I won't stand for Ardys Clark being with my daughter. I know she is helping you turn Marylyn against me. If you don't promise me right now that you will fire her I will take the baby home with me tonight. Promise me that you will kick her out of this house or I will take the baby away from you."

Astor knew there was no reasoning with the man and so agreed to let the woman go. To Astor, her former husband only thought about the baby in terms of his needs. Because Clark had been with the baby for a considerable time she knew this would be difficult for Marylyn.

A year later, hearing Thorpe use the same threat again, ten minutes into his harangue, Astor was just as angry as her former husband.

"I never did anything to turn the child against you. You should know by now I don't think it's a good principle to turn a child against a father."

A shouting match ensued, which reached its climax when Astor told Thorpe that she was no longer afraid of him and if he wanted a fight "there was going to be war." That night Thorpe went home without the baby and Mary Astor called Roland Rich Woolley. Eight days later Woolley filed papers in the Los Angeles Superior Court demanding a reversal of the original court order granting Franklyn Thorpe custody of Marylyn. Thorpe was charged with coercing Mary Astor into agreeing to that action by threatening to "publicly scandalize her and ruin her career as an actress."

If this announcement had made Hollywood perk up its ears, the following day the town was stretching its neck. Rich Woolley filed a second complaint charging Franklyn Thorpe with bigamy and demanded that his divorce to Mary Astor "be set aside and their marriage declared void" because they had never been "legally" married. Lillian Miles, the Tampa widow, was named as Thorpe's common-law wife.

On July 27 Franklyn Thorpe, through his attorney Joseph

Anderson, filed his answer. Thorpe announced that he had in his possession diaries written by Mary Astor which demonstrated "her continuous gross immoral conduct" and would brand her "an unfit and improper person to have the custody and care" of her daughter.

To say that the tabloid press ate this up would be an understatement. They devoured it. It was exactly the kind of juicy Hollywood scandal reporters and editors dreamed about. It pushed everything else off the front page and would become the "hottest" story to come out of Hollywood in more than a decade, leaving "the motion-picture industry in an uproar." The Astor-Thorpe custody battle had begun and, during the coming weeks, men and women all over America would be reading and talking about little else.

THE TRIAL

7

By any standard, Roland Rich Woolley was a remarkably gifted attorney. Not only had he successfully handled Ann Harding's custody issue but, ten years earlier, had represented renowned evangelist Aimee Semple McPherson in a case that was in the headlines for months. The celebrated evangelist faced criminal charges for fabricating her own kidnapping but, with Woolley's assistance, walked free. Three years later, representing Charlie Chaplin's second wife Lita Grey, Woolley earned his client a $750,000 divorce settlement—the largest at that time. Consequently, when Mary Astor walked into his office, Roland Rich Woolley was known in legal circles as a heavy hitter and a tenacious courtroom fighter.

Few knew that Woolley was a Mormon. His parents were married by Brigham Young and his maternal grandfather was one of the Church's twelve apostles. Woolley was a Mormon with a capital M. Although married to the daughter of the former governor of Utah, Woolley had worked his way through school and was a self-made man in the purest sense of the word. Raised to believe that a committed work ethic would not only earn life's benefits but that these achievements were nothing less than God's boon to all mankind, Woolley saw it as his duty to rise high in his profession. On a business trip to Southern California in 1920, he had immediately recognized the opportunities for success in LA, and during the succeeding sixteen years Woolley's skill, brilliance, and "steel trap" knowledge of the law helped him to become one of the city's leading attorneys.

In short, Mary Astor had not merely put her life in the hands of a skilled attorney, but as events would show, Mary Astor had found herself the perfect attorney.

Since Franklyn Thorpe's intention was to besmirch Mary Astor's reputation and destroy her career, Woolley intended to fight fire with fire. Woolley knew that everyone had skeletons in their closet. Thorpe had threatened to use the diaries to prove Astor was an unfit mother. If the good doctor could be threatened with the same sort of vilification, Woolley believed that the two would cancel each other out. So the attorney had set his private detectives to digging.

Now, with confidential reports in hand, Woolley's plan was to attack Thorpe's moral character so that when the contents of the two-volume diary were made public it would be Thorpe's reputation that would come out the worse for it. Consequently, the attorney's first move began on July 13 with the original filings submitted to Judge Dudley S. Valentine—the judge who had granted the original divorce—and it came in the form of three distinct but related petitions.

The first—and most crucial—was a request for the court to reverse the order granting Franklyn Thorpe custody of Marylyn. It claimed that Thorpe had coerced Astor into agreeing to it by threatening to scandalize and ruin her career. Thorpe was characterized as a "willful overbearing, domineering, gruff and abusive person claiming to be right in everything" which, when added to the demands on him as a physician, rendered him unfit to care for Marylyn. Astor also requested the return of $4,500 in securities that Thorpe had obtained by threatening to deprive Astor of the companionship of her daughter. The upshot was that, until the case was settled, Mary Astor was granted temporary custody of Marylyn.

At the time, the "scandalizing" accusation was interpreted as a threat to expose an affair, with one New York tabloid printing that "Thorpe was thoroughly upset by the interest Mary showed in a noted married playwright." This was an obvious reference to Kaufman.

The second petition, filed the next day, charged Thorpe with bigamy. It requested that the court nullify the Astor-Thorpe marriage as it was—due to a previous marriage—illegal. The petition named Lillian Miles as Thorpe's common law wife, having lived as husband and wife in both Florida and Los Angeles.

This petition was basically a diversionary tactic. It was dubious at best whether a California court would recognize a Florida common law marriage and grant the bigamy petition. Something else was at work here. In any custody hearing, the moral fitness as well as the moral environment provided to a child by the parent is crucial in determining which parent would be granted custody. Therefore, the burden of proof would be on Thorpe to prove that being raised by her mother would thwart Marylyn's opportunity to grow up into a normal, healthy, psychologically adjusted adult. To do this Thorpe would essentially need to prove that Mary Astor was no better than a "fallen woman" and therefore unfit to raise her child.

Nevertheless, in 1936, a man living with a woman outside the "bonds of matrimony" was considered so morally repugnant and so socially unacceptable that it could destroy reputations and ostracize everyone involved. The bigamy petition was a shot at Thorpe's position that, regarding little Marylyn, he held the moral high ground.

The third petition, also filed on July 14, was a request for the court to void the April 12, 1935, property agreement regarding the $60,000 worth of stocks and real estate. Astor had signed over control because Thorpe had threatened to deprive her of the companionship of her daughter. This petition was designed to paint Franklyn Thorpe as nothing less than a bullying blackmailer.

As all three petitions were fundamentally character assassinations, it was clear to anyone who understood the press that Woolley planned to fight Thorpe on two fronts—in the courts as well as in the court of public opinion. A rather surprised and equally dumbfounded Franklyn Thorpe immediately issued a carefully worded statement authored by his attorney.

> I regret Mary's attitude and feel that she has been very badly advised. Heretofore, I've always tried in every way within my power to shield and protect Mary from any adverse criticism or publicity. But now that she is raising the question of custody, my responsibility to the child demands that I use every means that lies within my power for safeguarding Marylyn's future.

Thorpe was making it clear that he would make good his threat to use the diaries. Regarding the bigamy charge, Thorpe stated that "it seems to be absurd. Until my marriage to Miss Astor I had never been married before." Those words would come back to haunt him.

Meanwhile, Woolley fired a second shot by returning to court on July 23 and obtaining an injunction from Judge Ruben Schmidt preventing Franklyn Thorpe from disposing the $60,000 worth of securities and property the doctor had gained control of. Thorpe's parents, Sam and Cora Thorpe, were included in the injunction, the implication being that Thorpe had secretly transferred some of these securities to his financially strapped parents. On top of everything else, Franklyn Thorpe was now accused of being a thief.

That same day Thorpe's demurrer—pleading for dismissal of the custody suit on the grounds that it had no legal basis—was dismissed. This meant that the custody suit was ready to go to trial.

• • •

Between July 23 and the commencement of the custody hearing on July 28, Roland Rich Woolley deposed Franklyn Thorpe and Lillian Miles in his office regarding the bigamy petition. By this time Thorpe had retained the services of an experienced trial attorney, Joseph Anderson. Although Ethel Pepin was a competent attorney, a trial is a highly adversarial proceeding requiring attorneys with specialized skills. Consequently, Pepin now became a member of Anderson's legal team.

Just as Woolley expected, Thorpe refused, under advice of counsel, to answer key questions regarding his Florida and Los Angeles relationship with Lillian Miles. Although the bigamy charge and custody petition were separate actions, they were inextricably intertwined due to the issue of "moral fitness." If Thorpe had answered yes to any of those questions it would automatically become admissible in the custody hearing. By not answering, Thorpe prevented Woolley from using his answers against Thorpe during questioning at the hearing.

Lillian Miles was another matter. She and Thorpe had had a common law marriage; that claim was absolutely true. In fact it was Lillian who, unwilling to deal with social ostracism, had led people to believe that the two were married. Now living in Los Angeles with her fifteen-year-old son and sick mother, the thirty-five-year-old widow of an Army officer desperately needed to maintain the aura of respectability.

Since a Florida common law marriage would not be accepted in California, Anderson's office had filed a second demurrer attacking the bigamy complaint, pleading for dismissal of the bigamy suit on the grounds that there was no legal basis for Astor's request. So, hoping that the bigamy suit wouldn't go anywhere, Miles had lied at the deposition—and planned to continue lying.

Woolley had hoped Franklyn Thorpe would be unwilling to perjure himself, thereby providing Woolley with ammunition. In not answering these questions an inference could be drawn by the public that the charges were true, and Woolley was now prepared to use that inference to his advantage.

• • •

Since attorneys at this time liked to file their answers to petitions at the last possible moment, Woolley knew that Thorpe's would be filed on Monday July 27, the day before the custody hearing was scheduled to begin. It was a purely tactical maneuver, giving the opposing side as little time as possible to digest the material.

Since Woolley knew what was in the diaries, he implemented a pre-emptive strike. Hours before Thorpe's reply was to be filed with the probate judge, Arthur Keetch, and with spectators and the press gaping, Roland Rich Woolley filed an Order To Show Cause as to why Dr. Thorpe should not be held in contempt for failing to answer the questions put him during the deposition. Judge Keetch gave Thorpe until August 10, to show why he should not answer the questions. Woolley then requested that, if Thorpe still refused to answer these questions, Judge Keetch hold him in contempt and have Thorpe immediately jailed until he did answer them. Playing legal hardball, Woolley was making it clear that possession of the diaries didn't automatically mean a slam-dunk in Thorpe's favor.

• • •

A few hours later Franklyn Thorpe and Joseph Anderson responded to the original July 13 custody petition. In their answer Dr. Thorpe "alleges that the petitioner has left writings admitting her gross immoral conduct" and "is an unfit and improper person to have guardianship of their 4 year old child." The answer even quoted passages from the diaries to support their claim:

> February 6, 1935: Why the hell I keep writing things down in this book I don't know. It seems to help me for some reason. I am such a muddle-headed person that I have to tie my thoughts down so that they won't go skittering off in all directions. Then too, maybe Marylyn someday would like to know what sort of person her mother was and maybe she will be consoled when she makes mistakes and gets into jams to know that her mother was a champion at making mistakes. I blush a little (very little) at the idea of her reading some of the stuff in this book. I have been and am such a fool.
>
> February 8, 1935: (Note to Marylyn) Never admit to anything to anybody. Honesty is not the best policy.

The introduction of that diary and those excerpts—with the implication that there was more to come—made banner headlines from one end of the country to the other. Within hours a media horde was preparing to descend on Los Angeles. Reporters would soon be flying in by the planeload to cover the trial, all of them "clamoring for the diary." In short, the media feeding frenzy had begun.

8

Five months earlier, Mary Astor had begun a five-picture contract with Columbia and was immediately rushed into two mediocre pictures. But the third picture, a loan out to Sam Goldwyn to appear in *Dodsworth*, would prove an unexpected blessing.

Dodsworth, based on the novel by Sinclair Lewis, tells the story of Sam Dodsworth, who after building a successful automobile company decides to sell it and, at age fifty, retire to tour Europe with his forty-one-year-old wife, Fran. Fran, a dutiful wife and mother for twenty years, cannot accept middle age, feeling that life is somehow passing her by. So, while in Europe, she takes up with a series of younger men, first in harmless flirtations and eventually in a full-scale affair. Sam weathers the storm by returning to the States and waiting for his wife's need to burn itself out. When Sam returns to Europe, Fran announces that she wants a divorce so she can marry a much younger, though impoverished, German count. While in Europe, Sam renews his acquaintance with Edith Cortright, an American widow living in Naples. Like Sam she is not impressed by titles and what both consider European pretension. They soon fall in love and plan a future together once Fran's divorce goes through. When the count calls off the wedding, Sam leaves Edith to rejoin Fran. Seeing Fran now, Sam immediately realizes exactly what a selfish, self-centered, and mean-spirited woman Fran has turned into. Because remaining with her will again suck the life out of him, Sam returns to Edith Cortright, anxious to begin their life together.

With Walter Huston set to repeat his acclaimed stage performance as Sam and Ruth Chatterton cast as Fran Dodsworth, Mary Astor was chosen to play Edith Cortright. Accordingly, during

Cast of *Dodsworth*: Paul Lukas, Ruth Chatterton, Astor, and Walter Huston.

May 1936, Astor reported to work at the United Artists studio for costume fittings, with actual filming set for June, July, and August.

When filming began Sam Goldwyn wasn't in Hollywood but in New York, where he had been since April. Diagnosed with intestinal toxemia following the removal of his appendix and gall bladder, Goldwyn's condition worsened, and the producer was given two hours to live. Fortunately, the medication took effect and, once he rallied, surgeons removed a substantial portion of his intestines. His health returning, Goldwyn was making a slow recovery. He'd be back in Hollywood in early July, when he planned to direct studio operations from his sickbed.

Directing *Dodsworth* was William Wyler, who brought to the set the sensibilities that would make him a legend in Hollywood. During his lifetime William Wyler would be nominated for more academy awards than any other director, and his films would earn their performers a total of thirty-six nominations. Wyler was a master of subjective cinema—using exterior means to bring the audience into a character's mind in order to understand and identify with a character in ways few directors could understand, much less achieve.

Wyler accomplished this by using subtle external gestures—a

look, a glance, a startled reaction, or even a small accident to which an actor would respond spontaneously. Unfortunately, Wyler was not a director who verbalized what he wanted. Rather, he knew what he wanted only after he had gotten it. If this required fifty takes, Wyler would shoot them, because for him, what was up on the screen was the only thing that mattered. Since Walter Huston had played Sam Dodsworth on Broadway, he was letter perfect and saw Wyler's endless takes as occasionally tedious, but simply part of the job. In addition, he and Wyler had already worked together five years earlier, and Huston's son, John, was one of William Wyler's best friends.

Because Astor's role wasn't large, she was able to sit on the sidelines and study the director's methods. She found Wyler intelligent and tough, a meticulous taskmaster who knew how to get what he wanted, even if it required outright bullying. In short, he "was not a 'that's marvelous, darling,' type." She thought his excessive takes "made actors sweat, it made them work harder in some cases. A scene might improve with repetition or it might deteriorate and Willy was seeking the one that was 'just right.'" Although he could be prickly and sharp-tongued, he and Astor "got into step very quickly." She would note in her diary, "I've struggled along now for years doing nothing outstanding but learning a lot. It has served its purpose in being a sort of apprenticeship but I think it's almost over."

After years of toiling on that "treadmill of trash," as she liked to call her earlier films, she now had the technical skill to work with a director of Wyler's caliber; a director who would do whatever was necessary to get the best out of her. Astor had come to believe that the greatest sense of fulfillment she could achieve as a film actress was to thoroughly communicate with her director. She would say, "You don't have to like him, but you have to respect his judgment or you're in trouble." Consequently, trying to give Wyler what he wanted, she found herself creating a character that was living and breathing; brought to life in ways that she had never been permitted to do in her sixteen years working in films. As another actress who also got into step with Wyler put it, "If he trusted actors he gave them a chance to be creative and we could do whatever instinctively we felt like doing."

In addition, Wyler was such an astute judge of his players that he immediately knew Astor would not respond to negative criticism, with its shades of her father. As she put it, "he could use spurs but not a whip. Willy simply expected an actor to know his job. He guided, rather than directed. He wasted no time giving lessons in acting." Wyler would set up the scene, and Astor did her best to give the director what he wanted.

• • •

Ruth Chatterton proved an entirely different matter. Chatterton was a strong-willed, opinionated woman who hadn't the slightest hesitation saying what she thought about anything, including Wyler's direction.

A Broadway star in her teens, by her thirties Chatterton was producing her own plays and pretty much controlled her career. Then, as her stage career waned, she found herself in Hollywood, where her film career flourished. Although her recent films hadn't done well, Chatterton was still a star of the first rank who intended to play Fran Dodsworth exactly the way she wanted and didn't anticipate any problems.

As Sinclair Lewis had written her, and Sidney Howard presented her on Broadway, Fran Dodsworth was a woman of superficial values who, exhibiting pretentious attempts at sophistication, was often embarrassed by her husband's plain-speaking midwestern American attitude. In other words, Fran was "a bitch" who eventually drove her husband into the arms of another woman, and that was how Ruth Chatterton intended to play her.

Wyler saw things differently. It made absolutely no sense to him that Sam Dodsworth would have been happily married to this kind of woman and, once retired, would want to spend the rest of his life with her. Therefore, Wyler interpreted Fran as a simple but multifaceted woman at a very sensitive point in her life who just couldn't "read between the lines." Desperate, like many women at her stage of life who could not accept aging and their lost youth, Fran got herself in too deep. Not really knowing her husband, she eventually lost him. Thus, as William Wyler saw it, Fran Dodsworth was a tragic figure for whom an audience would feel pity and certainly not as a bitch they would despise.

Chatterton wouldn't hear of it. From the first day working with Wyler to the last, each day was a pitched battle. Chatterton would, like many actors before her, come to hate Wyler and consider him a bully. Consequently, in the process of literally pulling out of Chatterton her greatest screen performance, Wyler likened it to pulling teeth, because "she played Fran like a heavy and we had momentous fights every day." Many have speculated that it was this tension between director and actor that made its way into Chatterton's edgy and nervous performance, which comes across as the temperament of a frightened and desperate woman. Mary Astor concluded that Chatterton detested Fran Dodsworth because "the character was that of a woman who is trying to hang onto her youth—which was exactly what Ruth herself was doing. It touched a nerve." In a sense, in playing Fran, Chatterton was playing herself. Consequently, Wyler bullied out of Chatterton a complex performance of a woman whose "tragic flaw" causes her to lose her husband and is the reason why Chatterton's performance is as luminous as it is.

Astor couldn't help being impressed, watching this strong-willed woman who never flinched or backed down. Astor often wished that she had the determination to take on life the way Chatterton did. Since the two women were intelligent, avid readers, appreciated good music, and enjoyed challenging and engaging conversation, Astor would recount, "I loved Ruth and we became close friends." Exactly how close, Mary Astor would soon discover.

• • •

During the *Dodsworth* shoot, Astor and Roland Rich Woolley prepared for the custody hearing. Astor recalled, "I spent many long hours talking to Woolley as it took a long time to tell him all that he wanted to know" and although she found Woolley "a genial, sympathetic man" he also had "a mind like a steel trap."

Writer Marcus Goodrich, Astor's current inamorato, was proving a great help. A friend of Ann Harding, the former newspaperman was in Hollywood earning easy money writing film scripts. He was bright and had been helping Woolley with suggestions and insights.

Although Goodrich could quickly knock out film work, he was laboring on his first novel, a fictional account of his time on a Navy destroyer during the war. No George Kaufman, Goodrich was good-looking, bright, well-educated and, still speaking with a slight Texas accent, had a sophisticated air enhanced by the ornate walking stick he carried. It was no great love affair—Goodrich was too much the womanizer—but more a friendship. He provided Astor the shoulder to lean on that she needed right then.

Learning about the upcoming trial, many whom Astor had considered good friends were now suddenly shying away from her. She had gotten the message early when she called English actress Evelyn Laye. Laye had been at the Toluca Lake house the night of the July 5 blow-up between Astor and Thorpe. But when Astor asked Laye if she could drop by Woolley's office to give her version of the events, Laye politely refused, telling Astor that "she was going to have a baby and the effort would make her too nervous." The actress was lying. In 1930 Laye had been involved in a very messy divorce in England. Knowing how ugly and very public these things could become, Laye didn't want any part of it.

Others didn't feel quite the same way. Before shooting began on *Dodsworth* Mary Astor—wanting to prepare her director for what might happen—told Wyler about the upcoming custody hearing and warned him that it "was going to make a big stink." Wyler shrugged it off, telling her, "What the hell, nobody's going to pay much attention."

William Wyler may have been a great director, but as a fortune-teller, he didn't have a clue.

9

Los Angeles is a company town. Accordingly, the city's court system understands that if stars are in court and not on set, it can cost film companies money. As the studios are among the town's leading employers, the courts make allowances. Consequently, the custody hearing was set for evening sessions beginning at 7:00 p.m.

Eleven hours earlier there had been a knock on the front door at 128 South Canon Drive in Beverly Hills. The door half opened and, dressed in her bedclothes, Mrs. Lillian Lawton Miles was startled to see an anxious gaggle of reporters. Asked whether she was *the* Lillian Lawton Miles, she nodded and, in a Southern accent, replied: "Yes, but I can't see you right now. You just got me out of bed. Can you come back in ten minutes?"

They could and they did. Since Miles's demurrer—and possible dismissal of the bigamy petition—would be ruled on in a few hours, she was optimistic that whatever she told reporters wouldn't come back to haunt her. Wanting to stave off social ostracism, Miles knew that when she lied regarding her time in Florida with Thorpe, she needed to be convincing.

Ten minutes later Mrs. Miles opened her front door, and reporters were invited into "a luxuriously furnished apartment by a pretty, fetching and vivacious blonde whose fluffing hair tumbled down her attractive face." Lillian Miles then skillfully conducted what is best described as an impromptu press conference.

When asked whether Mary Astor's charge that Miles was married to Thorpe was true her answer was emphatic.

"There is absolutely not a word of truth to it. There is no truth in any of Miss Astor's charges. I believe Miss Astor's charge that the doctor and I were married is her attempt to blacken the doctor's name before he gets into court." To show she meant business, Miles pointed her finger directly at the reporter. "I am ready for a real fight to protect my name."

Jotting down her answers, reporters plied her with questions.

"Is it true that you and Dr. Thorpe lived together in Florida and that after you both came here you occupied an apartment with him?"

"It is absolutely and viciously untrue; just as it is ridiculous that I was Dr. Thorpe's common law wife. Dr. Thorpe has been our family physician for many years. He is a splendid person. It is absolutely ridiculous for Miss Astor to charge that I was Dr. Thorpe's common law wife. I refuse to enter further into any discussion of details because as far as I am concerned, the whole thing is untrue. I have a fifteen-year-old son and my name means something to me, even though others' names don't seem to mean anything to them."

Miles couldn't resist getting in that dig at Astor. It was obvious to everyone in the room that there was no love lost between these two women.

"What are you going to testify in court?"

Having been coached by her attorney, she became evasive.

"I don't know what I will do in court but will act on the advice of my attorney. I must tell you, I loathe this publicity. My name has never been before the public before."

That would soon change. In less than twenty-four hours this impromptu news conference would become page-one news all over America. As Mrs. Miles would soon learn, talking to the press wasn't necessarily the best thing to do when one loathed publicity. As the next day's headlines would demonstrate, it has quite the opposite effect.

• • •

Later that morning Roland Rich Woolley and Joseph Anderson stood in Judge Reuben Schmidt's courtroom. Woolley had submitted papers requesting that the court consolidate the custody and the annulment suit into a single hearing. In this way Woolley could make the bigamy issue central in proving that Thorpe was morally unfit to have custody of little Marylyn. If the petition was granted, Woolley could question Thorpe on the witness stand regarding the common law marriage, and Thorpe would be forced to tell the truth.

In his answer Joseph Anderson argued that "different issues" were involved "and any consolidation of the two suits would confuse the proceedings." Judge Schmidt then set a date for his decision.

Soon after, in Judge Kenny's courtroom, the demurrer on which Lillian Miles had pinned her hope that the bigamy complaint would be thrown out was dismissed. Judge Kenny also overruled a second demurrer filed for Thorpe's parents concerning Thorpe transferring assets received in the original divorce settlement. The long and short was that the custody hearing was set to commence at 7:00 p.m. that evening.

• • •

Finished filming for the day, Mary Astor was alone in her studio dressing room changing for court. She and Woolley had worked out a legal strategy designed not only to give Astor custody but possibly save her movie career. Therefore, her choice of clothing as well as her courtroom conduct had been carefully worked out. Astor would follow certain strict rules: dress modestly, say nothing to the press, and at all times during the proceedings, keep her temper in check and her true feelings hidden. Mary Astor was to remain reserved— her demeanor under tight control.

Woolley knew that, when talking to the press, the press could distort. Woolley's baptism by fire had been the Amy McPherson trial ten years earlier, when newspapers printed whatever they wanted regardless of whether it was true or not. Then, once it was in print, the public pretty much accepted it as fact. This would not happen here. Until Mary Astor was on the stand giving testimony she would avoid the press, and Woolley wouldn't issue any statements unless they were absolutely necessary and pertained to what was coming out in the courtroom.

Mary Astor as Edith Cortright.

That first day Mary Astor chose a simple black tailored suit, visor hat with a white, ruffled lace blouse. Although she would not be called as a witness that day—merely sit at the counsel table beside her attorney—everyone's eyes would be focused on her. Being the principal attraction at tonight's proceedings, Astor knew that she needed to steel herself for what would be an extremely difficult time.

Despite sixteen years in the public eye, Mary Astor was basically a shy person who found public appearances difficult. Now, in front of the entire world, her private life was about to go public in the worst possible light. Therefore, Astor planned to get through this the only way she knew. Instead of a nervous, angry, extremely worried and frightened Mary Astor, the person sitting in that courtroom would be Edith Cortright—her character in *Dodsworth*.

"The person that I clung to as a close friend was Edith Cortright, the character that I was playing. She was three dimensional in my mind and I knew all about her. She has those rare qualities, wisdom and balance; two qualities which at that point in time I was sadly lacking. She was a lot of things that I wasn't, she was a lot of things I would like to have been. She had complete confidence in herself and I had very little. She was not talkative; she listened to everyone with a gentle, no comment smile. She walked tall; she made no unnecessary gestures or movements. She was cool."

It was in this way that Mary Astor fortified herself to endure what for her would be the unendurable.

• • •

Heading for the studio gate, Astor ran into Ruth Chatterton. Chatterton knew where Mary Astor was going; everyone did. Chatterton saw a woman in trouble for doing what she believed right, deserted by friends so frightened for their careers that they had lost sight of their common humanity. Astor looked half dead and desperately needed someone to stand with her. Chatterton also saw determination and courage. If there was one quality Ruth Chatterton admired, it was courage. Having taken a year off acting to become a leading American aviatrix, time and again courage and skill in the cockpit had saved her life. Thus, to Chatterton fear of Hollywood ostracism simply didn't exist. Seeing Astor, the world seemingly against her, Chatterton got right to the point.

"Do you have anyone with you?"

Astor nodded. "Mark Goodrich is working with Woolley."

"No, that's not what I mean. I mean someone to sit in the front row; someone you know is on your team and can give you a wink of encouragement. Someone that you know will be there for you?"

Knowing exactly what she meant, Astor shook her head.

"All right then, I'll drive you down and be with you!"

Chatterton had planned to spend the evening with German émigré director Fritz Lang who, along with Spanish musician-conductor Jose Iturbi, was a current "beau."

Ruth Chatterton was fascinated by the American judicial system. As a lark, Chatterton had worked as a crime reporter for a Los Angeles newspaper covering the murder trial of a man convicted of the gruesome killing of a twelve-year-old girl. Based on the evidence, Chatterton felt that he was innocent and his execution a miscarriage of justice. Since Lang's first American film was *Fury*, a powerful indictment of mob violence as well as the American court system, Chatterton was frequently on the set. Lang's second American film, yet another study of the pitfalls of the American justice system, would soon be shooting on the United Artist's lot. Therefore, it was logical that both Chatterton and Fritz Lang would be interested in the custody hearing. Evening plans now changed, and with Ruth at the wheel, the three headed for the courthouse.

Chatterton would prove an enormous help during the weeks ahead. Since Chatterton had a first-rate mind, analytical and incisive, she used it to pick Roland Rich Woolley's brain, compelling him to rethink his strategy. As Chatterton's independent expression of ideas could only benefit Woolley, during the coming days Chatterton's unstinting support of Mary Astor would prove crucial.

Years later Mary Astor would write of Chatterton, "Woolley said she should have been a lawyer; he seemed to enjoy matching minds with her, and they had many a heated discussion in the office."

10

The courthouse was worse than Astor feared; it was a circus. Not only were food venders selling snacks in the hallways, the courtroom was so packed that overflow crowds filled the corridor. Astor, Chatterton, Lang, and Woolley waded through the crowds without saying a word. The same could not be said for Franklyn Thorpe. Arriving thirty minutes earlier he had paused to make a brief, self-serving statement to the press.

"I had hoped to protect Mary. I'm sorry for what's going to come out."

Once inside the courtroom, flashbulbs popping, Astor took a seat at the far left of the single long counsel table beside Woolley. Chatterton and Lang sat in the front row directly behind her. Since America was experiencing one of the most severe heat waves in history, the room was sweltering. Nevertheless, Mary Astor gave the impression of a cool, emotionless, almost indifferent attitude to the brouhaha swirling around her. On the inside, it was a different matter. Although "it was all pretty hairy" and she was "under a great emotional strain," "walking a very thin line," never once during the trial did she let it show, and both the press and the public rarely found fault with her courtroom demeanor.

At the far left of the counsel table a stone-faced Franklyn Thorpe sat with his attorneys. Only six feet apart, neither he nor Astor made any effort to look at the other. Instead, as instructed, they kept their eyes straight ahead.

Mrs. Lillian Miles was also in the courtroom. This "Beverly Hills Matron," was dressed in black with a broad black hat and a white jacket. Subpoenaed as a witness, she wouldn't be taking the

LEFT: Woolley and Astor entering the courtroom.
RIGHT: Marcus Goodrich and Ruth Chatterton, her arm around Astor.

stand that day, and was not required to be here. Nonetheless, that bigamy charge hanging over her, nothing short of an act of god would have prevented her from sitting in that courtroom.

Presiding at the custody hearing was Superior Court Judge Goodwin Knight. At thirty-nine, Knight had been on the bench for about a year. A self-made man who had worked his way through school, Knight had practiced law for a number of years before taking a seat on the bench. In his year as a judge he had earned the reputation as a no-nonsense jurist who could easily handle a high-profile Hollywood divorce or a case involving the "average Joe." Knight was married with two daughters—one named Marilyn, and the second close to little Marylyn's age.

The first hour of the three-hour session was taken up with Woolley's second attempt to tie the custody, bigamy, and property settlement suits into a single hearing. During a procedural meeting a week earlier, Judge Knight had made it clear that the court was only interested in events occurring after the divorce—when Thorpe had custody of Marylyn. Woolley then asked for a continuance, or temporary suspension of the proceedings, to travel to Florida and obtain further evidence of Thorpe's previous marriage. As this was bigamy, it would invalidate the Thorpe-Astor marriage, rendering the custody hearing moot. As might be expected, Joseph Anderson was strongly opposed, arguing that this was merely a delaying tactic.

Once arguments were concluded, Knight, as he had done a week earlier, asked the attorneys if there was any possibility that, "for the best interests of the child," a compromise might be possible. The request had failed then and it failed today as well. Although Joseph Anderson was open to it, Woolley was not. Concluding that the common-law-marriage issue had lost Franklyn Thorpe the initiative, Woolley believed that the man was frightened of exposure and that his fear was the reason he was suddenly open to compromise.

Knowing they were in for the long haul, Judge Knight took a deep breath and announced he would render his decision regarding the consolidation and a continuance the following night. After signing a restraining order preventing either parent from taking Marylyn out of Los Angeles County, he called a brief recess and returned to chambers.

• • •

During the break Astor listened to Woolley's opinion on what had just occurred and then joined Ruth Chatterton. Arms around each other, Chatterton was announcing to the court, press, and public alike her unstinting support of Mary Astor. Not only did every newspaper in America report this, many also began calling Chatterton Mary Astor's best friend, which in truth, at this point in time, she actually was.

When Judge Knight returned to the crowded courtroom, everyone was talking and the courtroom had a party atmosphere. Bringing the court into session, Knight put a stop to that by announcing that under no circumstance would he allow any demonstration during testimony. That said, he turned to Roland Rich Woolley and nodded for him to begin. Woolley stood and called his first witness—Dr. Franklyn Thorpe.

• • •

Franklyn Thorpe rose from the counsel table and confidently strode to the witness box where, after being sworn in, he took a seat. Described as "tight lipped and hard eyed," Thorpe saw Woolley as the enemy and intended to treat him as such. This was the worst possible approach he could have taken. Unlike Thorpe, this was not personal for Woolley. Unhampered by emotions, he could play the chess board with a clear head. Consequently, Woolley conducted a methodical, carefully constructed, point-by-point examination.

In calling Thorpe as a witness, Woolley had three objectives. One: establish that, in direct contradiction to what was stated in the cross petition, Thorpe's actions in the preceding fifteen months did not demonstrate his belief that Mary Astor was "an unfit and improper person to have custody." Two: prove that, during the time that Marylyn was in the care of her father, Thorpe's actions had not been in the best interests of the child and thus it was her father, not her mother, who was unfit to have guardianship. Three: set the groundwork to prove that, while on the stand, Franklyn Thorpe was either misstating facts or, in some cases, lying, and in this way open to questioning the veracity of anything the man might state under oath or in paperwork submitted to the court. Asking a set of leading questions, questions containing specific information that Thorpe could either confirm or deny, this would enable Woolley to control Thorpe's overall testimony.

After some preliminary questions, Woolley asked Thorpe what circumstances had been involved in him finally taking charge of the child in October 1935, a full six months after being awarded custody.

"She told me that she wanted to go to New York and we agreed that I should have the child."

This was Thorpe's first lie.

"Is it not a fact she went to New York because you took the child?"

"It is not."

"Dr. Thorpe, considering you had signed an affidavit alleging that Miss Astor was not a 'proper person' to have custody of a child of 'impressionable age,' you permitted Marylyn to remain

Franklyn Thorpe on the witness stand.

with her mother this summer when the court gave you full custody last year. Could you please explain that to the court?"

"It was after I sold my half of our Toluca Lake house to Miss Astor."

"And how much were you paid?"

"$5,000."

Aware that the disparity between the doctor's income and his former wife's was a sore point, Woolley pressed forward. As any good trial attorney knows, if you attack a witness in an emotional area, it can make them distraught and confused. So Woolley attempted to get Thorpe's temper up.

"Did you turn Marylyn over to her mother because Miss Astor bought your half of the home?"

Angry at the implication, Thorpe answered in a flash of temper. "I did not."

"Then why did you not have the child?"

Temper having gotten the better of him, his "steel blue eyes were flashing," Thorpe answered without thinking. His reply was patently absurd.

"I hoped that she would be an influence for good over the mother."

Laughter rippled throughout the courtroom. Immediately realizing his gaff, once the courtroom was brought back to order, Thorpe clarified, "I felt that while Marylyn was with her mother, I could keep an eye on her."

Taking on Woolley head-on wasn't working. So Thorpe did his best to remain calm. Sizing up his witness, Woolley had also learned something. Franklyn Thorpe lied and lied often.

"And how long did the child stay with its mother?"

"From the time of our divorce until October 10 of last year."

"And is it not true that she paid the expenses?"

"Yes."

"It was not because Miss Astor had to bear the expenses?"

Anderson objected and, as Knight overruled, Thorpe fought to keep his temper in check as he once again lied.

"I let her pay all the expenses because she insisted on it. I repeatedly offered to share them. I offered to pay everything but she told me she wanted to feel she had something to do with the baby inasmuch as I have been given guardianship."

Woolley let the lie pass as he deftly guided the testimony.

"Was the child ever lacking?"

"No, she supplied the child with every material benefit."

"Did you visit the child during that time?"

"Yes. Three times a week."

"Did Miss Astor ever make this difficult?"

"No."

"Did you find the child cared for?"

"Yes."

"Did she treat the child in a motherly manner?"

Woolley's plan of attack was becoming evident. So, Thorpe was hesitant, trying to come up with an answer that wouldn't contradict his court filing.

"Well, no. I did not…. She did not appear devoted but acting from a sense of duty."

Woolley then set out to carefully prove an allegation in Astor's original petition.

"While your former wife was in New York, isn't it true that she sent your daughter all sorts of toys and gifts?"

Thorpe grew defensive. "Yes, but I also bought her clothes and playthings."

"Was there anything that you objected to while Marylyn was in the care of her mother?"

"Yes."

"And what was that?"

"The presence of nurse Ardys Clark."

"And what did you object to?"

"She didn't carry out my instructions."

"Regarding?"

"Marylyn's diet."

"And what happened to this nurse?"

"I demanded that she be dismissed and she was."

In the complaint Thorpe was described as intransigent and intemperate. In admitting that, during the Great Depression, he had a nurse fired merely to demonstrate his authority, Thorpe had just proven the claim in Astor's petition.

Having accomplished his first goal—disproving that Thorpe believed Astor unfit to care for the child—Woolley moved onto his second, the type of environment the father provided. Woolley now introduced Norma Taylor into the proceedings.

Norma Taylor was a showgirl who, with no discernible talent, had made her way in show business on her looks. Between 1931 and 1935 she appeared in six inconsequential B movies, in roles not much more than walk-ons. Prior to Taylor's Hollywood sojourn, her claim to fame had been her appearance in the Ziegfeld Follies, her scantily clad dancing in Texas Guinan's speakeasy, and her very public romance with playboy Tommy Manville, eccentric asbestos heir and publicity hound.

Woolley introduced Miss Taylor by bringing up the "relief" nurses utilized when Marylyn's regular nurse, Nellie Richardson, had her day off.

"That was Thursday, wasn't it?"

"Yes."

"On frequent occasions, didn't they stay in the house overnight?"

Thorpe was emphatic. "Never! They did not."

Again Thorpe was lying.

"Do you know a woman named Norma Taylor?"

Joseph Anderson vehemently objected but was overruled. Anderson was soon making objection after objection while, undaunted, Rich Woolley kept moving forward.

"Do you know Norma Taylor?"

"Yes."

"Did Miss Taylor ever act as a relief nurse for the child?"

"She was not. She did not act as relief nurse for Marylyn."

Thorpe grew uncomfortable. It soon would become apparent why.

"Didn't she sometimes take care of Marylyn? That is, prepare her dinner and put her to bed?"

"She might have helped me when I did those things. She used to come out and have dinner with me. But she wasn't a nurse and she didn't care for the baby."

"Was she not a frequent visitor at your home and did she not on occasion stay there all night?"

Thorpe struggled to keep his temper in check.

"She never stayed there all night!"

"All right then. Isn't it true that she frequently occupied the same bedroom with you, whether she stayed there all night or not?"

To control his temper Thorpe locked his hands together and gritted his teeth so hard that reporters could see his jaw muscles bulging in hard high knots beneath his ears.

"Norma Taylor never occupied any bedroom in my house."

Astor, sitting at the counsel table, casually stared at her shoe tops and then her fingers as she had done during most of Thorpe's testimony. Behind her Ruth Chatterton and Fritz Lang, like everyone else in that crowded, sweltering courtroom, couldn't take their eyes off Thorpe.

"Did she not share breakfast with you on several occasions?"

Anderson objected, and his objection was overruled while, no longer able to contain it, Thorpe's temper flared. He shouted vehemently.

"She did not!"

Woolley casually strolled over to the counsel table, picked up three snapshots, and entered them as evidence. Two were of Dr. Thorpe with blonde Norma Taylor in the garden of the Toluca Lake house embracing. The third was of Norma Taylor alone. In the first photo Thorpe and Taylor were kissing with Taylor's arms wrapped

Norma Taylor night clubbing with Tommy Manville.

around Thorpe's neck. Handed the snapshots, Thorpe immediately calmed. Staring at the photos in disbelief, it was obvious he had forgotten all about them.

"Is the woman in these snapshots Norma Taylor?"

Thorpe drew a deep breath. "Yes."

"Now, didn't you have some trouble with Miss Taylor on one occasion—a little disturbance at the house?"

"Well she was at a cocktail party across the street. She called up while Marylyn and I were having dinner. I could tell she was intoxicated, so I told her not to come to the house. But she did anyway. She forced her way in. So I called the police and they took her away."

Thorpe wasn't telling the whole truth, and Woolley called him out on it.

"Oh, that wasn't all, was it, Dr. Thorpe? Didn't you wrestle with her first—in Marylyn's presence?"

"No, she came into the dining room, and I told the nurse to take Marylyn to her room. Then I took Miss Taylor by the wrists and escorted her to the hall, by the front door. She grabbed a silver candlestick and smashed a window. She was intoxicated."

The packed audience was described as watching "goggle-eyed and gasping."

"As a matter of fact, you'd had a few, too, hadn't you?"

"No. Then the police came."

"But they didn't find the two of you in the hallway together, did they? Weren't you upstairs in the bathroom with Miss Taylor on the floor and you on top of her?"

"I don't remember the details."

"Oh come now Dr. Thorpe, please. Search your memory."

Many in the courtroom were grinning, as Thorpe's evasiveness was hopelessly ineffective. He finally looked up.

"Yes, I do recall that I tried to restrain her but she broke away from me and ran upstairs. She tried to lock herself in, but I got through the door and grabbed her. We fell down in a tussle."

"And the baby saw all this, didn't she?"

"Absolutely not! She was in her room."

Again Thorpe was lying. Marylyn had seen Taylor running down the corridor, but Nellie Richardson grabbed the baby and carried her into the bedroom.

"This Miss Taylor was your sweetheart, wasn't she?"

"No, just a friend."

Woolley wouldn't let up, not with those snapshots.

"But an intimate friend?"

Thorpe's voice rose along with his temper.

"No!"

"You saw her even after that occasion, didn't you?"

"Only once."

"When did this occur?"

"Toward the end of the year."

"Do you recall the date?"

"I don't remember the exact date. It was on Christmas while Miss Astor was in New York."

Even after what had happened, Thorpe still had this emotionally unstable woman to house while Marylyn was there. Woolley had deftly made his point. He now brought up another woman.

"Do you know Betty Grant?"

"Yes."

"Did she visit your home?"

"Yes."

"Often?"

"Several times."

"Was this in the capacity of a relief nurse?"

"Not exactly."

"And Madge Schofield. Did she also visit your home?"

Madge Schofield was the divorced wife of screenwriter Paul Schofield, with whom Thorpe had shared the house and was now sharing an apartment.

"Yes, she is the former wife of Paul Schofield."

"And did she act as one of these relief nurses?"

"Yes."

"Do you know a Mrs. Lillian Lawton Miles?"

Anderson shot to his feet. This objection was his most vehement of the day. Again he was overruled. As this was the woman accused of bigamy, every neck was stretched to hear. Mrs. Miles tried her best not to show any emotion. It proved difficult.

Woolley repeated the question.

"Do you know a Mrs. Lillian Miles?"

"Yes."

"Did she also come to your home?"

"Yes."

"Was this also in the capacity of a relief nurse?"

"Yes, on occasion, but her mother was always there as well."

"Did she ever spend the night?"

Anderson objected, was overruled, and Woolley repeated the question. "She sometimes stayed all night with you, didn't she?"

"She never did. Never!"

"Well, weren't there times when you and she had breakfast in bed?"

"We may have had breakfast together. But never in bed. It's your assumption that these things took place, but it's not the fact."

Woolley walked to the defense table, casually picked up a puffy, lacy Valentine card and, after introducing it as evidence, handed it to Thorpe. Seeing the card, Thorpe squirmed.

"Did Mrs. Miles send you this Valentine card?"

"Yes."

"Do you see the postscript written on the bottom?"

"Yes."

"Isn't that Mrs. Miles's handwriting?"

"Yes."

"Could you please read that inscription?"

Thorpe choked on the words. "How deeply do I realize that and how deeply do I love you, sweetheart…. Lillian."

Woolley gently took the card back. "Thank you."

At this point Judge Knight halted the testimony and adjourned until the following evening.

• • •

The courtroom erupted in absolute pandemonium. Reporters encircling them, Mary Astor, Ruth Chatterton, and Fritz Lang rushed out of the courthouse without saying a word. The same could not be said of Dr. Franklyn Thorpe. He was furious. Woolley had used Thorpe's own words to vivisect him.

"It is perfectly clear that the other side is making a deliberate attempt to frame me. Otherwise they would not bring up all these questions about myself and having other women at my house. Anybody knows me knows that such innuendoes are baseless."

Thorpe's attorney, Joseph Anderson, made a reference to the diaries by assuring reporters that, "when the time comes we will produce evidence against Miss Astor as damaging as that which has been given against my client."

Woolley had, with his deft questioning, put the other side on the defensive, and begun his campaign to neutralize the adverse affects the diaries might have if they were introduced as evidence.

With reporters filling their notepads, Woolley now used Thorpe's own legal maneuvering to paint Franklyn Thorpe as the real villain and Mary Astor as his helpless victim. Earlier, Woolley had asked for a continuance to travel to Florida and gather evidence regarding the common law marriage, but Joseph Anderson had forcefully argued against it. The question Woolley now posed to reporters was why, if Thorpe were innocent, would his attorney oppose a continuance. Woolley made it clear that Franklyn Thorpe had something to hide.

As expected, the press ate it up, as did almost every American who could read a newspaper. And this was only the first day.

11

The press was out hunting down everyone associated with the case, and no one was pursued more ardently than Mary Astor. They camped outside her Toluca Lake home as well as the United Artists studio. It had gotten so bad that Goldwyn executives had asked for and received extra police protection to keep out press and curiosity seekers. At Toluca Lake, Astor had engaged two armed guards. Because little Marylyn was now the most famous toddler in America, the guards were there to ensure that the little girl didn't fall prey to would-be kidnappers.

For Astor, dealing with the press had become such a nightmare that, following each day's filming, she didn't leave the studio. While Nellie Richardson cared for the baby at home, Astor set up temporary residence in her studio dressing room, essentially a small, self-contained bungalow with a bedroom, kitchen, and living room. It became a calm oasis where Astor could prepare for both her performance in *Dodsworth* as well as her court appearances.

• • •

Wednesday morning New Yorkers read the headline "Movies Fight Astor Exposé" and opened their copies of the *New York Daily News* to read that "persons who have seen the day-to-day entries in the brunette beauty's little book came the prophecy that $12 million worth of pictures would be ruined as box office attractions if the diary's contents were placed upon the record. Names of some of Hollywood's best-known actors are contained in the diary."

Only ten or so people had actually seen the two-volume diary, much less read it, as the diaries were locked in a safety deposit box. None who had read it had sufficient knowledge to report that its contents could cost the motion-picture industry $12 million. In short, someone had fed this fabricated story to the paper. As it made good copy, more newspapers latched onto it, and it was soon reprinted in newspapers throughout the country. Fiction had just transformed into fact.

• • •

If the courthouse had been a circus Tuesday night, by Wednesday it had become a Barnum and Bailey extravaganza. The courtroom was filled with women, who had been waiting in line for seats since morning, and reporters from all over the country were stuffed into the small jury box.

Mary Astor, dressed in the same simple black dress, was again accompanied by Ruth Chatterton and Fritz Lang. Also in court was Astor's mother. Astor's father, whether by choice or ordered by his daughter and her attorney, was not there, nor did he attend a single session of the hearing.

The crowds were now so thick that Astor and company had to push through the crush of people. Chatterton, Lang, and Astor's mother immediately sat together inside the railing, while Mary Astor took her usual seat at the far left of the single counsel table. Entering the courthouse, Astor had refused to comment on the previous day's testimony and made it clear that she wouldn't speak until she herself took the stand.

In addition to Lillian Miles, Cora and Samuel Thorpe—Franklyn Thorpe's parents—were in the courtroom, and they all sat together. The elder Thorpe now worked for the Federal Revenue Bureau. Having lost over a quarter of a million dollars during the stock market crash, between May 1934 and August 1935 he had been forced to live on state relief. Thorpe's parents said nothing to the press and neither did Lillian Miles. Because her Tuesday morning press conference and Thorpe's testimony had put her on front pages all over America, Miles wisely decided to keep her mouth shut.

Franklyn Thorpe had learned the same lesson. As he made his way through the courthouse, the press shouted questions about Norma Taylor and the photos of the two hugging and kissing. Not answering, Thorpe took his seat at the far right of the counsel table and spoke quietly to his attorneys.

Judge Knight brought court into session, and Roland Rich Woolley attempted to introduce into evidence a written agreement between Astor and Thorpe, signed prior to the divorce in which they agreed to divide custody. As Woolley explained, this was the reason why Mary Astor did not contest Dr. Thorpe's 1935 custody action. Since Mary Astor would have possession of Marylyn for six months each year, she did not plan to give up her motherly role in the baby's life. The document called into question the unfitness claim made in Thorpe's filing, since in it he had agreed to give Mary Astor partial custody.

On purely technical grounds, Judge Knight refused to admit it, as the agreement should have been submitted at the time of the original divorce. Woolley knew this would happen. What he wanted—and got—was for everyone to know that this document existed so that lingering questions as to why Mary Astor had given up legal custody would be answered.

Following this, Joseph Anderson submitted an extension of Thorpe's answer filed on Monday. Anderson also handed it to the press so it would make the morning editions. With Woolley tearing Anderson's client to shreds on the stand, this was Anderson's attempt to divert attention back to Mary Astor.

Because, at present, the hearing was only concerned with actions following the divorce, Knight denied Woolley's request to consolidate the petitions and for a continuance, as they fell outside this specific time frame.

· · ·

Franklyn Thorpe was recalled to the stand, and Woolley resumed his examination. After last night's debacle, Thorpe had been told by his attorney that his exhibition of temper hadn't done him any good. So, tonight, the doctor kept his temper under control. Unfortunately, the damage had already been done.

Woolley now attempted to elicit from Thorpe the actual reason for Astor commencing this custody action. He did this by bringing up the July 5 argument.

"And what did the argument concern?"

"She became angry because I was an hour late in getting the child home. I tried to reason with her and conciliate but she was so angry she wouldn't listen."

"What did Miss Astor say at that time?"

"She said, 'Now there's going to be war.'"

"Was there any other cause for the quarrel?"

"Miss Astor had been drinking."

Woolley couldn't let this pass.

"How do you know that Miss Astor was drinking?"

"I saw the glasses."

"And Dr. Thorpe, do you ever drink?"

"Occasionally I have a highball before dinner but, being a surgeon, I cannot afford to drink. My profession won't allow much of that."

Woolley realized that, unlike the night before, Thorpe had been better coached, as his answer had put him in the best possible light. So, cutting his losses, Woolley moved on.

"Dr. Thorpe, is it not true that since your marriage to Miss

Astor your medical practice increased, so much so that you really don't have time to care for the child."

"No. If anything, my business has fallen off during the last year."

Thorpe believed he was sidestepping an argument in Astor's petition—that he was too busy and had no time for the baby. What Thorpe hadn't realized was that he had given Woolley an opening.

"Dr. Thorpe, considering that you had signed an affidavit alleging that Miss Astor was not a proper person to have custody of a child of impressionable age, why did you permit Marylyn to remain this summer with her mother although probate court had given you full custody?"

"It happened after I sold my half of the house to Miss Astor for $5,000. Since this had been Marylyn's home I permitted Marylyn to stay with her mother."

"When was this?"

"May 1."

Woolley closed the trap by putting to him the same question he had asked the night before. "Did you turn Marylyn over to her mother because Miss Astor bought your half of the home?"

"I did not."

"That $5000 didn't have anything to do with relinquishing your daughter, did it?"

Realizing that Woolley was intimating that because his practice had "fallen off" he needed money and this was the reason why he had given his daughter to her mother, Thorpe was emphatic in his reply.

"Absolutely not! That was her final payment on my half interest in the home. I received $15,000 altogether."

"And Paul Schofield, when did he move out to live with you?"

"Immediately after the divorce. He was a close friend."

"And can you remember an exact date?"

"February 1 until May."

Woolley could have pursued the shared expense issue, proving Thorpe was short of funds, but he wasn't certain here and it might backfire. Since he had gotten what he needed from Thorpe the previous evening, Woolley was ready to begin his next line of attack and informed Knight that he had concluded his examination.

Judge Knight turned to Joseph Anderson, but Anderson declined to cross-examine as he planned to recall Thorpe as a witness for the defense.

Adjacent the courthouse, air compression drills were digging up the street, and the incessant noise was making it difficult to hear testimony. So Judge Knight ordered a recess, and moved the hearing to a courtroom on the other side of the building.

• • •

With everyone settled in their seats, court was brought back into session and Woolley called his next witness—John Walker, a Los Angeles police officer. With this witness, Woolley intended to prove that Thorpe had misrepresented key facts concerning the incident with Norma Taylor.

Officer Walker strolled to the witness box, was sworn in, and took a seat. After some preliminary questioning, Walker answered questions regarding the night of November 25, 1935, when he and his partner, Jack Meyers, were called to Thorpe's Toluca Lake home on a domestic disturbance complaint.

"And what did you see there?"

"The maid answered the door and told us that the doctor was upstairs having difficulty with a lady."

"Where was he?"

"On the second floor. She was screaming."

"When you got up stairs what did you find?"

"I found Doctor Thorpe sitting on Norma Taylor in the bathroom. She was intoxicated."

Woolley showed the police officer a photo of Norma Taylor.

"Is this the woman?"

"Yes."

"How did she appear?"

Walker referred to his notes. "She was blond, dressed in cream white lounging pajamas of a Chinese pattern and she wore sandals. Her toenails were painted red."

"What did Dr. Thorpe say to you?"

"Dr. Thorpe asked us to put her out of the house. He said that he had asked her to leave and that she got hysterical and then attacked him with a large carving fork and he was restraining her until we arrived as he didn't want to bring her out himself."

"What happened after that?"

"Dr. Thorpe took me into the bathroom, removed his trousers, and showed me two stab wounds, one on his hip and one on his leg, inflicted by Miss Taylor with a turkey carving fork."

Thorpe, having conveniently forgotten to mention this in his testimony, was now doing his best not to squirm in his seat. Not only had he misrepresented things, he had also failed to mention that Norma Taylor had assaulted him, a felony crime committed just a few feet from little Marylyn. Regarding those stab wounds, Woolley had a question.

"How do you know that?"

"Well, Dr. Thorpe said she did it."

"What else did he say?"

"He told me that he had met her a couple of times but couldn't get her out of the house."

"Did he press charges?"

"I asked him if he wanted to press charges, but he said no, he just wanted her taken away."

No way was Thorpe going to press charges. It would have made the papers, and that was the last thing the good doctor had wanted.

"Did Dr. Thorpe say anything else?"

"I asked him who she was, and he said he wanted her to get out of the house because of the child."

"And where was the baby during this time?"

"The child was sitting up in its bed in another bedroom across the hall."

Having gotten what he wanted from the officer—the close

proximity of the baby to a violent altercation—Woolley had no more questions. Joseph Anderson indicated that he did not wish to cross-examine. Anderson wanted the man off the stand as quickly as possible, as every word that came out of his mouth demolished Anderson's client.

As the police officer stepped down, Roland Rich Woolley called his next witness—Marylyn's nurse, Nellie Richardson. He was now ready to bring in the big guns.

12

Born in London, Marylyn's nurse, Nellie Richardson—described as a prim little woman wearing steel-rimmed spectacles—had immigrated to Los Angeles from Toronto three years or so earlier. She was twenty-eight and had dedicated her life to raising other people's children. First engaged by the Thorpes for a short period soon after Marylyn was born, she was rehired when Franklyn Thorpe took charge of Marylyn in October 1935. When Astor moved back to Toluca Lake in May, she kept Richardson on.

Nellie Richardson was a strict, inflexible disciplinarian who didn't allow the baby to deviate from the rules set down by the child's mother. Richardson's strong feelings for Marylyn were the principal reasons why she was appearing as a witness. A highly principled woman, she believed it best for a child to be with its mother and disagreed with Thorpe's efforts to undermine Astor's authority with the child. Appearing in court wasn't an easy decision, as the woman had been hired by Thorpe and both liked and admired the man.

• • •

After Richardson took the stand there were some preliminary questions concerning her credentials and previous history. Then Woolley asked questions that weren't so much bombshells as thermonuclear explosions.

Woolley showed her the photos of Thorpe and Norma Taylor. "Do you know who the woman is in the picture?"
Joseph Anderson objected and was overruled.

When she spoke, Richardson's words came out in clipped, precise phrases.

"Yes. They're pictures of Dr. Thorpe and Miss Norma Taylor." She pointed at the woman. "That's Norma Taylor."

"Was she ever at the house while the baby, Dr. Thorpe, and you were living with Dr. Thorpe?"

Anderson objected and once again was overruled.

"Oh yes, several times—many times rather. She was a frequent visitor."

"When did you first see Miss Taylor at Dr. Thorpe's home?"

"November 15, 1935, and she was a frequent visitor after that."

"Did she ever stay there overnight?"

Anderson objected; objection overruled.

"Yes. Many times."

"In what bedroom did she sleep?"

Anderson objected; objection overruled.

"In the same bedroom as the doctor?"

"Yes. Many times."

"How many times?"

"I couldn't tell you how many. I don't keep track of those things."

As the press furiously scribbled down every word coming out of the woman's mouth, Ruth Chatterton fought hard not to grin but couldn't help herself. She knew what was coming and relished the thought of watching Franklyn Thorpe's pose as Mr. Morality go flying out the courtroom window. Mary Astor also knew what was about to happen but, not wanting to appear to gloat, she did her best to remain expressionless, staring down at her shoes and rarely looking up.

Sitting at the opposite end of the counsel table, Franklyn Thorpe—in the middle of being labeled a liar—worked hard to control his temper by grinding his teeth. Sitting behind Thorpe, his parents shook their heads vigorously, denying everything coming out of Richardson's mouth.

Woolley continued. "When she stayed overnight where did you find her in the morning?"

Anderson objected; objection overruled.

"In the bedroom upstairs."

"Was that in the same bedroom doctor Thorpe occupied?"

"Yes, it was."

"Did you ever see Miss Taylor in bed?"

Anderson objected; objection overruled.

"Yes."

"How did that happen?"

"I served her breakfast in bed."

"Many times?"

"Yes."

"Was she alone?"

"Yes."

"Were there times when she wasn't alone?"

Embarrassed, Richardson lowered her voice. "Yes, when I served breakfast to her and Dr. Thorpe."

"You saw Dr. Thorpe and Miss Taylor together in the same bedroom?"

Anderson objected; objection overruled.

"Yes. Many times. I saw both Dr. Thorpe and Miss Taylor together in the bedroom many mornings."

"Do you remember the times?"

"Between eight and ten o'clock."

"And you served them breakfast?"

"Yes, many times. I served them breakfast in bed."

"Who made the bed?"

"I did."

In a patient voice, Judge Knight interrupted. Knight rarely interfered with questioning but it was obvious that he had didn't relish backstairs gossip functioning as testimony. So, he quietly asked Woolley if this questioning was absolutely necessary. Woolley assured him it was.

While this was happening Thorpe glowered while Mary Astor, sitting at the other end of her counsel table, kept her eyes fixed on her fingers.

Woolley continued.

"Did he sleep there those nights?"

"Yes."

"Was Dr. Thorpe's bedroom close to that of his daughter?"

"Yes, it was connected to the one in which the baby slept by a short hallway."

"Now, how many beds were in the doctor's room?"

"There were two."

"When Miss Taylor was there were both beds disturbed?"

Richardson was emphatic. "Only one bed was disturbed."

Judge Knight had heard enough. "Oh come on now, spare us that."

Sitting between his two attorneys, Thorpe wore a scowl, angry and embarrassed at being held up for public ridicule.

Woolley now brought up the November 1935 "turkey fork" attack. He wanted to establish that the baby had been aware of it.

"Was the child upset or frightened by what had happened?"

"The child wasn't frightened, merely curious as to what was happening in the house."

"After that bathroom event, did Miss Taylor come back to the house?"

"Yes."

Anderson objected; objection overruled.

"Yes, she did, once or twice."

"Where did she stay those times?"

"In the doctor's bedroom."

"Did you see her the next morning?"

"Yes and I served her a double breakfast there."

"In bed?"

"Yes. Miss Taylor was in bed and I served her and the doctor a double breakfast."

"In the bedroom?"

"Yes."

Finished with Norma Taylor, Woolley was now ready to move onto Thorpe's other lady friends.

"Between October 10 and May 1, did Dr. Thorpe have any other female callers who stayed overnight?"

Anderson objected; objection overruled.

"Yes."

"How many?"

"Several."

"Who were they?"

Anderson objected; objection overruled.

"A Miss Betty Grant and Mrs. Schofield. I believe Miss Grant slept twice in the doctor's bedroom."

"How did you happen to be there?"

"I took breakfast up to them."

"How did you notice them?"

"I saw her getting dressed in the morning when I took up breakfast. Dr. Thorpe was there."

"How many beds were in the room?"

"There were two beds. Twin beds."

"Were they disturbed?"

"Only one bed was disturbed."

"Do you know Mrs. Schofield?"

"Yes. She is the wife of the man who lived at the house for a while."

"Did she ever spend a night at the house?"

"Yes, several times. Once Mrs. Schofield came to the house and stayed in the doctor's bedroom. I saw her the next morning."

"What was the condition of the beds?"

"Both twin beds in Dr. Thorpe's bedroom had been slept in

when I made them up that morning, after serving breakfast to Dr. Thorpe and Mrs. Schofield."

At the counsel table, Thorpe was fuming. He whispered to Anderson loudly enough for the judge could hear, "He's my friend. It never happened. What do they think I am?"

Mary Astor made no reaction, but Judge Knight wanted clarification. He interrupted Richardson.

"This is the lady who was married to Paul Schofield?"

"Yes."

Woolley took up the questioning. "Although Mrs. Schofield was still married the two were estranged, weren't they, and no longer living as man and wife?"

What Woolley was implying was that even though Schofield was in the house, since the two were separated, the woman was free to sleep with Thorpe. Anderson objected but, before his objection could be ruled on, Richardson answered.

"Yes. I took breakfast to Dr. Thorpe and Mrs. Schofield the next morning."

Richardson had grown quite comfortable on the stand, now answering in a rush of words that prevented Joseph Anderson from getting in an objection. He complained to the judge. So, Knight leaned over and asked Richardson to allow Anderson to register his objection. Anderson objected that Richardson did not know the Schofield's marital status. This objection was sustained and Woolley continued the questioning.

Speaking about Miss Grant, Richardson repeated the same things she had said about Norma Taylor and Mrs. Schofield—stayed overnight, beds rumpled, breakfast in bed, frequent occasions.

"Was there another woman who stayed overnight?"

Anderson objected; objection overruled.

"Mrs. Lillian Miles also stayed all night."

There was dead silence in that courtroom. Everyone had their eyes glued to Richardson. Mary Astor lifted her head momentarily and glanced over at her former husband, who was struggling to control his fury. Her face was blank but one could imagine what she was thinking, since she detested Lillian Miles as much as Mrs. Miles detested her.

"Do you remember when?"

"I don't recall the date but, when she slept in the doctor's bedroom, I saw her getting dressed."

"Do you remember how many times she was there?"

"I think that she was there just twice. I served her breakfast in the bedroom. Dr. Thorpe was there."

"How many beds were disturbed?"

"Just one."

"And how would you know?"

"I always made up the beds."

Richardson then told the court that when Thorpe returned the baby on May 1 to its mother, Richardson had stayed on.

"How did you find the mother with the girl?"

"Loving and affectionate."

"How so?"

Richardson spoke in glowing terms. "She spent nearly all day playing with Marylyn. She showed considerable interest."

"And how was the child with the father?"

"The child was timid and afraid of him."

"And the reason for this?"

Anderson objected; objection overruled.

"I believe it was because he spanked her too much."

"Why did her father spank her?"

"Dr. Thorpe tried to make Marylyn play with a toy his way and when she couldn't do it, he spanked her. He wouldn't let her be a little baby. He wanted her to do things grownup babies did and he would spank her when she couldn't."

For the first time, Mary Astor reacted. Remembering how she felt seeing her child punished, tears filled her eyes.

"Did Dr. Thorpe spend much time with the child when she was in his care?"

"No, not very much. Dr. Thorpe spent no evenings at home to speak of."

"In your opinion, which parent did the child seem to prefer?"

Richardson answered without hesitation. "She preferred the mother."

"Thank you."

Woolley's direct examination concluded, Knight asked Joseph Anderson if he wanted to cross-examine.

Joseph Anderson had been anxiously waiting to do just that. Practically jumping out of his seat, he rushed towards Richardson, ready to pounce. He intended to force the woman to reverse the impression of Franklyn Thorpe she had just given the court. Voice raised, he planned to intimidate the woman by barking out questions in sledgehammer-like fashion.

"Is it not true before coming to court today that on four different occasions you had met with Miss Astor's attorney in his office and at the home of Miss Astor?"

"Yes."

Since judges know witnesses are prepped this was being asked to discredit Richardson with the public as well as unnerve and confuse her. "Isn't it also true that you told people you thought Dr. Thorpe was a wonderful man?"

"Yes, I did. I do think he's a wonderful man."

"Didn't you say you liked working for him?"

"Yes, because I did."

"Didn't you say that he was a fine father?"

"Yes, but Marylyn preferred her mother."

Before Anderson could continue, Judge Knight indicated the late hour and adjoined the court until tomorrow evening.

• • •

Having just had his reputation demolished, Franklyn Thorpe was so angry that he immediately left the courthouse without saying a word. Watching him storm out, it wouldn't have been much of a stretch to imagine that, if the doctor had his way, he would have gleefully strangled Nellie Richardson. What compounded his rage was the fact he had hired Richardson and saw her testimony as nothing short of rank disloyalty.

Richardson had shown that Dr. Thorpe hadn't been "framed" at all. In fact, what Roland Woolley had done was prove that Dr. Thorpe had not only misrepresented the truth but also outright lied, leaving the question open to exactly how much lying the doctor had done in general and calling Thorpe's credibility into question.

Astor, Chatterton, Lang, Astor's mother, and Marcus Goodrich immediately left the courtroom and headed straight to Woolley's office. Mary Astor was scheduled to take the stand tomorrow night, so Woolley needed to go over her testimony.

For Miss Richardson's efforts she would be labeled the tattling nurse and vilified by each of the women whom she had named in her testimony, testimony that made banner headlines from California to New York and all stops in between. The press now had a new name for Dr. Franklyn Thorpe: Hollywood's latest "gay lothario."

13

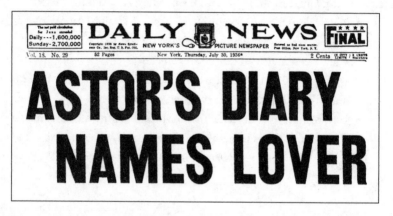

DAILY NEWS FINAL

NEW YORK'S ⬤ PICTURE NEWSPAPER

The net paid circulation for June exceeded
Daily --- 1,600,000
Sunday - 2,700,000

Copyright 1936 by News Syndicate Co. Inc. Reg. U. S. Pat. Off.

Entered as 2nd class matter, Post Office, New York, N. Y.

Vol. 18. No. 29   52 Pages   New York, Thursday, July 30, 1936*   2 Cents IN CITY / 3 CENTS Elsewhere

ASTOR'S DIARY NAMES LOVER

The affidavit Joseph Anderson filed on Wednesday night built on the answer he had submitted on the Monday prior to the start of the hearing. It charged, among other things, that Mary Astor "carried on a course of conduct which makes her wholly unfit to have custody of said minor child." It also alleged that Mary Astor, "when minor child was less than one year old and continuing up to the present time has carried on a course of immoral conduct detrimental to the best interests of the child."

Mary Astor was also charged with being in love with a married man and "with advice of counsel formulated a plan and scheme to allow the divorce to go ahead by default and later attempt to gain complete custody when the evidence of her immoral conduct would be old and more difficult to prove against her." Extracts from the second volume of the diaries were included to support the charges.

> February 8, 1935—I love George and the least I can do
> is to save him from a messy scandal... I could wait a few

months, let Franklyn think he won by telling him that George and I were through… bring it up again when he would have no grounds for cross complaint. It would be very hard for him to bring up an old affair against me. Later I can move to have custody changed to me. Got very drunk on Wednesday night and about 4:00 a.m. had to call the house doctor to give me a sedative.

February 19, 1935—For the sake of peace and a little respite from all this emotionalism I told him [Thorpe] I would do nothing at present. My main reason for saying that is quite, honestly, I want to be able to see George for the rest of his stay here without being all upset… I want to have the last few times of completely enjoying him and then when he has left town I can start it again.

The "George" mentioned in the extract was never identified. After being humiliated on the stand, Thorpe was telling Mary Astor that he was now fully prepared to do what he had promised to do— scandalize her.

In Astor's written response, she denied Thorpe's charges, stating what she had written were merely "thoughts and ideas, unformulated and unexecuted, and not so communicated to anyone." Denying she was in love with a married man she also stated that "any and all associations" she "had with any man was with the knowledge and consent of Dr. Thorpe… Dr. Thorpe has attempted to and still attempts to hurt and ruin my character and reputation."

The question the public was asking—who was "George"?

• • •

One person who knew was the mystery man himself. George S. Kaufman had been in town since the end of May. Registered at the Beverly Wilshire, he was in Hollywood writing a play with Moss Hart. Hart, weathering a serious depression, insisted on working here so he could attend daily sessions with his analyst. Kaufman also had an exclusive contract with producer Irving Thalberg and had not only co-written a second MGM Marx Brothers movie but was fixing the scripts for such diverse Thalberg productions as *The Good Earth* and *Marie Antoinette*.

In the morning Kaufman would work with Hart on their play, and in the afternoon, while Hart was with his analyst, Kaufman was at the studio earning a $5,000-a-week paycheck. His affair with Mary Astor over, Kaufman still kept in touch, and in early July the two had met at the Trocadero, where Kaufman was partying with the Thalbergs. Afterwards, they left together to spent the rest of the evening at a dinner party given by director Ernst Lubitsch. Truth was, Kaufman's main romantic interest right then was actress Luise Rainer.

Learning that Thorpe's latest affidavit mentioned an unidentified George, and knowing that sooner or later his name was bound to come out, Kaufman immediately wired his wife, Beatrice, then traveling in Europe and North Africa, to tell her what might happen. As Kaufman saw it, Franklyn Thorpe intended to involve him in a high-profile scandal as revenge for having been cuckolded. Knowing about the diaries, Kaufman was hoping for the best but definitely expecting the worst.

• • •

Meanwhile, in New York City, "turkey fork" wielding Norma Taylor had finally surfaced to become the comic relief in the unfolding drama of the Astor custody battle.

Miss Taylor's mother had called the newspapers to give her daughter's side of the story. After reading Nellie Richardson's testimony in the newspapers Norma became so upset that she was now in a "state of collapse" at her mother's Jackson Heights home.

The reason why Norma was so distraught? Every Hollywood contract had a morals clause stipulating that performers conduct themselves in a manner not in conflict with accepted public morality.

In 1936, sleeping with a man sans a marriage license fell under that provision, meaning that Norma might never work in films again.

The "actress" was so frantic that doctors had to be called in and Norma's mother "compelled to give her daughter a sleeping draught." Norma's mother insisted that her daughter was merely a patient of Dr. Thorpe and had accepted an invitation to recuperate at his home—a semi-sanatorium.

A few hours later, much to the surprise of the reporter receiving the call, Norma Taylor telephoned to state for the record that she and Dr. Thorpe were innocent.

"You know it isn't so. I went to his house—several times. He was my doctor. What's wrong with that? Dr. Thorpe operated on me and took care of me. But, heavens, we were just friends, like patients are with doctors. Thorpe is an awfully nice fellow and our friendship never went beyond that."

Norma also told the reporter that she would "throw a series of high explosive shells into the Astor trial" by personally coming to Los Angeles and "knocking Nellie Richardson's testimony into a cocked hat."

A few hours later, in a second telephone interview, Norma made an announcement.

"I got my lawyers working on this and some people better watch out."

"What about stabbing Dr. Thorpe with a turkey fork?"

"Ha, that's a good one. I don't even eat turkey."

"Well, the housekeeper testified you had breakfast in bed with him?"

"Not with him. I had breakfast in bed there lots of times and lunch and dinner. I was ill and getting ready for an operation. I was hysterical and worried about it and he took me to his house to rest up for the operation."

"But the housekeeper testified she served breakfast many mornings to you and Dr. Thorpe in the same bedroom."

"My goodness! That nurse, or housekeeper, or whatever you call her is going to get herself into a lot of trouble saying such things."

"How about the testimony that the police came in one night and found Dr. Thorpe struggling with you in the bathroom?"

"Yes, I remember them coming in when I was a little nervous once and the doctor was trying to quiet me. But stabbing him, say, that's Hollywood for you."

"What about the photos of you and Thorpe?"

"That was just a gag to make the doctor blush. We were kidding and it seemed like fun."

Interview concluded, Miss Taylor retreated to an unnamed location in the Catskill Mountains.

For the record, this wasn't the first time Norma Taylor was mentioned in a courtroom. In February 1933, she was named as co-respondent in a divorce initiated by a Mrs. Hutchins. It seemed that Norma was a "pupil" of Mr. Hutchins—a dramatic coach. While "studying" with Mr. Hutchins, she moved into his house and then proceeded to toss Mrs. Hutchins's clothes out of the woman's closet to make room for her own things, acting as if she were the lady of the house.

As might be expected, "Norma denied everything."

14

Los Angeles Times

R   FRIDAY MORNING, JULY 31, 1936.

Candid Camera Depicts Emotions in Actress' Child Custody Case

RUTH CHATTERTON,

MARY ASTOR,

ROLAND RICH WOOLLEY,

JOSEPH ANDERSON,

DR. FRANKLYN THORPE,

ETHEL PEPIN,

MICHAEL NARLIAN

At Thursday night's court session Mary Astor was once again accompanied by Ruth Chatterton. The session began at 6:00 p.m. rather than 7:00 as there was a lot of ground to cover. Fritz Lang wasn't with them, and neither was Mary Astor's mother. Woolley had asked the woman to stay home. During yesterday's session she had complained to the press about the difficulty of making ends meet on the pittance her daughter was giving her. The last thing Woolley needed was a two-year-old non-support story messing things up right now.

Astor would be taking the stand later that night. Dressed in a shiny blue taffeta dress opened at the collar, her sampan hat partly hid her red "Titian hair." Despite makeup, it was obvious that there were circles under Astor's eyes, as the pressure of the hearing was beginning to take its toll.

Lillian Miles—"handsome brunette" replacing "Beverly Hills Matron" in the papers—was sitting with Thorpe's parents. As for Dr. Thorpe, Hollywood's latest "gay Lothario" hadn't spoken to the press. Reputation pretty much in shreds, his private life had gone public in the worst possible way. Thorpe sat at his attorney's table stone-faced, tanned, and wearing a black and gray check sports coat, not saying a word to anyone.

• • •

As soon as the session began Woolley submitted his answer to Thorpe's affidavit filed the previous evening. Woolley then requested a subpoena for "two certain diaries in the handwriting of Miss Astor, one diary covering the period from September 1928 to January 5, 1930, and the other from March 25, 1930, to March 1935... said diaries would prove that Franklyn Thorpe threatened the defendant that if she did not do as he demanded with respect to the property settlement, custody, and divorce, he would publicly scandalize her." Judge Knight took the request under advisement, as he wanted to see where the case would take them first.

Woolley knew there were things in those diaries that Franklyn Thorpe didn't want made public. Therefore, Thorpe didn't want the *entire* two-volume diary brought in as evidence. But, if Thorpe didn't deliver the entire diary, then his excerpts would be excluded. In short, Woolley was telling Thorpe's attorney put up or shut up.

Preliminaries out of the way, Nellie Richardson was recalled to the stand and Anderson completed his cross-examination. Anderson needed to force Richardson to retract much of her previous day's testimony. Desperate to undo the damage she had done, he pounded at the woman incessantly, trying to intimidate her into reversing herself.

"Didn't you tell several people that Dr. Thorpe was a devoted father?"

Trying to avoid answering, Richardson kept silent. Judge Knight ordered her to answer.

"Yes I did. He was a fine father. She just preferred her mother."

"And would you say that while living with her father she received excellent care?"

"Yes."

"Did you ever say that it was a shame Marylyn's mother didn't take an interest in her child?"

Again Richardson had trouble answering and again ordered by Knight to do so.

"Yes, at the time I might have said that."

"Might?"

"I probably did."

Since Richardson was reluctant to answer, Anderson began barking out his questions. Woolley rose and objected to Anderson's obvious attempt to intimidate the witness. Richardson turned to the judge.

"Could you please ask Mr. Anderson to lower his voice? He's confusing me."

Judge Knight obliged. "Mr. Anderson, you really don't need to lift your voice when asking your questions, do you?"

"No, Your Honor."

Anderson turned back to Richardson.

"Didn't you once say to Dr. Thorpe's parents, 'Can you imagine a mother running away and leaving a baby like that?'"

Thorpe's parents nodded their heads emphatically.

"Yes. I might have. Miss Astor was not living there then."

"When Dr. Thorpe was staying in the house how many times was Mrs. Lillian Miles there?"

"About two times."

"Was she alone with the doctor?"

"Yes sir. I saw her twice in the doctor's bedroom in the morning."

"Was it not true that on one of these occasions Mrs. Miles stayed the night, her fifteen-year-old son was there also?"

"Yes he was."

"And Mrs. Miles' mother was there as well?"

"Yes."

"Now, about these four women. You saw both beds in the doctor's bedroom were rumpled only once during these alleged overnight visits?"

"Yes sir, when Mrs. Madge Schofield was there."

Judge Knight interrupted. He knew this was being done for the benefit of the press.

"I'm convinced all of these women were there. Can't we dispense with some of this and hurry things along? The doctor was not a married man at that time. It was his own home and it didn't matter what he did so long as the women staying all night didn't affect the child. Also, it is naturally presumed that both parents loved the baby."

Rebuffed, Anderson continued.

"Do you remember the date that Mrs. Miles stayed all night?"

"I can't remember the dates."

Judge Knight, growing increasingly impatient, leaned over and spoke to Richardson.

"Let's clear this up. Mrs. Miles was there at 10:00 p.m. when you retired, and the next morning you saw her in bed and brought her a breakfast?"

"Yes sir."

"And, you say that a Miss Betty Grant and Mrs. Schofield both were in the process of getting dressed when you saw them in the doctor's bedroom?"

"Yes sir."

"You saw Mrs. Miles in bed?"

"I didn't see her in bed. She was walking around the room when I saw her. She was dressed."

Anderson wasn't particularly pleased but, resuming the questioning, threw the witness a curveball.

"Miss Richardson, in a conversation with a friend when she advised you to stay out of what she called the 'Thorpe mess' did you say to her, 'Don't worry, I'll be taken care of?'"

"No. I didn't say that."

This perked Judge Knight's interest. Once again he leaned over to Richardson.

"Are you taking sides in this action?"

Put off by the question, Richardson hesitated before answering.

"No, sir."

Having done his best to "rehabilitate" Dr. Thorpe from Richardson's damaging testimony, Anderson decided to heat things up. He paused. He wanted everyone to hear him drop a bombshell.

"Do you know George Kaufman?"

In a single sentence Joseph Anderson had managed to answer the question America had been asking all day: who was the mysterious George mentioned in yesterday's court filings?

It was now obvious that Anderson intended to use this and other cross-examinations to introduce the contents of the diary even if he couldn't get the document introduced as evidence. Mary Astor would call this testimony by "innuendo." So Woolley objected whenever Anderson brought up a name, reinforcing what Mary Astor had asserted in her petition—Thorpe threatening to scandalize her and her friends. Jumping to his feet Woolley spoke in a loud, forceful voice.

"Your Honor I object. I protest against this as a trick. This is beside the point and merely an attempt to scandalize innocent people. It's immaterial and irrelevant. I protest against this as a trick to involve the name of a party not involved in this suit in a dirty scandal."

The objection was overruled, and Judge Knight turned to Richardson.

"You may answer the question."

"No, sir. I don't know him."

"Did you ever hear of George Kaufman?"

"Yes, sir, but he was never at the house."

Damage done, Anderson moved along.

"Did Miss Astor have parties when the baby was living with her?"

"Yes. Every other Sunday night."

In the 1930s, Hollywood had a six-day workweek. Sunday was the only day off, so everyone in town had Sunday parties.

"How long did these parties last?"

"The guests always left by eleven o'clock."

"Any liquor?"

"Yes. Highballs before dinner. But no one ever became intoxicated."

"Has any man visited Miss Astor from May 1 until now?"

"Several."

"Do you know who they were?"

"Some of them."

"What names of gentleman guests at Miss Astor's house can you remember?"

"Mr. Laughton was there with Mrs. Laughton. There was a Mr. Goodrich with a party of friends."

"Was there any gentleman ever alone with Miss Astor while you were there?"

"Yes. Mr. Goodrich was there with Miss Astor."

"How long did he stay?"

"He left at 11:00 p.m."

"How can you be sure?"

"I remember the time because I had to lock the gate after him."

Realizing that he wasn't going to get more out of Richardson, Anderson quickly terminated the cross-examination. Although Anderson hadn't altogether rehabilitated his client he had used Richardson to introduce George Kaufman into the proceedings.

Woolley now called Ardys Clark to the stand. Clark was "the pretty former nursemaid" whom Thorpe ordered Astor to fire. Also—and this was no small matter—while in Astor's employ, Clark had safeguarded the diaries. Woolley had only one point to make with Miss Clark. She told the court that Marylyn was disciplined "much more severely by the father."

"Dr. Thorpe tried to be very understanding with the baby, and the child was never treated badly by him, although I felt at times that Dr. Thorpe might have been too severe."

"How so?"

"Once when Marilyn objected to a cold shower he whipped her until she stood in the shower and took it."

"How old was the baby at the time?"

"Two and a half years old."

Woolley concluded his direct examination, and Anderson conducted a short cross-examination.

"Miss Clark, was John Barrymore ever a guest of Miss Astor's while she lived on Tower Road?"

Woolley shot to his feet and objected that Anderson was again using the witness to scandalize persons who had nothing to do with the case at hand. He was overruled.

Clark smiled. "No."

Anderson terminated the cross-examination, and Woolley then called Judge Dudley S. Valentine to the stand. Valentine had granted the Astor-Thorpe divorce fifteen months earlier. Woolley showed Valentine a secret agreement providing that Mary Astor could have her daughter if and when she posted a cash bond guaranteeing expenses Thorpe might incur if he needed to force Astor to return the child. It was further evidence of the undue power Thorpe had exerted over Mary Astor by threatening to take the child away.

A rather surprised Judge Valentine declared that he had "never seen it before" and that this was the reason why it had not been incorporated into the divorce decree.

Finished with Judge Valentine and, with Joseph Anderson declining to cross-examine, Roland Rich Woolley called his next witness—Mary Astor.

15

Mary Astor rose from her seat at the counsel table, crossed the floor to the witness box, raised her white-gloved hand and, giving her name as Lucille Thorpe, was sworn in. Everyone had been anxiously waiting for this moment, anticipating it as the dramatic high point of the hearing. Reporters, gathered from all parts of the country, flipped open their notepads, and spectators held their breath. The tension in the room was nothing less than electric.

Mary Astor knew that a great deal was at stake. It was a make-it-or-break-it night. Having learned to hide her emotions, Astor now had to show those emotions to a packed courtroom. She needed to express her deepest feelings so everyone would learn who Mary Astor really was, instead of what her former husband was trying to paint her as.

Astor would later recall that she was "numbed by the whole mad merry-go-round. I hated the headlines, the incessant flashbulbs and the gaping, curiosity-seeking mob. I was always exhausted after the sessions were over. So when I went into court and faced the bedlam of sightseers, newsmen, women, photographers, attorneys, and sat on the witness stand for long hours and answered questions that would have broken me up completely had I not kept the little pot boiling that was Edith Cortright."

Roland Rich Woolley had already set the stage by using Nellie Richardson's testimony to prove that Franklyn Thorpe had lied on the stand. Thus, if the man's veracity couldn't be trusted, then the question arose: could the man's claims levied against his former wife be trusted?

Woolley needed to mitigate the negative impact of the diary

Mary Astor's first day on the stand.

excerpts already made public and others that might come to light. To do this he planned to conduct Astor through a gentle, carefully modulated, nuanced two-day examination that would allow the actress not only to present her version of events but also give everyone a look into the heart of a caring and loving mother.

Although Roland Rich Woolley could ask the questions, it was up to Mary Astor to do the rest.

Woolley began with questions designed to paint Franklyn Thorpe in the worst possible light. So, he brought up Thorpe's claim that he had offered to pay for Marylyn's upkeep and education. In response, Mary Astor made it absolutely clear that at no time prior or after the divorce did Franklyn Thorpe ever offer to pay these expenses. On the contrary, he had ordered her to pay them as part of his demands, and if she didn't agree to those demands, he promised to embroil her in a scandal.

"Shortly after the divorce, did Dr. Thorpe threaten to take the child away from you?"

"Yes. He said, 'If you interfere with me in any way in the treatment of the child, I won't let her stay with you.'"

This was difficult for Astor to recount, and she kept twisting her handkerchief in her hand.

"Why did you give Dr. Thorpe the baby on October 10 last year?"

"Because he told me he expected me to give her up. I said I had hoped to have her longer, and he answered that if I displeased him in any way I wouldn't have her at all."

"What did you say to him?"

Tears welled up. "I said that because I wanted to keep the baby with me I would be a good girl or words to that affect."

Choking up and trying her best to stop herself from weeping, Astor found it difficult to speak, and Judge Knight called for a short recess. When she could speak Woolley resumed his questions.

"What did you do subsequent to October 10?"

"I went to New York and was gone three months before returning January 19."

"Between January 19 and May 1 of this year, did you visit your daughter?"

"Practically every day. If I worked late I stopped by to see if she was tucked in. On my days off I spent several hours playing with her. There was a time when I was very busy working hard on two pictures and sometimes I would come in late, after her bedtime. Even then, I'd go into her room to tuck her in and have just that little glimpse of her."

This expression of maternal love was so heartfelt that it brought tears to, of all people, Ruth Chatterton.

"Did Dr. Thorpe protest turning the child over to you on May 1 of this year?"

"No."

"You and not Dr. Thorpe made arrangements for Marylyn to attend a nursery school, didn't you?"

"Yes, just before she turned three. I wanted her to have a social life—to be a normal person. I don't want her being pampered like many Hollywood children."

"Did Dr. Thorpe play with the child?"

"He would attempt to play with her. He just didn't seem to know how to play with children. He thinks that to play with a child all he need do is say—" mimicking Thorpe—"'Now do this or do that. Pat Daddy's face,' or 'Tell Daddy what you did today.' He would say, 'Now, Marylyn, put your arms around Daddy's neck. Now pat Daddy's face. Speak up Marylyn.' It was a regular routine."

All during her testimony Astor never once looked at Thorpe, but Thorpe's eyes were glued on her. Dr. Thorpe did not like what he was hearing.

"Do you love your daughter?"

Astor hesitated as she tried her best to hold back the tears.

"Yes. I do very much."

"And what did you do about caring for Marylyn?"

"I did the usual things with her and looked after her wants. Marylyn was companionable, easy to get along with. I love her."

"How was she with you?"

Recalling her times with Marylyn elicited a smile.

"I find it fun to be with her. We play games together." Astor laughed. "She splashes in her little pool. She has a whole bunch of phonograph records—baby records, you know—and we have to play the whole set for her every night before she'll go to sleep."

"Did Dr. Thorpe object to the manner in which you looked after the child?"

"No."

"What was Dr. Thorpe's attitude toward all this affection between you and the child?"

Tears again welled up.

"Quite often he said that I spoiled her by paying too much attention to her and that I was turning the child away from him."

"Were you?"

"Certainly not."

"Between April 12 and October 10, 1935, did he ever discipline the baby?"

"Always. Always. It seemed to me that there was always something he thought was wrong in the way she acted."

"How did he discipline her? Did he ever discipline her severely?"

"Yes he did. He was not understanding with the child. Sometimes, if she didn't immediately obey him, he would jerk her roughly to her feet and, if she cried, he would order her to stop." Recalling this, Astor had to fight back tears. "I've seen him grab her by the arm and jerk and shake her so hard that her teeth rattled. It was so bad that once her lips were cut and her little body was covered with bruises."

Her throat choking off her words, Astor broke down again and Woolley needed to wait until she regained her composure. Even skeptical reporters were now having difficulty holding back a tear or two. As for the women in the room, most had out their handkerchiefs.

Sitting at the counsel table, Thorpe looked around and, seeing the affect this was having on the crowd, looked bewildered. Like a drowning man, he glanced over at his attorneys for help. They only smiled sardonically, trying to assure him that it was just a show. They may have believed this, but no one else in that courtroom did.

Woolley continued his questioning.

"Besides shaking her, what else would Dr. Thorpe do to the baby?"

Tears were again in Astor's eyes. "He would spank her sometimes and there would be bruises on the baby. Sometimes it was important that she be disciplined but I thought he always indulged in it at too great a length." Her voice began to break again. "The child was frightened of him. She was timid and afraid of him."

Judge Knight leaned over. "Did you ever say anything to him about this? Did you object?"

"Yes. I objected many times. I'd beg him not to be so hard on her."

"And his reply?"

"He told me 'I'll discipline my child the way I please and you mustn't interfere.'"

"Did you interfere?"

"Why no. I couldn't interfere, because if I did he would take my baby away from me. He said so on many occasions."

"What did you say to that?"

Astor hesitated and then looked at Knight, her voice choking up.

"What could I say Your Honor? He had custody of the child."

"I understand that, but was anything said?"

"I can't remember."

Woolley resumed his questioning.

"Were there any other threats?"

"Yes. In the middle of April 1935." Astor took a deep breath. "It was quite a scene. I can't use the language that was used that night but pounding the table he told me, 'I won't stand for Ardys Clark. Unless you discharge her I will take the baby home with me. She is turning Marylyn against me and I won't have it.' He told me to kick her out of the house or he would take my baby home with him."

Astor began to weep, and Knight again recessed until she

regained her composure. When she had, Woolley asked her, "What else did he say?"

"He pounded his fists and said that I was to remedy the situation or send the baby back to him."

"What did you say to him?"

"I said, 'I never did anything to turn the baby against you.' I wouldn't anyway, because I didn't think it a good principle to turn a child against its father, no matter how he treats the child."

Joseph Anderson finally stood up. "I object to that last sentence as being prejudicial."

His objection was sustained, with Judge Knight adding, "Strike that last sentence from the record."

Woolley continued. "At any later period did Dr. Thorpe renew his threats to take the child?"

"Yes, often."

"On last July 5 do you remember the occasion when Thorpe brought the child home very late?"

"I remember it very well."

"Did you have a visitor that night?"

"Yes, Evelyn Laye had stopped by."

"Did you have any conversation with Dr. Thorpe at that time?"

"We had quite an argument; once on the phone and once when he brought the baby home long past her bedtime. The doctor called up and said he couldn't get back and the child would have dinner with him. I told him to get her home as soon as possible because, she had been up late the night before to see Fourth of July fireworks. I told Dr. Thorpe, 'I'm getting tired of this. Whenever you take the baby out you bring her back late.' She had been up late the night before and I felt that she should have her sleep. I remonstrated with him and said he was breaking the child's schedule. I told him it was not right to interfere with a child's schedule and that he had caused her to miss a luncheon and her nap on various occasions. I told him that I wanted him to bring her home before her bedtime and that he was being selfish."

"What did the doctor say?"

"He said to me, 'You're the selfish person, Mary. All you are interested in is yourself.'"

"What did you reply?"

"I said, 'I am only thinking of the child and you're not. It is wrong to upset her schedule.'"

"His answer?"

"He said, 'I am going to do exactly as I please with the child and don't interfere with me.'"

"What did you tell him?"

"'You have your own interests at heart while I'm thinking of the baby.'"

"What time did he bring the child home?"

"He brought the baby home at nine o'clock in the evening. One hour past her bedtime after having her out all day."

"And what did he say, then?"

"He told me not to interfere or there would be trouble."

"At this point, did you say you'd give him a battle?"

"Yes. I said I was going to 'give battle' or 'fight' or words to that effect, meaning that I was going to cause trouble every time he did it that way. I also told him that I was no longer afraid of him. Before this I had always been afraid."

"Had you been drinking?"

"I had one highball at dinner but I was not intoxicated."

"At any later period did Dr. Thorpe ever renew his threats to take the child?"

"Yes, often."

At this point in the testimony Judge Knight interrupted, mentioning the late hour. When Astor left the stand Knight announced that from now on the court would be holding day sessions. He also informed both Woolley and Anderson that he planned to visit little Marylyn on Saturday morning at the Toluca Lake house.

• • •

Until now, Knight had ruled that only what happened following the divorce was pertinent to the hearing. Both Astor and Thorpe's testimony regarding moral unfitness *after* the divorce had pretty much cancelled each other out. Consequently, Knight needed to see for himself how well the child was doing. He wanted to both talk with Marylyn and determine by her surroundings and attitude the fitness of her parents to care for her.

If the child was doing well, Knight would have nothing sound on which to base his final decision. Then, and only then, he would require testimony concerning the parent's conduct prior to the divorce. This was not something Knight wanted to do. It meant submission of the diary and that would muddy up the waters. It was simply the only thing left for him to do.

Anderson couldn't repress a smile. It was a victory. If he got this ruling he could enter parts of what the press was now calling the "Misstep Diary" into evidence.

Knight then adjourned the court until 10:00 a.m. Monday morning.

• • •

What did the press think of Miss Astor on the stand? According to the newspapers, "Her testimony climaxed a day of sensations" and "filled the room with electric intensity." She made a "startling dramatic appearance on the stand bearing up under the strain." Her manner was "composed," "demure and lovely." "Although she appeared nervous, Miss Astor was in command" and "her demeanor spoke of complete confidence." "Her low, deep, strong, vibrant, and throaty voice, interrupted at times by gentle sobs, penetrated to every corner of the courtroom with perfect directness."

Despite the diary excerpts and their implication, Woolley's strategy was working. Mary Astor, and not Franklyn Thorpe, was winning over both the newspapers and the public. The judge, on the other hand, would be another matter.

• • •

Earlier that evening, when George Kaufman's was identified as the mysterious "George," reporters rushed for the telephones and called the Beverly Wilshire. It was a very annoyed George Kaufman who answered.

"There is no reason why my name should be linked with this case. I am just a friend of Miss Astor, like many others in Hollywood. I have attended several of her parties as a guest and a friend. I most certainly am not involved in her difficulties with Dr. Thorpe."

Kaufman's worst fears had finally been realized, and this was only the beginning. Once details of his affair with Mary Astor came to light, his very private love life would become very public and could adversely affect both his family as well as his career. Therefore, Kaufman did what he always did when he was in trouble—he called Beatrice in Europe and asked her advice. Beatrice counseled to wait and see as the case could still be settled before anything more came out. Unfortunately, as it would turn out, Kaufman's worst fears were about to be realized.

16

Norma Taylor was again in the news. The blond "actress," on the advice of three doctors, had been rushed to a Westchester County sanitarium, where she was now under the care of physicians.

According to Norma's attorney, Noah Braunstein, the "former night club dancer" was on the verge of a nervous breakdown. In a telephone interview Braunstein announced that he had requested "a full transcript of the testimony" because, once Norma recovered, she was ready to fly to Los Angeles and not only "throw a series of high-explosive shells into the Astor-Thorpe case," but she had also instructed Braunstein to prepare lawsuits "against all persons responsible for Miss Richardson's testimony."

Braunstein elaborated in a formal statement: "The charges against Miss Taylor by the witness Richardson are utterly perjurious. There are absolutely no grounds which would indicate moral turpitude on her part. The only relations between Miss Taylor and Dr. Thorpe were those of physician and patient. There is likely to be much more than a damage action involved. I intend to look into the criminal aspects of this situation."

Braunstein then dashed off a telegram to Roland Rich Woolley.

"My client Norma Taylor demands retraction of unquestionably false and perjurious testimony of your witness Richardson. My instructions are to proceed against all responsible for perjurious statements uttered by the witness. We shall hold you to strict accounting for any false testimony injurious to Norma Taylor."

Not wanting Joseph Anderson to feel left out, Braunstein wired him as well saying much the same thing.

Meanwhile Norma, after she had sufficiently recovered from her collapse—but before her nervous breakdown—called a newspaper to defend, of all people, Dr. Franklyn Thorpe.

"Dr. Thorpe saved my life and I owe my life to him, but this case is going much too far. I am determined to get this matter straightened out to clear my name of the slightest intimation of scandal."

When Norma was asked if there was any possibility that she and Dr. Thorpe might ever become more than just friends she answered: "Our friendship might have developed into something more serious, more lasting. However, with all this nasty mess, I don't know what to think. I like the doctor and he likes me. But that is all."

Interview concluded, the "vivacious blonde" was finally ready for her nervous breakdown.

• • •

Friday's *New York Mirror* had a quite different take on the Taylor-Thorpe relationship. According to the newspaper, there was "dignified Dr. Franklyn Thorpe being chased around his Toluca Lake house by a baby-faced blonde beauty, toenails painted red, wearing Chinese pajamas, waving a carving knife. And when the blonde caught up with the physician she sank the prongs into his hips and one of his legs." Apparently, as that newspaper saw it, the two had already become more than just friends; they had become enemy combatants.

• • •

Joseph Anderson was now ready to take the offensive with a one-two punch. The first blow occurred on Friday, when the attorney filed an affidavit asserting that Mary Astor had "willfully abandoned" her four-year-old daughter and disputing Astor's accusations that she had been forced into a divorce. "We can prove in her own handwriting that this was not the situation at all, but that she willfully abandoned the child for a married man—George Kaufman."

Anderson would attempt to introduce Mary Astor's diary

into evidence on Monday. He revealed that at least six men, all of them "outstanding leading men," would be subpoenaed to testify concerning exactly how well they knew Astor; six men whose "after dark" lives were far more romantic than anything they did onscreen. He added that Mary Astor's diary "is one of the most amazing and revealing documents" he had ever read and Franklyn Thorpe was resolved to let the "world know all." Anderson was asked whether John Barrymore was one of the six.

"I cannot make the six names public at this time, but believe me, when I do, it will be a bombshell."

Punch number two was planned for Saturday. Anderson would announce that he would file an affidavit on Monday asserting that at the time Miss Astor had obtained a temporary custody in the superior court, Thorpe held legal guardianship granted by the probate court. Accordingly, Mary Astor would be charged with perpetrating a fraud by "deliberately and fraudulently" concealing this fact. "If Miss Astor had informed Judge Dudley S. Valentine of Dr. Thorpe's guardianship letter, the judge would have been powerless to grant temporary custody of the child to the actress" and the current hearing on Miss Astor's custody petition would be "of no force, avail, or effect." It was a technicality, and a long shot at best, but cases can be won or lost on technicalities.

Learning this, Woolley pretty much concluded that Anderson's fraud accusation was a maneuver designed to demonstrate that Mary Astor, and not Franklyn Thorpe, was a liar. Woolley also knew that it wouldn't go anywhere and, frankly, was a rather pathetic attempt to counter the damage Woolley had done to Thorpe's reputation. As for the diaries, it should be remembered that Woolley had asked the court to subpoena the *entire* document and that request would remain Woolley's ace in the hole, since Franklyn Thorpe couldn't allow the entire contents of the diaries to come in as evidence. If the ruling was changed, allowing in evidence concerning what occurred before the divorce, Woolley's hands would be untied regarding the Florida common law marriage. Regarding this, Woolley's comment was brief.

"Hollywood and Thorpe will hear plenty."

•••

In Hollywood, the adverse affect that the custody case might have was finally settling in. Consequently, "Astor Sensations Scare Film Moguls" was the front-page headline of a *New York Daily News*. In part the story read, "Movie moguls sweated freely as the sensational Mary Astor custody case threatened to destroy the reputation of many highly placed in the industry."

The *New York Evening Journal* saw it this way: "At least six men whose love-making has quickened the hearts of millions of women in the world's motion picture theatres were reported in a condition bordering on panic as a result of Mary Astor's determined fight for custody of her small daughter."

The *New York Mirror* was a bit more dramatic. "There is—everybody in the movie colony agrees—no preventing the earthquake which Mary's diary threatens, and movie producers, as well as the half-dozen perfect lovers of the screen, will be affected… in a trial threatening Hollywood with the greatest series of shocks in its history."

Whether these or any other newspapers were printing the truth, a partial truth, or merely inventing as they went along had become irrelevant. What did matter was that it all fed into Franklyn Thorpe and Joseph Anderson's evolving legal strategy. It was their intention to put the fear of God into Hollywood and, by doing so, manipulate the industry into putting pressure on Astor to cave.

At the beginning of the hearing, Thorpe's tactic had been merely

Mary Astor and her daughter.

to intimidate and scare his former wife into withdrawing the suit by mentioning that the diaries existed. Then, after Thorpe had been eviscerated—first under Woolley's questioning and then by Nellie Richardson's testimony—the stakes had risen. Feeling that Astor and her attorney had become emboldened, Thorpe and Anderson's next step was to increase the pressure by submitting diary excerpts and bringing in George Kaufman's name. Then, after Astor's brilliant recital of her version of events on Thursday, Thorpe and Anderson were ratcheting it up even further by threatening both to submit additional diary extracts as well as subpoena the men mentioned in them. It was their hope that this would generate enough pressure to force Astor to drop the suit while any potential damage to her career was still minimal.

What Anderson and Thorpe didn't understand was that Mary Astor no longer cared about her reputation or even her movie career. What concerned her was the upbringing of her daughter, which she believed was being sabotaged by Franklyn Thorpe undermining her authority as a mother while also raising the terrifying specter that at any moment her child could be snatched away from her. Mary Astor wasn't bluffing. She had pushed all her chips into the pot and was going for broke.

17

On Saturday morning, not surprisingly, Norma Taylor was in the news again. It was reported that while a very melancholy Miss Taylor was still resting in a private sanatorium under an assumed name, her attorney had informed reporters that he had conferred by telephone with Joseph Anderson, and that Anderson had promised to recall Nellie Richardson to the stand for further cross-examination.

"Miss Taylor did not retain me to get money, but to get vindication for her good name. Charges have been made by innuendo against Miss Taylor and her good name shall be kept clear of scandal."

How melancholy was Norma Taylor? On Saturday, the woman didn't phone a single reporter to give an interview.

• • •

Meanwhile, at Toluca Lake, Mary Astor, dressed in a white summer suit, was standing in front of her home, little Marylyn playing beside her. They were waiting for Judge Knight. During the last two weeks, despite a tsunami of publicity, Astor had "tried to maintain a normal life and a semblance of calm with Marylyn." Today was different. The two were not alone. In addition to an attorney, Frank Rank from Woolley's office, there were scores of reporters and photographers milling about. Woolley and Astor had agreed to allow the press in so the public could glimpse the loving home in which Mary Astor was raising her daughter.

On Thursday evening, the actress had used Edith Cortright

to help her to open up. Today would be different. Today Mary Astor needed to be herself.

Franklyn Thorpe also knew what the judge needed to see. Thorpe had to prove that his daughter not only loved him but also loved being with him. Fortunately, when Thorpe—Anderson beside him—parked in the driveway, Marylyn, playing with a kitten, lit up and, shouting "Daddy," ran over. Thorpe grabbed hold of the little girl and, after kissing her, bounced his daughter up and gave her a tight hug. Pulling

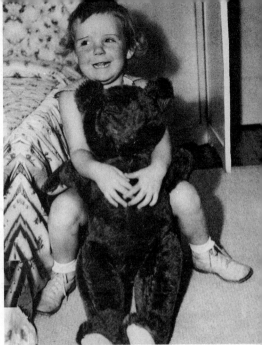

Little Marylyn in her bedroom with her oversized teddy bear.

away, the little girl took his hand and led her father to her sand pile where they made sand pies together. Astor joined them.

"We can never get enough toys for Marylyn's sand pile."

Thorpe didn't respond. He was angry and he wanted Astor to know it. Astor, aware that their every gesture and every word would find its way into the newspapers, felt they should at least be civil with each other. Realizing that Thorpe wasn't going to play along, she looked away and concluded it best to keep her mouth shut.

• • •

At around 11:00 a.m., Judge Knight finally arrived by auto and, surrounded by reporters, Mary Astor walked over, shook hands, and attempted some small talk.

Knight knew that testimony given in court by the parents about a child was, for the most part, extremely biased. He had learned that he needed to see how a child interacted with his or her parents to ascertain what the child really felt. Knight also believed that it was best to see a child in their home environment, where a child felt free to be him or herself.

Since little Marylyn was a real attention getter, as soon as she saw the judge smile at her, the little girl left her father and walked over to her mother. Wrapping her arms around her mother's knee, she looked up at her mother, smiled, and then hugged her mother's legs even tighter. Instead of being shy around strangers, Marylyn was laughing and clapping—not only enjoying all this attention but actually playing to it.

When Astor introduced her to the judge, Knight's smile broadened and, crouching down, he shook the little girl's hand and told her that he had two little girls, with the oldest also named Marilyn.

When Thorpe joined them, the four posed for photographers. While flashbulbs popped, the baby took hold of first her mother's hand and then her father's and, standing between them, pulled her parents until the three stood close together. This was typical of a child with divorced parents but it only served to make Marylyn's parents uncomfortable. While Astor tried her best to smile, Thorpe frowned. Unlike his former wife, Franklyn Thorpe did not hide his feelings.

Marylyn was soon showing off in front of photographers—giggling while the flashbulbs popped. She even demanded that her oversize teddy bear be included in the photos. It was evident that the child's openness and lack of trepidation with strangers suggested one thing: Marylyn Thorpe was a well-adjusted and happy child. That is what the judge hoped to see and what he, indeed, did see.

Thorpe, annoyed that he wasn't able to interact with his daughter, headed down to the lakeside. Not seeing her father for a while the child made an announcement.

"Come, see the baby swans."

Carrying her oversized teddy bear, she led everyone to the lakeside where her father was standing. Thorpe saw her coming and she shouted.

"Daddy!"

When Marylyn reached her father—reporters at a distance—

father and daughter were alone together for a few minutes. Since the swans wanted to be fed, Mary Astor walked down from the house carrying some stale bread. She handed her daughter bread slices, then gave slices to the lawyers, and even offered bread to Thorpe. Having just proven that Marylyn was neither afraid nor timid around him, Thorpe was in good spirits. Taking the bread, he actually made some small talk with Astor.

While everyone was tossing scraps of bread to the swans, on the side of the lake the sun shone through the tall trees. Judge Knight turned to Mary Astor.

"What lovely surroundings."

She agreed. Bread depleted, lead by Marylyn, everyone headed back up to the house. The judge, lawyers, photographers, and reporters all walked up to the second-floor nursery. With everyone comfortable, Marylyn yanked open her closet and, one by one, took out all her dolls. Sitting them in a row on the bed she introduced them to the judge, naming each one. A few minutes later, Judge Knight sat on a chair and placed the little girl on his knee.

"Do you like Mickey Mouse better than Minnie Mouse?"

Marylyn smiled. "I like 'em both."

"Do you love your mom?"

Marylyn nodded vigorously. "Uh-huh. I do."

"And do you love your pops?"

Marylyn nodded once again. "Uh-huh."

The truth was that this little show was being conducted for the benefit of the newspapers. Knight could discern how the child felt about her parents by the way she interacted with them and her emotional state by how well she interacted with everyone else. What he and everyone observed that morning was a happy, stable and well-adjusted child. So, once this bit of "theatre" was out of the way, Judge Knight and the assembled reporters were given a tour of the house.

A short time later, the judge and lawyers holed up inside a spare bedroom with the door shut, participating in an off-the-record conference. Astor and Thorpe remained with Marylyn and

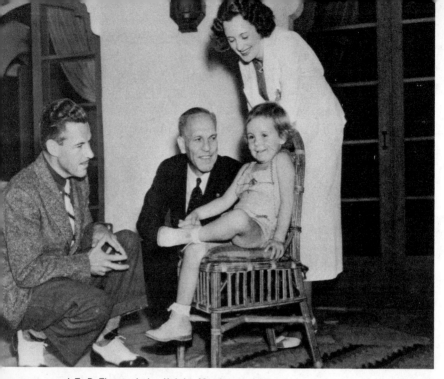

L To R: Thorpe, Judge Knight, Marylyn, and Astor.

the press. During the ten minutes they were together Knight hoped he might persuade the lawyers to settle out of court. He had decided to admit into evidence testimony regarding events prior to the April 1935 divorce. What now concerned Knight was the salacious, embarrassing, and potentially damaging evidence that would come into his courtroom and how it might taint the baby for the rest of her life. Unfortunately, his pleas fell on deaf ears.

Having just heard the judge's decision, Joseph Anderson felt he now had the trump card—the diaries. Therefore, Anderson saw no reason to compromise. Franklyn Thorpe wanted full custody. Compromise was also unacceptable to Mary Astor. Talks going nowhere, the three men left the bedroom to face reporters. Judge Knight spoke.

"The attorneys declare their principals are adamant. There can be no settlement. It's too bad. Such lovely parents and such a wonderful house. It's like the irresistible force meeting the immovable object."

Judge Knight also took this opportunity to announce that he would resume evening deliberations before the end of the week, as Mary Astor was needed back on the set of *Dodsworth* to complete her role.

A few minutes later a jubilant Franklyn Thorpe bent, kissed his daughter, and spoke to reporters.

"I've got the plans all drawn for a home that we'll live in if we get custody. It's got a swell little nursery and all and it's within walking distance of a grammar school and a high school. We'll live there a long time if I get her."

Judge Knight made his goodbyes and walked to his car. The reporters, photographers, and lawyers did the same. Meanwhile, Marylyn, her mother holding one hand, used her free hand to wave good-bye to her father. She appeared disappointed that all the excitement had come to such an abrupt end.

Judge Knight had been in the Toluca Lake house for a little less than an hour.

18

On Sunday morning it was announced that Norma Taylor, that vivacious "platinum-blonde Hollywood and Broadway beauty" was not only "getting ready to bolt" from a Westchester sanatorium and fly to the coast but intended to burst into the Superior Court of Los Angles and demand that her name be cleared. When exactly Norma would be making this dramatic appearance depended on how soon she could pull herself out of her nervous breakdown. Attorney Braunstein promised to keep the press informed.

• • •

The real news that Sunday was George S. Kaufman. Kaufman—to escape reporters camped outside the Beverly Wilshire—had spent Thursday night, Friday, and much of Saturday with Moss Hart at Hart's rented house in Beverly Hills. Unhampered, the two worked on their still-untitled play. It was almost finished and scheduled to open in the fall. Kaufman couldn't leave Hollywood—at least not right then. His contract with MGM legally obligated him to remain until August 8, and he and Hart needed to finish the play as soon as possible.

Then, on Saturday, hearing about Anderson's subpoenas, Kaufman secretly made his way to Catalina Island, where he checked into the island's luxurious St. Catherine Hotel, hoping to keep both the press and possible process servers at bay. Kaufman immediately sent off five telegrams. One was to wife Beatrice, still in Europe, giving her an update. Another was to his wife's relatives in Rochester. That telegram was brief.

"Don't believe what you read in the tabloids."

For Sunday, Kaufman had plans to go yachting with producer Irving Thalberg and Thalberg's wife, actress Norma Shearer. Thalberg was about to set up his own independent production company within the MGM facility. As head of an MGM production unit, Thalberg had signed Kaufman and others for his exclusive use but, once it was up and running, Thalberg would transfer these contracts to his independent company.

Since Kaufman was also one of Broadway's most successful directors Thalberg wanted Kaufman to direct films for his company as well. Kaufman relished the idea since he could, as he wrote his wife, earn "a hunk of money where our old age security will come from." Now, finding himself embroiled in a scandal that could upset these plans because of the morals clause in all Hollywood contracts, George Kaufman had a lot at stake.

• • •

Sunday morning, the playwright was anticipating a pleasant day yachting with the Thalbergs. Thalberg's yacht, the Melodie, was docked beside a pier a short distance from the rear of the hotel. While Thalberg and Shearer were waiting on the dock to greet Kaufman, Joseph Anderson's brother, William, suddenly popped up. An attorney himself, William Anderson was standing in for a process server.

"Are you George Kaufman?"

"Yes."

Anderson handed Kaufman the summons, and a very surprised George Kaufman glanced down at it.

"What is this, a subpoena?"

"Yes it is."

Kaufman was upset. "Well, that's too bad, isn't it?"

Boarding Thalberg's yacht, he was both angry and flustered. Before heading to his cabin he paced the deck and, after a long groan, cried out that he was being crucified. Presumably the person doing the crucifying was Dr. Franklyn Thorpe. Kaufman later told a friend, "It was so maddening that I was ready to throw myself overboard and let the sharks finish me."

This was the "bombshell" Joseph Anderson had promised and the next day it made headlines. George Kaufman's private life was about to go public. Instead of heading out to sea, Kaufman, Thalberg, and Shearer returned to Los Angeles.

Reaching his hotel, Kaufman rushed past reporters and barked out a one-sentence statement.

"I have nothing to say about this case."

• • •

After William Anderson telephoned his brother, Thorpe's attorney immediately announced to the press his plans regarding Kaufman.

"We will question him very thoroughly about his friendship with Miss Astor. This is only the beginning of our attempt to show that Miss Astor is not a fit mother for little Marylyn. There will be many others subpoenaed here, many of them prominent persons. You may depend on it and that I will cross-examine Miss Astor thoroughly."

"Do you plan to introduce the secret diary?"

"If Miss Astor's answers give me an opportunity, the diary most certainly will appear."

"The entire diary?"

"No, Kaufman's place in the diary will be established without introduction of the entire document. Passages involving him will be read into the record."

Under cross-examination, Anderson would "endeavor to force Miss Astor to admit her child is devoted to her father and relinquished the little girl because she thought it would be in the best interests of Marylyn."

Using the testimony of Mrs. Lillian Miles and other witnesses, including a cross-examination of Nellie Richardson, Anderson intended to prove that Richardson's claim that Miss Taylor, Mrs.

Miles, and other women were overnight guests in Dr. Thorpe's bedroom was a figment of the woman's imagination. Presumably this was what Anderson had told Norma Taylor's attorney. The truth was that Joseph Anderson had enough on his plate without having to worry about Norma Taylor's antics.

19

On Monday morning, upon decamping from an unnamed Westchester Sanitarium, Norma Taylor announced through her attorney that she felt much better after her rest over the weekend. Her lawyer felt that Norma was now ready for a speedy trip to the coast to safeguard her reputation. The "vivacious blonde" wanted her name cleared and was threatening legal action "against all persons responsible for the thoroughly perjurious testimony" involving her with Dr. Thorpe. It seemed Norma had made a miraculous recovery not only from her bout of melancholia but also from her nervous breakdown.

• • •

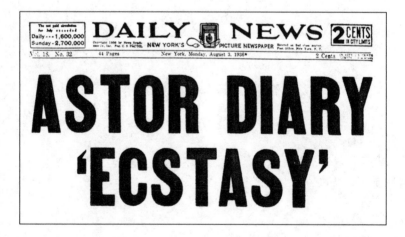

In New York, the front page of the *New York Daily News* proclaimed, "Astor Diary—'Ecstasy'" and part of the lead story read, "If Mary Astor wanted to spare her adored 'George' the embarrassment of

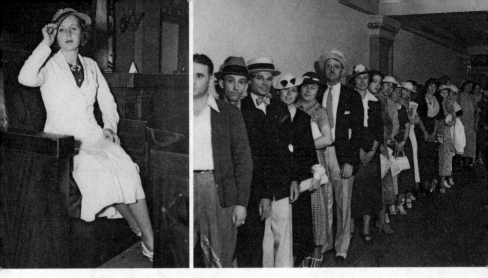

Mary Astor's second day on the stand.

a public revelation of their love she should have not confided to her famous diary the story of her complete capitulation the first time she met him and of the 'thrilling ecstasy' that followed." The meeting was in a swank Manhattan bar, described in her diary as 'our 21' underlined at each reference. The diary recounts how the growing friendship was cemented by several rounds of champagne and brandy cocktails. During the late afternoon they made a round of other bars, spent evenings at the theatre, and wound up in an apartment on East Seventy-Third Street. Miss Astor's prose in describing the experiences at Seventy-Third Street would make a writer of romantic fiction envious.

As this generally resembled diary entries that Anderson intended to submit into evidence, there is little doubt that his office was the source. Attorney Anderson was preparing the press and public for his cross-examination of Mary Astor.

• • •

In the Los Angeles superior court, the hearing was about to begin its fourth session when a mob of several hundred sweating, anxious people poured into the courtroom to find seats. Expecting portions of the diary to be read made the hearing an even "hotter ticket" than usual. Soon the courtroom was packed, and crowds filled the corridors, where vendors sold ice cream and hot dogs. Judge Knight was forced to move the hearing three times to ever-larger courtrooms. None proved large enough, and the overflow crowds listened from the hallway.

Mary Astor arrived with Ruth Chatterton, Roland Woolley, Nellie Richardson, and Astor's mother—with strict orders to not speak to the press. As the five pushed through the crowds, reporters shouted questions about the diary, but Astor didn't respond. Following a Sunday at home with the baby she looked rested and refreshed. Wearing no makeup except a bit of lip rouge, she had on a two-piece white linen suit with a sheer dark blue V-neck blouse and a brown felt hat. She carried a white handbag under her arm. Wedding and engagement rings worn on the small finger of her right hand, she was described as "a cool figure in white as beautifully poised as though enacting a role for the camera."

Ruth Chatterton, also dressed in white, sat in the front row. Nellie Richardson and Astor's mother sat close by. The very blonde Mrs. Lillian Miles was sitting patiently with Thorpe's family.

One person who wasn't in court was George Kaufman. Closeted in his hotel suite, he and Moss Hart were completing their play. In New York, a newspaper printed that he and Beatrice had "long been living their own lives," code words meaning the two had affairs with the other's consent. One intrepid reporter even interviewed an employee at the 21 Club who remembered how intimate Kaufman and Astor had been when they were there. Kaufman's private life was rapidly becoming very public.

Accordingly, Mendel Silberberg, an influential Los Angeles attorney on retainer by MGM, was also in court. Known as a "fixer," almost immediately after Kaufman was handed the subpoena Mayer and Thalberg met with Silberberg concerning the legal consequences of any actions Kaufman might take. Because Kaufman was a valuable asset to the studio, Silberberg in court to advise Mayer and Thalberg. Since Kaufman was under contract with MGM until Saturday, there was also the question of possible legal ramifications for the studio.

• • •

Mary Astor and her attorney as well as Franklyn Thorpe and his attorneys were required to wait patiently behind the guardrail while Judge Knight cleared his calendar. This involved granting two divorces and an annulment of a Tijuana marriage. There were no witnesses, and simple statements made by the plaintiffs proved sufficient for Knight to grant the decrees.

That out of the way, Astor and Thorpe and company stood up, walked inside the railing, and made themselves comfortable at the counsel table. First on the agenda was a request made by H.F. Selvin representing Samuel Goldwyn, the producer of *Dodsworth*. The producer asked for the hearing to be delayed a week so that Astor could complete her role in the film. Subsequently Selvin, Woolley, and Anderson followed Judge Knight into chambers, where Selvin explained that five hundred extras were on the United Artists lot costing several thousand dollars a day if Miss Astor was not in front of the cameras.

Judge Knight offered to hold night sessions, but Selvin told him that in some of last week's footage Astor had looked exhausted. Consequently Knight had no problem with the delay, and neither did Woolley nor, surprisingly, Joseph Anderson. This would give Woolley more time to gather additional Florida common-law-marriage evidence, and Anderson needed the time to ferret out the men he wanted to subpoena.

When Judge Knight returned to the bench he announced that he had just agreed to a one-week continuance following today's session so that Miss Astor might complete "urgent work at her studio." The next session would be held the following Monday, August 10.

Then, as Anderson had promised, he submitted his motion alleging that Astor had obtained temporary custody fraudulently.

Judge Knight heard Woolley's argument in opposition and immediately dismissed Anderson's motion.

Undaunted, Joseph Anderson dropped another one of his bombshells by announcing that he had obtained a subpoena for John Barrymore and process servers were searching for the actor.

Hearing this, Roland Rich Woolley immediately shot to his feet and, with Astor nodding her approval, spoke to the court.

"John Barrymore has nothing whatever to do with the case. And to call him as a witness would be just as consistent for them to subpoena former Governor Landon or President Roosevelt. We regard this as another move in the desperate and futile effort of Mr. Anderson to throw up a smokescreen around an unjustified attack upon Miss Astor's charges and a character assassination program involving matters not material to this issue."

Barrymore, described by the press as "the greatest screen Romeo of all time," had legal problems of his own. With two lawsuits pending—coincidentally both before Judge Knight—there was a question whether the actor was well enough to attend his own legal proceedings. Barrymore was at the Mar Vista Sanatorium drying out, where his doctors described him as "seriously ill." So ill, in fact, that his doctors had made it clear that to bring him into court might actually endanger the man's life.

So, Judge Knight recessed the court for a few minutes to discuss the Barrymore issue with all the attorneys, Barrymore's as well as Astor and Thorpe's. After listening to arguments, Judge Knight determined that Barrymore could be served but whether he was physically able to appear would be determined later. That out of the way, Knight resumed the hearing.

• • •

Mary Astor was finally recalled to the stand and, "beautifully dressed and speaking in a low voice, played to a sympathetic audience." She smoothed out her dress, and Roland Woolley picked up his direct examination where he left off on Thursday.

"Did you have a conversation with Dr. Thorpe about the end of March 1935 concerning a divorce?"

"Yes."

"What was said?"

Astor's voice dropped a bit and, handkerchief on her lap, she kept pulling it through her fingers. "He said that unless I allowed him to obtain a divorce and custody of the baby and to do with the property as he pleased, he would scandalize me in the eyes of the public; that he would blacken my name and the names of many of my prominent friends. That he would plaster me all over the front pages of every newspaper in the country and wreck my reputation and ruin my career as an actress."

"What did you say?"

"I said that I thought it was a pretty horrible thing to do. I was thinking of my child. I told him that if he wrecked my career and ruined my chances of making money as a motion picture actress, I couldn't earn money to support the baby and I said, 'Something you can't—or won't do.'"

"Did he ever repeat these statements?"

"Continuously. That went on for days and nights… until well… until the divorce."

"What was the condition of your health at the time?"

"I was ill. I was in a state of semi-hysteria. I was too ill to talk. I was heartsick. I was licked. I was deathly afraid of him."

"You feared Dr. Thorpe at that time?"

Her voice shook a bit. "Yes. I was mortally afraid of him. He struck me once. I did not know when he would do it again. He could get me into a hysterical state. I had to get away. I couldn't stand the everlasting torment of his threats. I knew he would try to carry out his threats if I resisted him. He has no shame and he'd do anything of that sort. I was definitely afraid of him."

Sympathetic sighs were heard throughout the courtroom. Realizing he was being painted as a wife beater, Dr. Franklyn Thorpe—who had been sitting with his fingers tightly interlaced—

suddenly rose half out of his seat and, face flushed, turned to Anderson.

"That's nuts."

Judge Knight brought down the gavel and warned Thorpe that he wouldn't tolerate that sort of behavior in his courtroom. A contrite Franklyn Thorpe sat back down.

Woolley continued.

"In the pre-divorce agreement a trust fund was even set up for Dr. Thorpe to fight any attempts you might make to recover the baby?"

"Yes."

"Why would you sign something like that?"

"I was sick. I was semi-hysterical, heartsick, and too weak to fight. He threatened to blacken my character and to destroy my friends. He said I would never act again in films. He could get me into a hysterical state. He had a form of hypnotic control over me."

Anderson stood up. "Objection! Dr. Thorpe is a physician, not a hypnotist."

Judge Knight agreed. "Strike the reference to hypnotic control."

Although stricken from the record, this didn't stop Americans from reading "Husband Hypnotized Me" in banner headlines.

Woolley continued. "Did you move away from your Toluca Lake home on or about April 1, 1935, and take the baby with you?"

"Yes. I couldn't stand his tormenting me with these continuous threats that he was going to ruin me, blacken my name, and wreck my chances of ever acting again."

"Did you believe that he would?"

"I knew that he would try."

"Why did you believe that?"

"He said it and I believed him. He would do anything. He seemed to have no shame."

"Did you have the flu at the time?"

"I was in bed part of the time, up until the time that I moved."

"Were these threats, which you have related, the reason you gave Dr. Thorpe guardianship of the child?"

"Yes, exactly the reason."

Woolley handed her a copy of the trustee agreement prohibiting her from taking Marylyn out of state without Thorpe's permission.

"Is that your signature?"

"Yes."

"Why did you sign it?"

"Because I was told to by Dr. Thorpe."

"At the time you signed it, were you fearful that Dr. Thorpe would carry out the threats you have told us about?"

"Yes. He told me I would have to sign it."

"Were you afraid of him at the time?"

"Definitely afraid, yes. I knew he would carry out his threats to scandalize me."

"Do you remember a conversation with Dr. Thorpe and his attorney, Miss Pepin?"

"Yes. It occurred in the library, where I had made up a bed because I was ill, about March 28, 1935."

"At that time did Dr. Thorpe make any further threats?"

"Yes. He said, 'This thing is going to be the way I want it. I'm going to get the divorce and the custody of the child and the distribution of the property the way I want it.' I said I would do as he pleased. There was nothing else that I could do. I was ill and heartsick over the way things were turning out. I was licked."

"What, if anything, did Miss Pepin say?"

"She said, 'I don't think it's very fair deal for Mary; especially the declaration of trust.' And Franklyn said, 'Ethel, you are going over to Mary's side. It's going to be the way I want it. I'm running this show.'"

"How did you feel, then?"

"I realized that I was licked. I was ill. I was heartsick over the way the thing was turning out. I knew that he would try to do the things he said he would do. I left then and moved to 1122 Tower Road in Beverly Hills and took Marylyn with me."

"Who brought up the subject of divorce first?"

Anderson objected and was overruled.

"I did."

"What did you say?"

"I brought up the divorce question and he said he would allow me to have a divorce. We had been discussing divorce since March 1933."

At this point, Judge Knight brought the gavel down and announced a recess for lunch. Knight retired to chambers and Astor and Chatterton pushed their way out of the courtroom through rows of excited spectators.

• • •

With reporters gathered around, Roland Rich Woolley informed them that Joseph Anderson was scandalizing perfectly innocent people. Overhearing, Anderson shouted at Woolley in a voice everyone could hear.

"I'm not going to take the time to answer all these incriminating and phony statements. I am going to prove conclusively before I'm through—"

Woolley cut him short. "Be careful what you say and be prepared to prove any allegation. Have you forgotten the Supreme Court's ruling? As an attorney, you're responsible for scandalizing statements that are not proven."

Woolley was referring to a Supreme Court decision whereby an attorney is required to prove the validity of statements made concerning persons who could suffer harmful repercussions if these statements could not be proven. In 1936 an attorney could be sued for false statements and even, depending on the severity, disbarred. So Anderson, considering it the better part of valor, shut his mouth and, like everyone else, marched off to lunch.

20

At 2:00 p.m., Knight brought court back into session. Mary Astor resumed her place in the witness box and Woolley—following a few questions that allowed Astor to clarify several dates—concluded his direct examination. As Woolley sat, Joseph Anderson rose, ready to begin his cross-examination.

Mary Astor was prepared. Woolley had warned her that the questions asked would be designed to make her lose her temper and say things detrimental to her case. Therefore, Astor steeled herself for what the newspapers would later call a "merciless cross-examination." She'd write, Edith Cortright "was my shield; without her I would have been shattered emotionally."

Joseph Anderson needed to accomplish two things. Because Astor's testimony had left everyone thinking Thorpe was a wife beater, Thorpe wanted that charge immediately discredited. Second, and most importantly, Anderson needed to get the diary into evidence by having Astor contradict what she had written so he could use it to impeach her testimony. Once the diary was in evidence he could attack Astor's character. Hence, right at start Anderson—as it was reported—"hurled his questions" "like a bullwhip."

"Did Dr. Thorpe strike you on March 28, 1935?"

"Yes."

"Where?"

"In our bedroom."

"How?"

"He sort of pushed me into a chair."

Astor demonstrated with a pushing motion using her left hand.

"With his open hand?"

"Yes."

"Were there any bruises?"

"I don't recall."

Anderson had gotten the clarification he wanted and moved on.

"Why were you in such dread of him?"

"Because I knew my husband wanted to shame me."

"Did you provoke him—had you told him of your affair with George Kaufman?"

Every eye was on Mary Astor. Every ear straining to hear what she would say. The air in that room was charged. But, instead of answering the question, Astor sidestepped.

"It was during one of his intimidating conversations. I had protested. I said: 'You can't do this dreadful thing to me.'"

"Well, did he mention any names?"

"Yes. Many names. Names of my prominent friends."

"Was there any reason for his threats?"

"Yes, because he wanted to shame me, so he could get control of the child and the property."

Because Astor's answers were not what she had written in the diaries, Anderson felt he could impeach her testimony. Walking to the counsel table, he was handed several diary pages. He handed them to Astor.

"Do these pages belong to your diary?"

Studying the pages, she nodded and her anger flared.

"Yes, they are part of the diary which was stolen from me by Dr. Thorpe by stealth through a discharged servant."

Anderson turned and spoke to the court as well as the press.

"We're going to impeach this woman's testimony with her own handwriting."

Woolley intended put an end to this immediately. Because he had told Astor that, when diaries came up, to announce that they had been stolen, Woolley objected that a stolen document was inadmissible.

Joseph Anderson was prepared. He cited a California appellate ruling permitting the introduction of a document regardless of how it was obtained.

As Anderson spoke, Woolley studied the detached pages. He had guessed correctly. They were separated. Franklyn Thorpe didn't want the entire diary submitted. So, Woolley cut Anderson short.

"It's been tampered with and mutilated. It's a two-hundred-page document and the pages reflecting on Dr. Thorpe have either been torn out or mutilated in their entirety. If he wants to do this then the diary must be introduced in its entirety."

Woolley handed Knight the sheets and then he and Anderson argued back and forth. Mary Astor's diary was in two volumes, but it was the second volume—with entries from March 25, 1930 through March 1935—that contained the Kaufman passages and from which these pages had been removed. In mentioning a two-hundred-page document Woolley was referring only to the second volume.

Woolley said that the court had the right to learn where the rest of diaries were and why it had been mutilated. Anderson suddenly accused Woolley of attempting to steal the diaries, declaring that over the weekend two attempts had been made to break into his office. Outraged at the accusation, Woolley denied it, and the two began a heated argument.

Meanwhile, Judge Knight—after skimming through the

pages—wanted to know how Anderson got hold of the diary pages. He dismissed Astor and recalled Franklyn Thorpe to the stand.

Thorpe said that he had given the complete diary to his attorney Ethel Pepin. Taking the stand, Pepin said that she had given the books to Joseph Anderson. Anderson testified next and told the court that he had given the diary to his brother, William. Called to the witness box, William Anderson told Knight that he had separated the pages in order to make photostatic copies of the "pertinent pages."

"I put all of it in my safety deposit box except possibly one or two pages."

"And where are those pages?"

"I don't know."

Judge Knight looked at William Anderson skeptically. It was obvious that they were attempting to exclude pages. Judge Knight wasn't pleased.

"Regardless of what you consider pertinent to this case or not, I want the rest of the diary in this court room next Monday including the missing pages. All portions of the diary that are relevant will be admitted into evidence unless opposing counsel can cite authorities which would prohibit their introduction. After reading these eight pages I am satisfied of their relevance." Knight turned to Woolley. "I will take the responsibility that all innocent persons mentioned in the document will be protected."

Woolley sat down. With the judge taking responsibility for what was or wasn't going to be admitted as evidence, Woolley had won the first skirmish. He turned and whispered to Astor that "he had an answer to the diary problem."

• • •

Mary Astor took the stand and the cross-examination resumed. Anderson, certain that the diary would be admitted, brought up things discussed in the diary so he could impeach Astor's testimony if she contradicted what she had written.

"Is it not a fact that the reason that you let the divorce go through in April 1935 by default was because you were in love with a man named George Kaufman."

Woolley jumped up. "Objection! This is nothing but an attempt to introduce scandalous, scurrilous matter into this hearing in order to injure Miss Astor, and indirectly her child; as well as scandalize someone not involved in this hearing."

Woolley's objection overruled, Anderson shouted.

"Is it not a fact?"

Bringing her gloved hand to her face, Astor, eyebrows raised contemptuously, looked at Anderson with total contempt for a few seconds before answering.

"That is not a fact."

Later, Astor would describe her courtroom strategy. "I often confused the attorney for the other side by taking a long time before answering his questions, eyebrows slightly raised. 'Do you really mean I should answer such an imprudent question' in my thoughts. I wasn't smart or clever but I was completely rattle-proof thanks to Edith Cortright."

"Were you in love with George S. Kaufman at the time the divorce was filed?"

Hearing this, Woolley was back up. "Objection to this entire line of questioning. This question has no bearing on this proceeding."

Judge Knight agreed and sustained. Anderson continued.

"Isn't it a fact that you sought the advice of an attorney before you discussed the divorce with Dr. Thorpe?"

"Yes."

"Did you go to La Jolla in the early part of 1935?"

Astor's answer reeked with sarcasm. "Yes. I am not a prisoner."

Unfazed, Anderson continued.

"At that time did you come to some conclusion as to your own rights and what you were going to do?"

"Yes. I considered it my right to be free of the brutality of the man—" her voice rose—"and from his constant association with Lillian Miles."

In her seat Mrs. Lillian Miles did her best not to show any emotion. This was an even worse accusation then the one made by Nellie Richardson. And the worst part about it was that it was absolutely true.

"When did you first discuss divorce?"

"Early in February."

"Did you give him any reason for the divorce at that time?"

Woolley objected that it was irrelevant because it hadn't been acted on, and Judge Knight sustained. Anderson continued.

"Who was present when you discussed the divorce in February?"

Woolley objected to this entire line of questioning, as "a definite effort is being made on the part of the defendant to scandalize this witness by delving into matters not pertinent to the issue. I would just like some of this cleared up."

Once again, Judge Knight overruled.

"Who was present?"

"I can't remember."

"Isn't it a fact that you knew in February 1935 that Dr. Thorpe would fight for the compete custody of the baby?"

She shook her head. "I don't remember."

"Isn't it a fact that at that time you also knew that Dr. Thorpe was going to name George Kaufman in a divorce action against you?"

Woolley jumped up. "Objection! The question is designed to scandalize someone not involved in this hearing and the witness is being asked to testify as to the state of mind of Dr. Thorpe."

"Objection sustained."

Anderson continued. "Well, didn't you have a discussion with Dr. Thorpe about a call he made on George Kaufman at his hotel suite?"

"Yes. That was discussed among other things."

"Where did this discussion between your former husband and yourself take place?"

"It may have been in my bedroom, living room, or any other part of the house. I don't remember."

"In your own words, what was said?"

Showing her disdain for the man, Astor looked Anderson directly in the eye.

"I said, 'You know George Kaufman has nothing to do with this divorce.' I told Franklyn that by living with me as man and wife, after he knew of my association with George Kaufman, he had condoned it."

"Your exact words?"

Astor glared at Anderson in disgust. "I told my husband that George Kaufman had nothing to do with any arrangements we had made for a divorce. I told Franklyn, 'You've known about George Kaufman and me since last October. Since then, we have been living together as man and wife and in that way you have condoned it. Now that the divorce matter has come up and we are miserable and fighting for our child you throw George Kaufman at me when I want to get a divorce so you can get Marylyn.'"

"And what did Dr. Thorpe say, then?"

"He said, 'I don't care. I'll use any means I wish to get custody.'"

Mouths dropped while reporters frantically filled their notepads. Mary Astor had admitted in open court that while married to Franklyn Thorpe, she had had an affair with George Kaufman. This was adultery with a capital A and adultery was a very serious matter in 1936. Thirteen years later, Ingrid Berman would have an adulterous affair with director Roberto Rossellini, and her career in Hollywood evaporated overnight.

Anderson continued his questions.

"Had you consulted an attorney about a divorce?"

Before Woolley could object, Astor lost her temper and lashed out.

"I wanted to be free from Dr. Thorpe because of his constant association with Lillian Miles."

This reply wasn't as hot tempered as it might first appear. Although Mary Astor had just admitted to adultery, with this outburst she had announced that Dr. Thorpe was also an adulterer. It was an open attack on both Thorpe's hypocrisy and the double standard—woman committing adultery, that's horrible, but a man committing adultery, that's "boys will be boys."

Nevertheless, Anderson wouldn't let up.

"Is it not a fact that you had already selected a place to live in Beverly Hills before you discussed the divorce?"

Astor shook her head firmly. "It's not a fact."

"Had you looked for a place in Beverly Hills?"

"I had not—not before we discussed the divorce."

At this point Judge Knight brought his gavel down and adjourned until next Monday.

• • •

Mary Astor had scored a hit with the press. "The dazzling film beauty's testimony" "electrified the courtroom with high drama." "The slender and frail dark-eyed wisp of a girl weighing barely a hundred pounds" "faced the crowded courtroom with utmost composure" and spoke "in a hesitant but carefully controlled voice." Under Anderson's "sledgehammer blows" "her voice was firm and level" so that "when the ordeal was ended" "Miss Astor emerged as the freshest woman" in the room.

If there had been a jury in that courtroom, they would have most likely carried Mary Astor out on their shoulders.

• • •

Reporters crowded around as Anderson's associate A.P. Narlain spoke.

"We're going to have to let the whole thing come out now. Miss Astor's own statements make it necessary. We had hoped to pass over some parts of it, but we can't, not with her statements about Dr. Thorpe hanging there."

"Let the whole thing come out" was Narlain referring to the entire diary, implying that they weren't concealing anything, just trying to protect Mary Astor.

• • •

Leaving the courthouse on Woolley's arm, Mary Astor was smiling and let it be known that, "I want the judge to read the entire diary. I want him to see all the things that I wrote about my former husband. They are worse than anything they can say about me."

This was strategy. Woolley was now certain he could keep the diary out. Earlier, he had hoped to do this by demanding that the entire document be included, but now, with it mutilated, he could keep it out for that reason. The new line was that it was Mary Astor who had nothing to hide, that Franklyn Thorpe was doing the hiding. Woolley and Astor had cleverly turned the specter of damaging diary revelations loose on Franklyn Thorpe.

• • •

Earlier, reporters had caught a glimpse of the diary pages in the courtroom, and it was reported that Astor used "purple ink." Some newspapers even added that the pages were scented. Concerning this purple ink revelation Mary Astor would recall, "I had a fancy for an ink called 'Aztec Brown'; the combination of colors seen at a distance by members of the press gave them the impression that it was written in 'purple ink.' They were no doubt confirmed in this opinion by their supposition that the diary recorded events of that passionate hue."

• • •

Shortly after court adjourned, George Kaufman, leaving his hotel, was told by members of the press camped outside that his name had again come up in court, and he was asked if he had, indeed, been Miss Astor's lover. This time it was a very annoyed, very worried George Kaufman who hurriedly made a two-sentence statement.

"I have nothing to say. I am not interested in anything Miss Astor may have testified to."

21

As fiction editor for *Harper's Bazaar*, Beatrice Kaufman was, technically, a member of the media and, therefore, knew far better than her husband how to manipulate the press.

Personally, "Beatrice was totally shattered" that her husband's affair with Astor had gone public as it pointed out her limitations as a wife. But Beatrice was not one to run from adversity. Instead, she understood the necessity to implement immediate damage control to counter her husband's increasingly negative public image. Therefore, in her position as the "wronged woman" she had to tell the world that she didn't consider herself "wronged," she was an understanding wife, everything was fine between her and Kaufman and, finally, George Kaufman loved her.

Arriving in London, Beatrice immediately telephoned the *London Daily Express*—the newspaper with the largest circulation in England—and requested a reporter come to the Park Lane Hotel. The interview would be an exclusive and the only one Beatrice Kaufman would give on the subject. Eventually, it would be reprinted in every newspaper in America.

Beatrice had been vacationing in Europe and North Africa with her boss, Carmel Snow, editor of *Harper's Bazaar*. She was planning to visit Paris and then Amsterdam before returning home. When Beatrice met with the *Daily Express* reporter in her hotel suite her hair was streaked with gray and she was dressed in silver pajamas. Just then the telephone rang. It was Kaufman calling from Los Angeles wanting to know how she was holding up. Following a brief telephone conversation, Beatrice began eating some tureen soup.

"This is the first food I've tasted in forty-eight hours." She nodded to a photograph. "That's our daughter, in Central Park. She's our only child."

Finishing her soup, Beatrice took out her cigarette holder, lit a cigarette and, chain smoking, nervously walked about, talking nonstop.

"I don't know why I'm seeing you. I really don't want to talk about this and don't plan to talk to any other reporters. I am more than anxious to have this unpleasantness forgotten and over with as quickly as possible. Really, Hollywood sensationalism has no place in my life. Whatever comes out in evidence and whatever may be said is something which I already know, or is something which is completely apart from the important thing—the relationship between my husband and me."

Beatrice lit another cigarette as the reporter asked a question.

She answered: "There is nothing more I can say than that our life will continue as in the past. I knew all about this case before it caught the limelight. I know Mary Astor. My husband met her just about this time a year ago. I was in Honolulu. He was working in Hollywood. They had a flirtation. I can't see any terrible harm in that. Is it unusual for a husband to flirt with an actress? We have been married twenty years. We are adults leading our lives in an adult fashion."

She was asked about Kaufman as a husband.

"George is a good husband. I love him very much. He is in love with me despite the things that may have happened. I heard about the Mary Astor business a year ago when I returned to our home in New York. I entertained Mary Astor there. I had heard her husband wanted custody of the child and had threatened to use my husband's name. But somehow I didn't think it would ever become a lawsuit with the eyes of the world focused on it. I plan to rejoin my husband at the end of August. And when I get to New York, George will be there to meet me. My life with my husband will go on as usual."

Beatrice puffed on her cigarette.

"You know, George is worried, really worried, for my sake. In two days I've had five radiograms from him. They are to reassure me, to stop me from worrying, and to shield me from this publicity. That is sweet of him, isn't it? But of course I cannot help being anxious."

"And the diary?"

"Please don't ask me to discuss Mary Astor. She is a film actress. She kept a diary. Very stupid, that. But I prefer to remain outside this affair. I would like to preserve some dignity."

• • •

In Los Angeles—in an effort to preserve his own dignity—George Kaufman had dropped out of sight. Labeled by the press the "perfect lover," reporters inquiring at his hotel or the MGM studio were told Kaufman was out of town visiting friends. In truth Kaufman had escaped to the house Moss Hart had rented in Beverly Hills, where, undisturbed, the two would finally complete their play.

Despite the distraction of the custody brouhaha, George Kaufman was so disciplined a writer that he and Hart were only a few days away from finishing the play. This, despite the fact that Kaufman couldn't eat, couldn't sleep and, by his own admission, was absolutely miserable. Right now, if there were anyone George Kaufman wanted to feed to the sharks, no doubt that person would have been Dr. Franklyn Thorpe.

• • •

Joseph Anderson was regularly issuing updates on the progress of his subpoenas. Having inferred that practically every major male film star in Hollywood was discussed in the two diaries, a lot of people were praying for a quick resolution of what was becoming an extremely messy business.

Consequently, although the custody hearing was postponed until the following Monday, fueled by both Joseph Anderson's flow of statements and a scandal-mongering press, instead of dying down, the story was transforming into a media firestorm, threatening to destroy everyone in its wake.

The best example of the fear sweeping across Hollywood can be seen in English actress Evelyn Laye. With Joseph Anderson talking subpoenas, Laye and her husband, English actor Frank Lawton, were preparing to put themselves out of reach of process servers. Packing furiously, the two had virtually "barricaded" themselves in their Beverly Hills home. Laye paused only long enough to answer her phone and speak briefly to a reporter. Laye had been at Astor's home the night Astor and Thorpe had their blow-up and Astor announced "there will be war."

"There is nothing I can say about the Astor case. My husband and I are making a very rapid departure to England so I haven't time to talk. There's really nothing I can say about it. My husband and I are hurrying to catch a plane for New York, en route to England."

That said, Miss Laye hung up the telephone, and later that day she and her husband flew out of Hollywood. Two days later they were in England, six thousand miles from Judge Knight's courtroom and Joseph Anderson's subpoenas.

• • •

John Barrymore, presently "holed up" at a Culver City sanitarium, had a less drastic means to keep process servers at bay. Outside, at the facility's entrance, baseball-bat-wielding guards were ready to ensure that no process server made it past them.

Inside Barrymore, dressed in silk pajamas, was being examined by a court appointed cardiologist as part of his own lawsuit. Regarding the Astor-Thorpe custody case Barrymore was emphatic.

"I know nothing about Miss Astor's affairs. I'm in no way mixed up in the Astor affair."

It had been ten years since John Barrymore had ended his affair with Mary Astor and much had changed with the actor. Barrymore's hedonistic lifestyle, his drinking, his carousing—it had all finally caught up with him. At age fifty-four his body had begun to give out, his face prematurely aged, and his mental state best described as diminished. An actor who had always been letter perfect with his lines now needed them written on massive chalkboards.

To play Mercutio in MGM's *Romeo and Juliet,* Barrymore was required to move into in a sanitarium, where he couldn't touch a drop of alcohol. Due to a weakening heart, Barrymore had trouble with the film's dueling scenes, occasionally lost his voice, and costly hours were lost coaxing the actor to read his lines correctly. Barrymore had become such a problem that producer Irving Thalberg would have fired him if not for the intersession of the film's director, star, and fellow performers. It was the beginning of a decline that would, in a few short years, turn the once great John Barrymore into an industry joke—a man more to be pitied than admired. For anyone who had seen and known Barrymore at his peak, as a larger than life actor and personality, it was proof that, indeed, the mighty had fallen.

• • •

The court-appointed cardiologist informed Judge Knight that the actor had a damaged heart muscle. Enlarged, it was causing muscular contraction and "galloping rhythm." Today this is called congestive heart failure and Barrymore had been suffering from it along with chest pain for the past four years. Due to the limitations of 1936 pharmacology, the only thing to do was keep Barrymore stationary and give him medication that would reduce the liquid in his blood stream. With the strain on his heart reduced, his lungs would eventually clear and he would receive sufficient oxygen.

The cardiologist made it clear that the actor needed absolute rest. "If Barrymore follows his physician's instructions to the letter he may be able to appear in four or five weeks. If he does not cooperate, he may never be able to appear in court at all." In other words, if John Barrymore were dragged into court he'd most likely drop dead before he completed his testimony.

Accordingly, Judge Knight granted a continuance in Barrymore's lawsuit but announced that he would eventually "dispose of this case, even if it is necessary to bring John Barrymore into court on a stretcher."

Immediately following the examination Barrymore's attorney Aaron Sapiro secreted the actor to an unnamed institution, where he could be ensconced until the custody hearing had played itself out. When Joseph Anderson reached Sapiro by phone, Sapiro refused to tell him Barrymore's location. In fact, Barrymore was so well hidden that when process servers questioned Elaine Barrie—the actor's twenty-one-year-old fiancée in residence with her mother at Barrymore's Tower Road home—even she didn't know where the actor was. Barrymore, like Kaufman, had pretty much disappeared.

22

Norma Taylor was again in the newspapers, but with a new twist. Her former boyfriend, Tommy Manville—millionaire asbestos heir—had just arrived from Europe on the Normandie and, as one newspaper put it, like a "knight errant rushing to the aid of his fair maid in distress" informed the press that he was pledging his "fortune, his social position, his time and personal efforts" to support Norma Taylor in clearing her name.

This was typical Manville. The personification of the 1930s playboy, Manville frequently had his photograph in the newspapers with a beautiful blonde on his arm. So when this publicity hound learned of Norma's Taylor's situation, and seeing an opportunity to once again get his name in the papers, Manville immediately sailed back to the States. Reaching New York, he quickly called Norma's mother. Then, after telling her to tell Norma that he was 100 percent behind her, Manville immediately contacted the newspapers.

• • •

As promised, Roland Rich Woolley was back in court on Tuesday in front of Superior Court Judge Carl A. Stutsman obtaining a commission to travel to Tampa, Florida and take depositions of six witnesses to prove that Dr. Thorpe had been married before moving to Los Angeles. The issue was crucial—whether the bigamy charge stuck or not—in proving that Franklyn Thorpe was both a liar and a moral hypocrite and thus unfit to retain sole custody of his daughter.

Woolley offered the court affidavits recently obtained from

Florida residents. In one affidavit, Dr. William M. Rowlett—Thorpe was Rowlett's assistant in Rowlett's practice—remembered that in 1925 Dr. Thorpe married Mrs. Lillian Lawton Miles. In addition, there was the question of a wedding reception given following a trip to Jacksonville. Woolley informed the judge that he planned to fly to Tampa as soon as the custody hearing concluded so that he could depose these witnesses.

Joseph Anderson's associate counsel A.P. Narlain—Anderson was busy with subpoenas—told the judge that he also planned to fly to Florida to question these witnesses. Stutsman told Narlain that he would hear his application for a commission on Friday.

Upon leaving the courtroom, Narlain told reporters that Norma Taylor and Lillian Miles would also be testifying. Apparently, that would be when Miss Taylor would storm into Judge Knight's courtroom and demand vindication.

With the names of potential Florida witnesses now public, Dr. Rowlett informed reporters in Tampa that a female attorney representing Miss Astor had visited him a few days earlier. He told her that, to the best of his recollection, Dr. Franklyn Thorpe married Mrs. Miles in 1925. Contradicting this was Richard D. Morales, an attorney recently retained by Joseph Anderson to represent Dr. Thorpe. Morales told reporters that Dr. Thorpe lived in a modest neighborhood in Tampa with his parents Mr. and Mrs. Samuel S. Thorpe. Morales knew nothing about any marriage.

• • •

On Tuesday Mary Astor was on the United Artists lot, shooting the scene in *Dodsworth* where Edith Cortright meets Sam Dodsworth in Naples and they begin their affair. It was a critical time for Astor. During the coming week she would complete her work on the film, in scenes designed to be the most emotional and memorable of the film. Because Astor's character would dominate the latter part of the movie, this work required her total concentration.

With the activities of a busy film studio swirling around her,

Mary Astor—described as "relieved and happy like a little girl on her first picnic"—was giving an interview to a group of invited reporters. Between a camera set-up, she sat comfortably just outside a soundstage. This interview was her first since the legal battle had begun and would be her only interview during the entire custody hearing. Approved by Woolley, it was being given to drive home the issue of missing diary pages—inconvertible proof that Franklyn Thorpe, and not Mary Astor, had something to hide.

A few miles away, seated in his lawyer's office, Dr. Franklyn Thorpe, "bronzed man of the outdoors," was also being interviewed. Woolley and Astor's statements that the diary contained incriminating evidence against Thorpe needed to be countered. In both interviews the two discussed much the same subjects only, as might be expected, from quite different perspectives.

Regarding the custody hearing:

> Mary Astor: "I'm only interested in the truth coming out. I don't care if some of it hurts me. I'm not afraid. I can take it. I'm going to keep fighting. I am making this fight for only one reason—to recover my baby for myself. I've got to for the sake of my child. For that end, I will undergo any suffering."

> Franklyn Thorpe: "Sure, I'm on the spot in this case. But I want my baby and I don't think Mary is the person to have custody. I could not think of Marylyn being brought up in that atmosphere. Her life is an unwritten page."

Regarding Marylyn Thorpe:

> Mary Astor: "Nothing in life matters so much to me as Marylyn."

> Franklyn Thorpe: "My responsibility to our child demands that I protect and safeguard Marylyn's future. I want her to become a normal person."

Regarding the tampered diary:

Mary Astor: "In my case, there is very little, indeed, to tell. I can assure you I'm not afraid to have anything that I wrote in my diary come out. But others are afraid. They've probably taken out of the diary everything derogatory I wrote about Dr. Thorpe. I'm not surprised at this. There are events described in it which I am sure Dr. Thorpe wouldn't like bruited about publicly. Some of the things I discussed would get him into difficulty with the law regarding medical services he provided to Lillian Miles." This was an obvious reference to the abortion Thorpe had given Miles. "I didn't want to throw any dirt in this case, but since they started it, why not let the dirt fly."

Franklyn Thorpe: "What else could you expect? They'll charge that we removed a lot of things from the diary, but that's all rot. The judge will see when the book is brought into court that all the pages are there and numbered and the continuity is not interrupted."

Regarding George Kaufman:

Mary Astor: "I testified that my friendship with Mr. Kaufman was well known to my husband and that by the mere fact that my husband continued to live with me he condoned anything that may have happened."

Franklyn Thorpe: "Kaufman was scared of me. I thought that I could straighten things out. I thought that things weren't as bad as I had imagined them."

Mary Astor was called back to the set. Heading into the soundstage, she was told that Kaufman had said, "I am just a friend of Miss Astor and I am not interested in any testimony given by her."

She smiled. "Well, that's interesting, isn't it?"

"Have you heard from Kaufman?"

"No, I haven't."

"You mean Kaufman hasn't called you and wasn't angry when he was served with a summons?"

"Oh, no, it's nothing like that. I haven't heard from him in months."

Franklyn Thorpe: "The trouble with Mary is that she learned thoroughly the doctrines of moral irresponsibility. You know, I thought a long time, debating the matter before we were married. Our temperaments were bound to clash. Remember that old Greek myth about the centaur and the mermaid? They met on a strand by the sea. They fell in love one night and then came the time they had to part. That in a measure, I guess, is the story of Mary and me."

Referencing Greek mythology, Franklyn Thorpe still rationalized that he held the moral high ground. Even as the evidence piled up, even as his sexual indiscretions came to light and his deceptions labeled him a liar, the man simply couldn't let go of this image he had of himself. It would prove Thorpe's Achilles' heel because, sooner rather than later, Franklyn Thorpe's past would come back to haunt him in newspaper headlines that even he couldn't rationalize away.

23

On Wednesday morning August 5, New Yorkers purchasing the *New York Daily News* read the following excerpt from Mary Astor's diary concerning George Kaufman.

"He is perfect. I don't know how he does it? He is perfect."

The newspaper reported that Miss Astor described Kaufman as "the superman" of the bedroom and went on to print that "page one of the candid confessions was written when the affair with the elderly master lover of the movies was in full flower." This was clearly a reference to John Barrymore. "Although Miss Astor in her diary does not credit the recipient of her first extra-marital favor with the extraordinary gift of entertaining her as she later discovered in George S. Kaufman, this early adventure nevertheless had its moments of ecstasy... Mary's avowed intention, on the first page of her day-and-night journal, was to tell things as they are and not as they appear to be. She addressed her diary as her 'perfect friend' and 'Oh so discreet!'.... While she accorded her first friend the title of 'complete man' she did not endow him with the superman characteristics that so surprised and thrilled her while she and Kaufman shared an East Seventy-Third St. Manhattan apartment."

Several of these quotes had been printed in the same newspaper two days earlier, but they were not Joseph Anderson leaks. They were fabrications, and would mark the beginning of not one, but two diaries. There would be the actual diary held in a Los Angeles safety deposit box, and a fabricated diary that became more and more tantalizing as time went on. As newspapers—reprinting the fabrications—used other newspapers as sources, the real diary and the fake fused in the public's mind so that distinguishing fact from fiction became virtually impossible. What this did was fire up the public's imagination even more, ensuring that the custody battle would dominate the public consciousness.

• • •

Norma Taylor, that "famous carving-knife girl," was enjoying her favorite pastime—calling newspapers and giving interviews. This time Tommy Manville was also on the line. Norma was staying with Manville at Bon Repos, Manville's estate in New Rochelle. She, Manville, Manville's pretty blonde "secretary" Dolly "Honeychile" Goering, and a Miss Jacqueline Dahlia—a "beauteous brunette French teacher"—were now sharing Manville's twenty-nine-room, vine-covered mansion.

"Sure, I got Norma Taylor with me. Norma needed a real rest after her ordeal so I invited her out just as soon as I got off the boat."

Norma added, "Tommy knew I needed a rest and he was sweet enough to ask me and I came."

"She's a darling girl. We're going to the Westchester Bath Club today for a ride in one of my speedboats."

• • •

While Norma was boating on Long Island, Mary Astor was working on *Dodsworth* twelve hours a day inside a Hollywood soundstage. There was talk that producer Samuel Goldwyn was worried about the negative impact the custody hearing might have on the film's potential box office. Truth was, this was the least of Sam Goldwyn's worries. Having almost died from intestinal toxemia four months earlier, he was presently recuperating at home. As for *Dodsworth*, having viewed the rushes, Goldwyn thought Wyler was doing a brilliant job and the producer had high hopes for the film.

George Kaufman was now officially in hiding, secretly residing with writing partner Moss Hart, rushing to finish their play.

Franklyn Thorpe wasn't in hiding. He was treating patients in his Hollywood Boulevard medical office and making house calls.

As for Thorpe's attorney, Joseph Anderson, he was telling reporters that, besides Kaufman, a dozen other "world-famous men" were mentioned in the diary, men he was ready to subpoena in a series of courtroom bombshells. Regarding Woolley's allegation of a wedding reception in Florida, Anderson told reporters, "You can go tell Roland Rich Woolley for me that's a lot of poppycock!"

Earlier Anderson had filed an answer to Astor's demand that the property settlement be set aside. Franklyn Thorpe denied that he had coerced Astor into agreeing to the settlement and "stated that he benefited from the settlement only through a $4,250 profit participation on telephone stock." Following this Anderson obtained an order requiring Mary Astor to appear in Judge Douglas Edmonds's court on Saturday at 10:00 a.m. to answer questions at a deposition regarding the bigamy and annulment suit. This was retaliation for Woolley's request that Thorpe be cited for contempt regarding deposition questions asked about the Florida common law marriage.

• • •

Thursday morning, Norma Taylor suddenly had an epiphany. Taylor told reporters that *they* were the reason she had decided to remain longer at Manville's New Rochelle estate.

"I wanted some peace and quiet and to get away from the reporters. I was tired of all the hubbub and excitement."

"And what about the Astor trial?"

"I think it's definitely disgusting and it should never have been in the newspapers. I don't know what's going to come out of it all."

• • •

As for Mary Astor's "misstep diary," the fabrications were flying. The *Los Angeles Evening Herald Express* reported that "Mary Astor was an unofficial scorekeeper in Hollywood's tournaments of love. Four pages of the voluminous two-hundred-page document contain her charm ratings of the 'first ten' among the male celebrities of screenland. Kaufman was definitely the tops and no rival ever stirred Miss Astor's salty prose to the heights she attained in describing her appreciation of him."

The *New York Evening Journal* printed that "the most panic-stricken persons in the film colony are not alarmed so much about being called to testify about their acquaintance with Miss Astor as they are about their position on the list."

According to the *New York Daily News*, Astor had written that Kaufman "fits me perfectly. This makes for many exquisite moments. Twenty, count 'em diary, twenty."

Having read these fabrications, Franklyn Thorpe was so outraged that he issued a statement announcing that he was no longer speaking to the press.

"Every time I open my mouth they print a column. Many of the things published as purported excerpts from the diary are not phrases from the book. As a matter of fact, the only real quotes from the diary are those used by my attorneys in papers on file with the court in the law suit."

True though that might have been, it didn't stop the newspapers from continuing to print the falsehoods.

• • •

The press also reported that Kaufman had made a plane reservation for a "quick dash back to New York" where, according to Kaufman, New York "would seem as peaceful as a virgin forest after all the excitement in Hollywood."

As for this "virgin forest," as much as Kaufman was the talk of Hollywood, he was also the talk of the town in New York, the general sentiment being regret that Mary Astor had confessed to her affair with Kaufman.

Restaurateur Arnold Reuben was incensed. "Kaufman was often

here. He's a quiet man who minds his own business. In the twenty years I've known him, there hasn't been any stain on his character."

One friend remarked, "Everyone on Broadway knew the two were together. I know he must be awfully upset. It must have come down on him like a ton of bricks."

On this Kaufman would have wholeheartedly agreed.

• • •

```
Sch 1911 E Emma
Thorpe Franklin (Lillian) phys 201 La-
   fayette Arcade  h111  S. Moody-av
   (HP)
"  John P (Hattie) mgr h310 S West-
```

On Thursday Roland Rich Woolley announced that he had additional witnesses willing to testify that Dr. Thorpe was married to Mrs. Miles. He added that Dr. Franklyn Thorpe and Lillian Miles were even listed in the Tampa City Directory as husband and wife.

One neighbor recalled, "I'd frequently seen them taking sun baths together right in their back yard, Dr. Thorpe wearing only a gymnasium strap and the woman in a scanty bathing suit." Two physicians who worked with Thorpe were certain Lillian was his wife, while the secretary of the Florida Board of Medical Examiners believed that "if there is anything unconventional about them, it was not apparent." Dr. G. C. Ranklin remembered that "Dr. Thorpe introduced Mrs. Miles to me as his wife, and her conduct certainly indicated this was true." Others remember the two living a normal married life—attending country club dances and inviting friends to play bridge, and they found it hard to believe that the two had lived together without benefit of clergy. Or, as one neighbor told Woolley's investigators, "If they weren't married, they certainly fooled me."

• • •

As for Hollywood, the trial and the diary were major topics of conversation. About Mary Astor opinions were mixed. Some thought "she was pretty stupid ever to have jotted down with such amazing candor her two-volume diary." Others thought "she is showing astonishing courage in fighting her case though in the face of such defamatory developments. It seems now that she will continue even at the cost of her career." Nevertheless, everyone agreed that she was a tenacious fighter.

The studio where Astor was working on *Dodsworth* continued to bar reporters from the lot while she worked on her part, which, according to the Samuel Goldwyn Company, would be completed on Saturday.

Many at the studio who had seen rushes were saying that, in *Dodsworth*, Mary Astor was giving the performance of her career.

24

On Friday, it finally came to light why Norma Taylor was so passionate about "clearing" her name. It appeared that Miss Taylor's involvement with the custody hearing was causing profound anguish to a "well-known Hollywood man" who was about to ask her to marry him. Oddly, Norma did not telephone a single newspaper to comment. Apparently it had finally dawned on Miss Taylor, as it had to almost everyone else, that it was best to keep one's mouth shut. Only with Norma, for some strange reason, it had taken a bit longer.

• • •

But the real news on Friday wasn't Norma Taylor. A few days earlier, Mrs. Ethel Maclean of Intervale, New Hampshire had called a newspaper, and a reporter was immediately dispatched. Mrs. Mclean had quite a story to tell.

"Franklyn Thorpe married my daughter, May Maclean, in 1917, when May was seventeen and he was in his twenties. He was a medical student at Columbia University when he eloped with May. After that they got their own apartment."

Although Thorpe eventually transferred from Columbia to Tufts University Medical School, he was home with his "wife" summers and on holidays.

"Then, early in 1919, my daughter became ill. May was operated on but it did not help. She died on August 9, 1920, holding my hand and Franklyn's. Franklyn was weeping. We buried her in Woodlawn Cemetery in the Bronx. When he proposed three days after her death to May's cousin, naturally I was surprised, knowing how he

May Maclean "Thorpe" in 1917.

loved May. When I asked him about it, he said to me, 'Mother, I did this because she reminds me so much of May and I would like someone with me always who would keep her in my thoughts.'"

In addition to photographs, Mrs. Maclean showed the reporter letters written by Thorpe to May. They were all addressed to Mrs. May Thorpe. In part one of them read:

> February 22, 1920
>
> Whenever I think of you in any danger or sickness it is just as if a cold icy hand had closed around my heart and was squeezing the blood out of it. Anything that affects you makes a coward of me. It is not manly or courageous perhaps but the thought of you ill or in danger seems to take my manhood from me. I have often thought of this weakness of mine and tried to reason out the cause and I think it must be because of my dread of being left here in the world alone without you. Maybe in years to come I will grow stronger but life seems to mean little to me except with you, dear. It is just as if you were the real heart of my heart. No lover ever loved his ladylove any more tenderly or deeply or passionately than I love you. When I think of holding you in my arms up close to my heart I burn and thrill and ache all over for you. I don't know how to express it—it is beyond words but it is almost as

if you were a part of me, only a thousand times dearer. I never knew I could love a woman as completely as I do you. Lots of love from your old hubby, Franklyn

Corroborating the story was May's cousin, Mrs. William G. Many. "He proposed to me three days after May died. I did not feel flattered and told him so. But, he was a peach of a fellow in his way."

A second corroboration came from May's cousin, James R. Powers. "Franklyn told the family that he had eloped with a widow with two children but that his family had the marriage annulled because Thorpe's family wanted him to continue his medical education. Thorpe eloped with my cousin May when she was seventeen. They wrote us from Atlantic City that they were married. Naturally we did not ask to see the marriage certificate for it never occurred to any of us to doubt their word."

According to undertaker Nathaniel Morrow's funeral records May was buried on August 11, 1920. Mrs. Morrow told a reporter, "The bill was sent to Franklyn Thorpe. It was for $290. $200 was paid in advance and $30 on October 11, 1920. Our records do not show further payments." On the billing record there was a written notation, "Deceased, Mrs. May Thorpe. Send bill to Franklyn Thorpe of Tufts Univ., 45 Hemenway St. Boston—husband's address, 2074 Seventh Ave."

Roland Rich Woolley must have lowered his eyes in a silent prayer of thanks. Rarely are lawyers in the middle of a case handed such a gift.

For Thorpe it was his worst nightmare come true.

Joseph Anderson knew that immediate damage control was necessary. This story proved his client a liar. Worse, Thorpe had lied to his attorney. If Anderson had known early on he could have framed it for the press so it wouldn't have been so damning. Having gotten wind of the story on Thursday, Anderson contacted Thorpe to find out the truth and, hopefully, dilute the impact of this press disaster. So, "late Thursday Thorpe was summoned for an 'urgent' conference" with Anderson and, after the two talked, Anderson made an announcement to the press regarding Miss Maclean.

"The tale that Dr. Thorpe was married to May Maclean is false and absurd. Before he married Lucile Langhanke, Dr. Thorpe had been married only once. I have a certified copy of the divorce decree. May Maclean was merely a friend of the doctor's. The rumor that Dr. Thorpe was married to a widow with two children is false. That's all I can say about it now."

When Franklyn Thorpe's mother, Cora, was asked about the stories concerning her son's marriage to May Maclean, all she would say was, "I'm not saying yes or no. I can't. I will have to refer you to Dr. Thorpe's attorney. Why not let the dead rest. It was just one of those boyhood romances. It had nothing to do with this case."

Reading Thorpe's denial, May's mother, Ethel Maclean, was so upset that she informed Mary Astor's attorney that she was willing to appear as a witness and do "anything in her power" to help Mary Astor regain custody of her baby.

• • •

There was also an interesting development in the Tampa, Florida marriage story. A key witness had disappeared. What made this interesting was that this key witness was an Anna Miller, AKA Mrs. Richard Morales, former wife of the attorney recently hired by Joseph Anderson to collect affidavits disproving the common law marriage claim. It appeared that Mrs. Morales had been hostess at the "wedding reception" given by Dr. Thorpe and Mrs. Miles following their reputed marriage. Attorney Morales commented:

"I don't know anything about it. My former wife gave lots of parties—sometimes two or three a day."

If this wasn't absurd enough, Joe Carter, president of the Tampa Patrol and Detective System, had obtained affidavits from a number of Tampa citizens claiming that Thorpe and Miles were husband and wife. The absurd part was Carter announcing that he had nothing but the highest respect for Dr. Thorpe and lauded

Thorpe's skill as a physician. In fact, Dr. Thorpe had been Carter's family doctor and delivered his granddaughter. Carter also added that Dr. Thorpe and Mrs. Miles had had some "pretty wild parties" back then when Carter was still chief of detectives. When one of the neighbors complained, Carter had to send detectives to Miles's home. He failed to mention if, on that occasion, anyone had been running around waving a turkey fork.

• • •

It didn't take long before Joseph Anderson, Franklyn Thorpe, and Lillian Miles realized that the common law marriage accusation would soon be proven. As a result, they met in Anderson's office late Friday to discuss strategy, and a decision was reached. Deny, deny, deny until, hopefully, Joseph Anderson could pull off a miracle.

This miracle depended on two things. One: pound home the message that the diary—if made public—would do harm to the film industry hoping that the industry would pressure Astor to cave. Two: pound at Mary Astor during cross-examination until she admitted to its contents. If the diary couldn't be submitted into evidence, Anderson still had an ace up his sleeve. While the diaries were in his possession and not the court's, he was free to use their contents any way he saw fit. Accordingly, the possibility of submitting sections to the press for publication was also discussed.

Meeting concluded, Lillian Miles left Joseph Anderson's office for what had been announced as some pre-testimony preparation. Then, with her mother standing beside her, Mrs. Miles spoke to the press for the first time in almost two weeks. This time her comments were brief.

"I will testify of course that I never entered into a common law marriage, or any other marriage with Dr. Thorpe."

As for Thorpe and Anderson, they made statements of their own. The first came from Dr. Thorpe.

"Mary is proceeding in the face of the gravest danger to herself and to the child. We didn't want to drag in the names of all the celebrities listed in Mary's diary unless we were forced to it. But she is leaving us no course but to go through with the fight."

The second came from Joseph Anderson.

"If the text of Miss Astor's diary is revealed in court, it will split the movie industry wide open. The tragedy of it is that many of the persons named in the manuscript are innocent victims of the determined wiles of a beautiful woman who experimented with love as a scientist experiments with test tubes. Miss Astor's diary is but one weapon the doctor has at his command. There are others even more sensational than the diary. We have just started to fight."

At about this time a newspaper story appeared claiming that "it was said that Miss Astor regards herself as a modern goddess of love, picking her partners in romance from the dizzy heights of a Hollywood Mt. Olympus" and "the quaking Casanovas, fearing revelation of their names, are said to have joined forces to raise a settlement fund, in an attempt to persuade Dr. Thorpe to withhold the diary he plans to present in court Monday."

When Joseph Anderson was told the ten were going to bring in lawyers of their own to suppress the book, he couldn't help himself, and laughed at this newspaper fantasy. His strategy was working.

. . .

In court on Friday, Woolley and Anderson had a faceoff in front of Judge Knight regarding the deposition Anderson wanted to take of Mary Astor on Saturday. Woolley argued against it, informing Knight that his client was in poor health due to the strain of the custody suit and her long hours at the studio. Joseph Anderson accused Woolley of trying to evade the issue. That was when H.F. Selvin, representing Samuel Goldwyn, informed Knight that Miss Astor would not finish her work on *Dodsworth* in time to permit her appearance in court anytime Saturday. Judge Knight then ruled that she could answer questions before the case resumed on Monday.

Business concluded, Knight had something else to say to both attorneys, and he hoped they were listening.

"Marylyn will not be awarded as the revenge prize in a family row. My decision shall not be swayed by the lawyers or principals using as weapons the mistakes of either Dr. Thorpe or Mary Astor. The welfare of this sweet, healthy, happy, dimple-faced child is the only issue in which I am interested. When I visited Marylyn at her beautiful home I obtained a picture of a vigorous, happy, normal youngster with a keen interest in her surroundings and I hope the outcome of this case will ensure the child growing up with the unbiased, happy outlook to which all children are entitled."

As these two lawyers and their clients would soon learn, Judge Knight meant every word he had just said.

25

On Saturday, August 8, John Barrymore's attorney Aaron Sapiro suddenly had a change of heart. After being bombarded by phone calls from Joseph Anderson, Sapiro no longer had any objection to Barrymore accepting a subpoena. There was one catch. Sapiro would only allow it to be served after Barrymore had left the sanatorium. This was legal maneuvering aimed to thwart any attempt by Anderson to file a contempt charge against Sapiro for not cooperating with the court. Sapiro was betting that by then the Astor custody case would have run its course, making Barrymore's appearance moot.

As for George Kaufman, after days of searching, not only had the press finally located the playwright, but Kaufman had actually given an interview—well, sort of. While staying at Moss Hart's house, where the two had just finished their play, reporters suddenly appeared at the door. One enterprising newsman actually crept around to the side of the house and began talking to Hart through an open window while Kaufman, "all nerves," hid behind the curtain trying his best to "suffer in private." Hart served as intermediary.

"Is Kaufman going to testify in regard to his love affair with Miss Astor?"

Hart asked Kaufman, Kaufman answered, and Hart repeated.

"I am hoping that I will not be called; it is highly probable that I may not be forced to take the witness stand at all."

"Are you going to protect her?"

Hart-Kaufman-Kaufman-Hart.

"I can't say. I have been advised by my lawyer not to talk."

"Have you seen Miss Astor frequently, since it's been asserted that you promised Dr. Thorpe that you would not visit her anymore?"

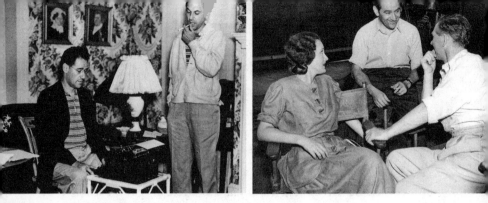

LEFT: Kaufman and Hart working.
RIGHT: Astor and Huston on set with William Wyler.

Hart-Kaufman-Kaufman-Hart.

"I refuse to answer."

"Are you afraid of physically meeting Doctor Thorpe?"

Hart-Kaufman-Kaufman-Hart.

"I can't say. I have made every effort to avoid an unpleasant scene."

"Would you resort to fists, epigrams, swords, or pistols, if you were challenged to a duel?"

Hart-Kaufman-Kaufman-Hart.

"I refuse to answer that."

"Are you not interested in what Miss Astor has to say about you and herself as you formally stated?"

Hart-Kaufman-Kaufman-Hart.

"I have nothing to say."

"Did you keep a diary?"

Hart-Kaufman-Kaufman-Hart.

"I have nothing to say."

"How would you handle this situation in a play?"

Hart-Kaufman-Kaufman-Hart.

"It is not—" pause—"I have nothing to say."

"Are you making a stand against questioning to protect others supposedly named romantically in Miss Astor's diary?"

Hart-Kaufman-Kaufman-Hart.

"I have been told to answer no questions."

"Are you coming back to Hollywood after all this blows over?"

Hart-Kaufman-Kaufman-Hart.

"I can't say."

Moss Hart shut his window, and even though an intermediary George Kaufman was no longer speaking to the press.

• • •

Joseph Anderson met again with reporters and told them that, if Mary Astor were willing to drop her suit and let her former husband retain sole guardianship, the diary not already in evidence would be given back to her. Instead of "trial by newspaper" it had now become "negotiation by newspaper."

When Roland Rich Woolley met with the press he announced that Mary Astor would be finishing up her role in *Dodsworth* sometime that evening, and then handed out a statement from Miss Astor.

"I'm going to see this thing through no matter what happens. After all, Marylyn is more important to me than anything else in the world, including my career. I'm sorry that this is the only means for me to gain custody of my child but I have no other course."

This statement was for the benefit of Thorpe and Anderson and was, essentially, a no to the deal.

• • •

During the preceding week Mary Astor had been working on *Dodsworth* almost twelve hours a day while living in her dressing room on the lot. Isolated from the public and the press she had become totally immersed in her part and, emotionally, it had been her salvation. In the process, despite the turmoil surrounding Astor outside the studio, on the United Artists Studio soundstages Mary Astor was finding her greatest fulfillment as an actress.

The last scene in the film was shot that week and was work that Mary Astor would be proud of for the rest of her life. In the scene, Edith Cortright is alone on the terrace of her home in Naples. Sam Dodsworth, after having lived with Cortright, has returned to his wife. Now, with Sam gone, and knowing she would once again be relegated to a life of empty drifting, Edith Cortright is utterly desolate. She turns, looks out at the water at a small skiff. The skiff suddenly veers, and she sees Sam Dodsworth on it. Realizing he is coming back, the desolation on her face is immediately replaced by a look of sheer joy as she ecstatically waves to him.

The scene took a while to set up. After Astor worked out a few technical issues with the carpenters and the set decorator, Director Wyler told her what she needed to do—when and where to look. Then, Astor gave herself completely to the character, and that was what William Wyler captured on film.

When she was done with that first take, Astor looked over at Wyler, expecting him to ask for another. Instead she heard, "Cut and print." Astor was astonished, as Wyler never did a shot in one take. She was so astonished that she remembered, "I made my way through the maze of cables, the confusion, to where Willy was talking casually to a couple of people. I touched him on the arm. 'You kidding? Willy, did you, uh—did you just give up?'"

"What? Oh!" Wyler shrugged as if the answer was obvious. "It's good, you'll see. It was fine, just fine."

When Astor saw the rushes she realized that the director had been right. It was perfect. Mary Astor had become Edith Cortright. In their emotional intensity, those last few moments of *Dodsworth* have been compared to the final moments of Charlie Chaplin's *City Lights* in how they bring the viewer into the soul of a character. At long last, Mary Astor had become the great actress she had always wanted to be.

• • •

On Saturday night, after completing her role, Astor was on her way to Walter Huston's dressing room where the two planned to celebrate by enjoying some champagne together. But, before she got there, Astor was asked to stop by Sam Goldwyn's office.

Walking into the room, the actress was surprised to see "an assembly of producers from all the studios, with their lawyers." In that room were A.P. Giannini, Irving Thalberg, Louis B. Mayer, Jack Warner, Harry Cohn, Jesse Lasky, and other studio heads. It was a collection of the most powerful men in Hollywood. They were here to plead their case to Mary Astor. In fact, this meeting was deemed so important that Sam Goldwyn had left his sickbed to host it.

Astor sat down, and Roland Rich Woolley stood beside her. She hadn't been told about the meeting because Goldwyn wanted to make sure that, if there were any problems, she would have already completed her role in *Dodsworth*.

While Astor sat there she would later recall, "Everyone was whispering and conferring, and I sat there wondering what all the furor was about."

Irving Thalberg spoke for the group.

Thalberg was chosen to act as spokesman for several reasons. He was not only a superb mediator but, six years earlier, when Mary Astor was married to Kenneth Hawks, Hawks' brother Howard was married to Athole Shearer, Thalberg's sister-in-law. So, Thalberg and Astor had been—so to speak—family. In addition, prior to his marriage, Thalberg had caroused with Ken and his brother Howard. So, there was a possibility that some of these extracurricular activities might have found their way into her diary. Since Thalberg was planning to start his own independent production company, he didn't need to be involved in a scandal that could impede his plans. Combine this with the possibility of losing George Kaufman's services, and Thalberg had the most to lose if the diary went public.

Speaking in his deep, resonating voice, Thalberg argued the moguls' case. He had five points to make. One: he told Astor and her attorney that they had made a grave mistake bringing this suit to trial because the diary's pornographic content would "create a vicious scandal" that would adversely affect everyone who worked in the film industry. Two: Thalberg told Astor that she would irrevocably damage her career, as the public would turn their backs on her after learning about her bedroom activities. Three: this scandal would "give the industry a bad name." Four: in all probability, once the diary became public, she would lose the suit and not obtain custody of her little girl. And, finally, it "would be wiser" to "drop the case or at least attempt an out-of-court settlement."

Astor thought Thalberg a bit pompous by making it seem as if the entire movie industry would collapse simply because of what she had written in her diary. Then, when Thalberg finished, everyone turned to Astor, anxious to hear her answer. As the only person in the room who had actually read the diary's contents, Astor was surprised hearing what they believed was written in it.

According to Astor, "They had heard of or seen certain pages that contained descriptions of sexual acts with almost every well-known actor in the business—with box score performance. All I could say was that it just wasn't true and if there were such pages they had to be a forgery." When the box score was mentioned again, "I could only beat my fists… and cry futilely, 'There wasn't any box score and I never called the damned thing dear diary.' I was not believed, naturally."

When again asked to drop the case, Astor looked at Roland Rich Woolley. Woolley did not want to give away his courtroom strategy—that a mutilated document was inadmissible. So, he shook his head. Since Astor relied unconditionally on her lawyer's advice, she turned to Irving Thalberg and everyone else in the room.

"I'm sorry, gentlemen, but I will proceed with the case, as my lawyer has just advised me."

That said, she got up, left the office, and joined Walter Huston in his dressing room, where the two enjoyed their celebratory champagne. Celebration concluded, Mary Astor returned to her dressing room, packed her things, and headed back to Toluca Lake to spend Sunday resting with her daughter. She would now be living at home.

Sam Goldwyn, when asked if he might exert pressure on Astor by using the morality clause standard in all Hollywood studio contracts, shook his head.

"A woman fighting for her child? This is good."

Meeting over, Sam Goldwyn returned to his sickbed.

26

Stepping into his limousine, Irving Thalberg was driven directly to Moss Hart's house in Beverly Hills, where an anxious George Kaufman was waiting. Thalberg gave Kaufman the bad news. Astor's refusal to settle meant a good possibility the diary would be introduced into evidence and Kaufman called to the stand.

Kaufman had already been advised of his legal options. He could remain in Los Angeles and be dragged into court where, if he refused to testify, he would be hauled off to jail for contempt. If he chose to leave California—his contract with MGM had ended just hours earlier—he would be out of the jurisdiction of a California court and thus avoid testifying. But, if he did this, a bench warrant would be issued for his arrest, and if he returned to Los Angeles he'd be thrown in jail.

It was a serious decision for George Kaufman because if he skipped town it would mean he wouldn't work in Hollywood again for a long time. This would "deep six" his plans to write and direct for Thalberg's independent company, and all that Hollywood money would evaporate. On the other hand, *Stage Door*—a play he had written with Edna Ferber—was scheduled to open in October with rehearsals ready to begin in a few weeks. As he was set to direct, this meant Kaufman would need to be in New York week after next.

Before Thalberg had arrived Kaufman had already made up his mind, but the when and how depended on what transpired at the meeting. Now, knowing for certain that Astor was not going to settle, Kaufman immediately shifted into gear.

Once Thalberg left—giving the producer plausible deniability—Kaufman had himself checked out of the Beverly Wilshire and then arranged for a friend—a woman—to pay his hotel bill. That out of the way, and to avoid reporters, the playwright was driven to San Bernardino where, in the wee hours of the morning, George Kaufman boarded the Santa Fe Special. Locked in a private compartment booked under an assumed name, the playwright was soon on his way back to New York.

• • •

By Sunday morning the papers were printing rumors that Kaufman had skipped town, as well as the results of Saturday night's mogul meeting. The information was sketchy and none of the names of the film executives were mentioned, with the exception of Irving Thalberg and his wife Norma Shearer—and she hadn't even been there. It was claimed that Thalberg and Shearer had spent Saturday trying to broker a settlement between Astor and Thorpe. Some newspapers had Thorpe and Anderson attending and one paper even had George Kaufman at the studio pleading with Astor to settle, with Astor in tears.

Holding his daily press conference, Joseph Anderson was asked about this "conciliation" meeting.

"I do not care to be quoted one way or another. I will say we are ready to go ahead with the cross-examination of Miss Astor and the introduction of at least enough of the diary to refute statements she has made on the stand."

Anderson's strategy to frighten the film industry into pressuring Astor having failed, the only course of action left him was to pound at Mary Astor on the stand until he could use her statements to impeach her testimony. If he couldn't get the diary introduced, the attorney still had his contingency plan—using photostats handed out to the press of the "pertinent passages"—to force Astor to drop the suit or face a perjury charge and its legal ramifications.

With rumors flying that Kaufman had left town, Anderson was asked what he would do if Kaufman didn't show up in court on Monday. The attorney was blunt.

"Well, he'd better be there. I'll seek a bench warrant for Kaufman's arrest for contempt of court."

· · ·

Mary Astor was home with her daughter when Woolley called with information about last night's mogul meeting. As Astor would recount in her autobiography, "A certain person who knew that he figured prominently in the diary was not at all happy at the thought of it being admitted as evidence and had substituted a forged version, and his lawyer had shown it to the producers in an effort to pressure us into dropping the case or rejecting the diary as evidence." Fragments of this forgery were leaked to the press, which gleefully quoted them. It was the forgery that "contained a 'box score' of practically every male big name in the business, and it was loaded with pornographic details."

Astor knew the man well. Six years earlier, while still married to Kenneth Hawks, Astor had acted as an intermediary between an actress friend with whom this man was involved. One day, when Ken wasn't home, this older man came by, and as she would write, "I was becoming uncomfortably aware that I and not my friend was the object of his visit. Subtle evasive tactics availed for only a time; then it became one of those ridiculous La Tosca pursuits around a couch. When he grabbed me and kissed me, I slapped him and almost literally kicked him out of the house."

Astor told her friend, and the friend told the man, who, infuriated at being exposed, confronted Astor with a report about her affair with a film producer. He threatened to give it to her husband. When Astor asked the man why he had made the pass, he answered, "Because I knew you would be easy to make a pass at." Hearing herself being labeled a tramp, Astor suddenly felt a total, all-consuming fury and stared him straight in the eye.

"Why wait? Let's call Ken now. He's in his office."

Seeing that she meant business, the man backed down. Now, six years later, he had guessed correctly. Astor had written about this incident in volume one of her diary. Since he didn't want all this to go public and sully his reputation, he had created a forgery and blown "up the importance of that document to the point where it had the entire motion-picture industry in an uproar."

• • •

By day's end, several newspapers had printed that, because a dozen careers would be ruined by Astor's "book of secrets," an Association For The Suppression Of The Diary had been formed by the Great Lovers Protective Society. These Casanovas had approached Astor and "asked her to spare them the revelations which they fear will hurt their careers, their current wives, and sweethearts." On and on this nonsense went, as newspapers printed anything remotely related to the Astor custody hearing whether it was true or not. By now the freedom of the press had descended into a tabloid free-for-all.

27

Monday morning, Irving Thalberg issued a statement. "Mr. Thalberg is interested, as everyone is, in bringing about a settlement of the matter. Mr. Thalberg considers this an unfortunate affair and deeply regrettable from any viewpoint." Later asked about reports that he and wife Norma Shearer were intervening, he told a reporter, "I know no more about this case than anyone in Hollywood." Technically, he was telling the truth—sort of.

• • •

Before session, outside in the corridor, Joseph Anderson and A.P. Michael Narlain were handing reporters photostats of pages from Mary Astor's diary for publication. The pages concerned George Kaufman.

This had been in the works since Friday. Because Anderson had been ordered to bring the complete diaries to court, he wasn't sure whether Knight would take possession. If he couldn't submit the pages as evidence and impeach Astor's testimony, then their publication would open the possibility of perjury charges.

Regarding the complete diary, A.P. Narlain told reporters, if submitted into evidence "there are eighteen names of well-known people who would be affected adversely should the contents of the journal become public record."

Arriving at the courthouse, Roland Rich Woolley was told about the photostats. He reiterated that he would demand that the entire diary be entered into evidence, including portions removed that concerned "Thorpe's amorous adventures."

Astor with her mother.

• • •

The sweltering courtroom was so packed that some spectators were forced to sit on folding chairs in the aisles. When Mary Astor entered—her mother and Nellie Richardson beside her—the noise increased dramatically. Wearing the tailored black suit she had worn during most of the trial, Astor made her way through the crowds and sat at the counsel table. Immediately surrounded by photographers, she smiled and posed for photographs. She told reporters that Ruth Chatterton was on set working but had promised to come to court during her lunch break. Standing in for Ruth was Ruth's mother. The two chatted and the older woman even patted Astor on the back reassuringly.

Franklyn Thorpe sat grim-faced at his end of the counsel table. Behind the railing were his mother, his sister Clara, Don McMullen—Thorpe's best friend since they were twelve years old and attending military school—and Mrs. Lillian Miles. For some reason, Thorpe's father wasn't in court that day.

• • •

At 10:00 a.m., Judge Knight brought the court into session. Joseph Anderson looked around. Not seeing Kaufman, he asked Knight to issue a bench warrant. Knight had a question.

"Have you properly subpoenaed him as a witness?"

William Anderson stood and explained that he had personally served Kaufman. A.P. Michael Narlain also rose and said that he had just spoken by telephone with Irving Thalberg. Thalberg told him that Kaufman had disappeared and that he didn't know Kaufman's whereabouts, as Kaufman "had completed his writing assignment at MGM." Knight looked at Anderson.

"You really don't need him because you are examining Miss Astor today."

"I know, but I expected him to be in court this morning and he is not here. I would like the process of the court to go out immediately so we will have him here when I do want to call him."

"Have you your return service?"

"Yes, it is on file with the clerk."

Judge Knight signed a form, officially issuing a bench warrant for the arrest of George S. Kaufman. The bail was set at $1000 and a deputy sheriff was dispatched to bring the playwright back in handcuffs. Dashing out of the room, reporters immediately phoned their editors and, within hours, it was headline news all over the country. The following morning the story would even make the front page of the *New York Times*.

Meanwhile, George Kaufman, halfway to Chicago, was safely locked in his private compartment. In bed, under the covers, he was completely oblivious to the furor his disappearance was causing.

Back in court, Roland Rich Woolley requested that Knight ask Anderson if, in his cross-examination, "he would attempt to impeach Miss Astor based on anything that she may have written." If Anderson answered yes, Woolley would ask how, and the moment Anderson mentioned the diary, Woolley would charge that the diary was inadmissible citing legal precedent that a mutilated and or altered document was inadmissible. That done, the diary would be—in court at least—a dead issue.

"All the News That's
Fit to Print."

The New

Copyright, 19

VOL. LXXXV.....No. 28,689.

NEW YORK,

ROOSEVELT'S ALLIES IN LABOR PROPOSE 1940 LIBERAL PARTY

Nonpartisan League Speakers See 'New Political Alignments' in a Few Years.

GREETED BY PRESIDENT

Referring to Courts, He Says History Shows Return to Reaction Is 'Short-Lived.'

LANDON CALLED A 'PUPPET'

Lewis, Hillman and Berry Declare Roosevelt Victory Vital —Hope to Swing 5 States.

Text of the President's letter appears on Page 10.

By LOUIS STARK
Special to THE NEW YORK TIMES.

WASHINGTON, Aug. 10.—State chairmen and committeemen from forty-eight States today formed a permanent body Labor's Nonpartisan League, enthusiastically endorsed the candidacy of President Roosevelt and planted what speakers referred to as the possible seeds of a liberal party, if one is deemed necessary, in 1940.

Greeted warmly by President Roosevelt, who, in a letter, declared his pride in the league's endorsement, the delegates heard predictions that labor would hold the balance of political power this year in West Virginia, Pennsylvania, New York, Illinois and Kentucky and would come close to such a desired condition in other States if the or-

Warrant Out for Kaufman As Witness in Astor Trial

Playwright Fails to Answer Subpoena and Dr. Thorpe's Counsel Says He Has 'Disappeared'—Star Testifies in All-Day Session.

By The Associated Press.

LOS ANGELES, Aug. 10.—A bench warrant was issued today for George S. Kaufman, the playwright, when he failed to obey a subpoena calling for his appearance as a witness at the trial of the action in which Mary Astor, film star, and her former husband, Dr. Franklyn Thorpe, are struggling for the custody of their daughter, Marilyn.

A. P. M. Narlian, of counsel for Dr. Thorpe, who had subpoenaed Kaufman, stated that he talked over the telephone to Irving Thalberg, motion picture producer, and that Thalberg informed him that Kaufman had "disappeared." Thalberg did not know where Kaufman was at present.

Kaufman recently completed a writing assignment at Metro-Goldwyn-Mayer, the studio of which Thalberg is an official, and had been a guest on Thalberg's yacht.

At the continuation of the trial today, after a week's lapse, visits by John Barrymore, a holiday party in Havana and meetings with Kaufman in New York and elsewhere were described by Miss Astor.

Over and over again Kaufman's name bobbed up as Joseph Anderson, counsel for Dr. Thorpe, continued his questions.

Miss Astor replied: "I am not sure," "That is untrue," "Not that I remember," and "I don't recall" as he asked her if she "had been living with George Kaufman in various places in the United States."

The names of Bennett Cerf, a New York publisher and former husband of Sylvia Sydney, and Daniel Silberberg, a New York stock broker, were mentioned in the testimony.

Miss Astor testified that Barrymore visited her at her Hollywood home to tell her his troubles "after that famous transcontinental trip of his."

She apparently was referring to Barrymore's trip from New York to Los Angeles, when his protégé, Elaine Barrie, followed him. There were two visits, she said.

After the termination of her contract with Warner Brothers in October, 1925, the actress testified she went to New York where, during

Continued on Page Fourteen

DEWEY JURY CIVIC 'VIGIL TO SMASH R

Mayor Calls Leade Today on Plan fo War on Crime

CITY-WIDE STUDY

Strengthening of of Law and Prote Witnesses Are

Text of the grand ju ment on rackets, Pag

Disturbed by the exter eering and other orga and by the "appalling" business men giving fi sive testimony in fear the special New York C jury that was dismisse has taken the initiative ganization of a perman tisan committee of pro zens to combat these co

Recommendations con presentment filed wit Wednesday and made pi day embraced a city-wi investigate criminal cou activities of prosecutin to assure protection to and to compel hesitai men to give testimony.

Copies of the present sent to Governor Le Mayor La Guardia. T the committee will be and will develop its ow ship and program, with officials on its member However, the Mayor yesterday to hasten the

SMITH WILL SHUN STATE CONVENTION

Omission of Ex-Governor as a Delegate Indicates Wider Breach With Old Allies.

LIMA MOB STONES GERMAN CONSULATE

City in Turmoil When Peru's Soccer Team Quits Olympics, Refusing to Replay Game.

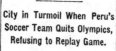

Anderson knew what Woolley was planning so he sidestepped by informing Judge Knight that his questions were merely preliminary. So Roland Rich Woolley sat down, and Mary Astor was called back to the stand.

• • •

Joseph Anderson's plan was to hammer at Astor, asking her about things mentioned in the diary. If her answers contradicted the diary he could use these lies to impeach her testimony, and if she admitted the truth, he'd have evidence of her unfitness to regain custody. But, to the detriment of Anderson's strategy, Mary Astor was up for the challenge and would once again prove herself "completely rattle-proof."

First up was George S. Kaufman.

"Mrs. Thorpe, you testified that your husband condoned your actions with Mr. George Kaufman. At that time was anything said as to what conduct you had with George Kaufman?"

Woolley shot up to object. He was overruled, and Knight explained, "The burden of proof rests on Miss Astor. Miss Astor should explain why she signed the contract at the time of the divorce."

Anderson continued. "Was anything said to you by Dr. Thorpe as to what sort of conduct you had with Mr. Kaufman?"

"I wasn't aware that it was concerned with my conduct."

Woolley was back on his feet and, after stating his reason for objecting—Anderson introducing a line of questioning designed to impeach the witness—Anderson countered that the direct examination had opened this area for cross-examination. Woolley's objection was again overruled.

"I can answer no—inasmuch as it had no bearing on the issue. He possibly mentioned it—that he would use it against me."

Astor had skillfully sidestepped the question.

"Now, what was said by you to Dr. Thorpe about George Kaufman?"

"I don't recall."

"Did you tell him that you had had an affair in New York with George Kaufman?"

"I don't recall discussing any such matters."

"Was anything said by Dr. Thorpe as to what your conduct had been with Mr. Kaufman?"

"I am not sure."

"Don't you remember Dr. Thorpe telling you that you had been living with Mr. Kaufman in various parts of the United States as man and wife?"

Astor's voice dropped. She glared at Anderson.

"No! Because that isn't true. I don't remember any such thing."

"Was anything said about what your conversation with Kaufman was about?"

"I am not sure."

Although Anderson was referring to information contained in the diary, Astor refused to give him a direct answer when an "I don't remember" or "I don't recall" would suffice. And then, when she couldn't do that, she gave him an answer that made it clear he didn't know what he was talking about. If that weren't bad enough, when the opportunity availed itself, Astor would turn Anderson's questions around on him.

"Did you say anything during that conversation with Dr. Thorpe other than what you have testified to?"

"Yes. I recalled to his mind the conversation we had six months previously, when I was quite frank with him about my friendship with Mr. Kaufman and my husband said to me at the time, 'I understand this friendship between you and Mr. Kaufman. It is a wonder you haven't turned to somebody else long before, after the way I've treated you. I wouldn't be much of a physician if I didn't understand it. I haven't kept my word with you under our agreement of two years ago when I was going to get a divorce. I've given you a raw deal. I have been expecting something like this.'"

With Astor referring to Thorpe's infidelities, the whispering in the courtroom rose considerably, and Franklyn Thorpe frowned. The noise finally grew so loud that the bailiff was required to rap for order. For the next thirty minutes, Anderson asked about Kaufman, but between Woolley's objections and Astor's brilliantly evasive answers, Anderson failed to establish that George Kaufman was the reason for the divorce, and Astor did not contradict anything in the diary. Completely stymied, in an attempt to prove she neglected the baby, Anderson began asking Astor about her stay at Tower Road after the divorce.

After another series of nos, and denials regarding leaving the baby alone all night while she was out on the town, Anderson was forced to move on.

"How did Dr. Thorpe treat Marylyn just prior to the divorce?"

Astor again turned the question around.

"He allowed her in the room while he quarreled with me, while he shook his fist in my face and while he pushed me down in a chair. I asked him to wait until the child had left the room, but he said to the maid, 'Let her sit there.'"

Realizing that Astor would probably do the same with every question asked about Thorpe, Joseph Anderson turned to her three-month vacation the previous fall and winter. He planned to bring up names of men, implying they had been her lovers.

"Isn't it a fact that you told George S. Kaufman in March 1935 that you would meet him in October 1935?"

Following some more questions about Kaufman, Anderson introduced another name.

"Did you meet Bennett Cerf?"

"Yes, I saw Bennett Cerf."

It was obvious what Anderson was up to, so Woolley was up on his feet.

"This is an attempt to scandalize innocent people. I object to this entire line of questioning. The child was here at that time, not in New York."

Judge Knight looked at Anderson. "Where are you going with this?"

"Your Honor, the question was only preliminary."

On these grounds the objection was overruled, and Anderson continued.

"Did you go out with Bennett Cerf while you were in New York?"

"Several times."

Woolley was again on his feet. He was outraged. "These events occurring in New York have absolutely nothing to do with this child custody phase of this case. The child was here, not in New York."

Again Judge Knight overruled, and Anderson asked about the Christmas trip to Havana.

"Did anyone go with you?"

"Yes."

"Who?"

"Several people."

"Tell me their names?"

"Carlos Paraga, his sister, Danny Silberberg, and then we were joined in Miami by some other people."

"And Daniel Silberberg?"

"Yes. Some of us went to Havana and others stayed in Miami. It was just a Christmas party of friends."

"Did Danny Silberberg go to Havana?"

"Yes, I think. Possibly. Among others."

"Well, wasn't Mr. Silberberg there all the time?"

"No."

"With whom did you stay in Havana?"

"I didn't stay with anyone."

"How did you register at the hotel in Havana?"

"As Mrs. Mary Thorpe."

"Did anyone occupy the room with you?"

"No."

"When you returned to New York, where did you stay?"

"At the Seville Biltmore."

"How did you register?"

"Mary Thorpe."

"Did anyone stay with you?"

"No."

"When you came back to California, did you have a conversation with Dr. Thorpe?"

"Many."

"Where did you have your first conversation with Dr. Thorpe?"

"At the train in Pasadena."

"Did you tell Dr. Thorpe about your trip and your affairs in New York?"

Annoyed at Anderson's use of the word "affairs," Astor's feelings became evident in her caustic response.

"I can answer part of that question."

"Well, answer it."

"I told him a great deal about my trip."

After a few more questions another name came up.

"Didn't you mention the name of a doctor you saw in New York?"

"Yes."

"What was his name?"

"Dr. Mortimer Rodgers."

"Did you see him in New York?"

"Yes. I was continuing treatment I had started in California."

"Did you ever go out with him socially?"

"I had lunch with him once or twice."

"Did you ever go to dinner with him?"

"I don't remember that I did."

"Did you ever go to any shows with him?"

"I don't recall."

"Did he come to the hotel to see you?"

"Yes."

"How many times?"

"Twice, when it was inconvenient for me to go to his office for treatment."

"Did you tell Dr. Thorpe about your affairs with any of these men?"

Woolley objected to the inference Anderson was making.

"He keeps using the word affairs…."

Judge Knight sustained and told Anderson to curtail his inappropriate use of the word.

"Now Mrs. Thorpe, while you were living on Tower Road, did you ever drink liquor in the presence of the child?"

"I might have had a dinner highball while she was around."

"Did any of your guests?"

"I suppose so, but no one was ever drunk while she was around."

"Had you been drinking intoxicants?"

"Possibly, I had a cocktail before dinner."

"Did you drink in the bedroom?"

Wanting no more of this, Astor put a stop to the implication. "There never was any drinking in my bedroom. Nothing improper ever took place in that bedroom while the child was in the house."

"Didn't Jack Hirsh, your former servant, serve you a fifth of a gallon of Galantine's scotch whisky every day."

Astor, temper rising, snapped at Anderson. "No! That is not true."

"Isn't it a fact that John Barrymore visited you there while the baby was present?"

Woolley objected. "This is a contemptuous effort to bring in the names of persons who have nothing to do with this proceeding."

Judge Knight leaned towards Anderson. "I take it that Mr. John Barrymore wouldn't be any particular menace to a child."

The entire courtroom burst into laughter. The bailiff rapped for order. When the room quieted Anderson replied.

"Agreed, but we shall hear more of Barrymore later—a lot more."

"I take it, Mr. Anderson, that you have some evidence pertaining to this case. This man is prominent in the theatrical world and there is no need of bringing his name into this matter unless he has something to do with the proceedings."

"Your Honor, I will connect them up."

Knight turned to Woolley. "I can't see the relevance, but the attorney has promised to connect this up, so I will permit an answer."

"Did Mr. Barrymore visit when the child was present?"

"Yes."

"When did he visit you for the first time?"

"I don't recall the date."

"How long did he stay?"

"About an hour."

"How many times did he visit you on Tower Road?"

"I don't remember exactly. It seems to me he came up twice with Mr. Camomile. He wanted to talk over his troubles."

"At that time, did you serve him liquor?"

"No!"

"Isn't it true that he was intoxicated on these visits?"

Woolley objected as the question was leading. His objection was sustained.

"Could you tell if he was drinking?"

"No, he had not been drinking."

"Do you remember the time that you brought Marylyn out while Mr. Barrymore was there?"

"I didn't bring her out. She was in the patio playing and I took him out to see Marylyn."

"Was she ever in the room with Mr. Barrymore?"

Woolley was on his feet objecting to this "insinuating and contemptuous reference to the actor."

Judge Knight overruled.

"No, she wasn't. I took Mr. Barrymore out to meet my daughter."

"Is it not a fact that when you took him to the patio he fell over her?"

This elicited laughter throughout the courtroom.

"That is ridiculous."

"Don't you remember you tried to rescue Marylyn when Barrymore was falling over her?"

"No, because it never happened."

"Was that the only time that Mr. Barrymore was in the presence of the child?"

"As nearly as I can remember."

"How long was he there the first time?"

"About an hour."

"How long the second time?"

"Not very long. Ten or fifteen minutes."

"On what visit did he tell you about his troubles?"

Woolley objected that this had nothing to do with this case. Agreeing, Judge Knight sustained.

"Was there anyone with him beside Mr. Camomile?"

"There might have been someone in the car."

"Did Barrymore ever come alone to your home?"

"Mr. Camomile came both times."

"Did you ever serve drinks in the presence of Marylyn while Mr. Barrymore was there?"

"No."

At this point Judge Knight pounded his gavel and recessed the court until 2:00 p.m.

• • •

If Joseph Anderson had wanted to wear down Astor and confuse her into impeaching herself he had failed dismally. Mary Astor did not fall into a single trap that Anderson had set; instead, he had fallen into several of hers. The miracle that Thorpe and Anderson were hoping for had simply not materialized.

28

Not wanting to lose their seats, many spectators had brought lunches and munched away during the recess. At 1:30 Ruth Chatterton appeared. She hadn't had time to remove her stage makeup and would need to leave by 3:30. Wrapping her arms around Astor, Chatterton told her that everyone on the film set wished her luck. Turning, she answered a reporter's question.

"I'm just here to lend Mary moral support. It is no little thing for Mary to put aside her pride and modesty to fight for the thing she loves best—her child. I admire Mary very much for her courage. I am with her all the way."

Chatterton then gently shoved her mother towards the reporters and joked that, since her mother was eager for a Broadway career, maybe they could help by interviewing her instead.

• • •

At 2:00 Judge Knight brought the court back into session and Mary Astor took the stand. Anderson now tried a different approach. He began asking questions in machine-gun fashion, often asking a question before Astor had finished answering hoping she wouldn't have time to think of an evasive answer. In response, Astor took her time, whether she was interrupted or not.

"Did anyone else visit you at the Tower Road beside Mr. Barrymore?"

Astor grinned. It was a stupid question.

"Yes. I do have a great many friends."

"Name some of them who visited you."

Woolley was on his feet. "I object to this whole line of questioning. It is a brazen effort to scandalize innocent parties."

Judge Knight agreed and looked at Anderson. "Are you referring to anyone in particular? If that's the case, then please name him."

Anderson turned back to Astor. "Did George Oppenheimer visit you at Tower Road?"

"Yes."

Oppenheimer, a film writer, was a close friend of Kaufman.

After some questions about Mr. Oppenheimer, Anderson introduced another name.

"Did anyone visit you at Tower Road while the baby was living there named John Eldredge?"

"Yes."

"How many times?"

"Several times while making a picture together I brought him home for dinner."

"How long did he stay?"

"Not very late because both of us were working."

"Did he ever accompany you to the bedroom?"

"No."

"Were you ever served drinks in the bedroom with Eldredge?"

"No."

"Were you ever served drinks in the house?"

"Yes."

"How late?"

"Before dinner."

"Any after dinner?"

"I don't think so, no."

"Did Count Alfredo Carpegna ever visit you at the Tower Road address?"

"Alfonso Carpegna? Yes."

Carpegna was a European playboy fond of the company of beautiful women. Anderson asked almost the same set of questions about him. Since Astor wasn't the least bit flustered by any of this, Anderson concluded this line of questioning with one last question.

"Did you ever keep at that place for many hours male visitors in your bedroom?"

Astor glared contemptuously first at Anderson and then at Thorpe.

"I never did. Nothing ever went on in that bedroom with a child in the other room."

"How did Dr. Thorpe treat Marylyn just prior to the divorce?"

"He allowed her to be in the room while we quarreled, while he was threatening me, shaking his fist at me, and pushing me into the chair. I said that we should take her out of the room before we went on, and he said to the maid, 'Let her sit there. She's got to learn to sit still.'"

In repeating a question he had asked earlier, Anderson was attempting to turn her answer around at her.

"Then, if he was so cruel to the child, why did you allow him to gain custody without a contest?"

"I didn't understand the meaning. He said he would just have the say-so."

"Did he say he was going to take the child?"

"Yes, but he said he might give me the baby for extended periods and I hoped he would change his mind about taking her away from me."

"How often did Dr. Thorpe visit the child at the Tower Road address?"

"Two or three times a week."

"Did he ever discipline the child while he was there?"

"Practically every time he was there."

"Did you ever discipline the child?"

"Yes I did, but not in the manner he did."

"How did he discipline her?"

Astor took a long time to answer, so Anderson turned to Knight. "I would like you to ask her to answer my question as to how?"

Judge Knight spoke up. "How did he discipline the child? Tell us how he disciplined her the last time you remember."

"Your Honor, what I'm trying to say is whenever he disciplined her it was in a burst of vile, maniacal temper. He would take hold of her and jerk her and spank her roughly."

Anderson resumed the questioning.

"How often did this occur?"

"I can't fix the time—it happened often. He would spank her while he was in a rage, which I contend is bad for a child. When he was in a rage he would treat her in a manner he would not treat her if he was in his right mind."

"Did you speak to servants about the manner in which Dr. Thorpe treated his child?"

"I wasn't allowed by Dr. Thorpe to criticize his treatment of the child."

"Did you tell anyone about the brutal treatment of the child by the doctor?"

"Yes. I went up to Miss Ann Harding's and told her about it. I told Marcus Goodrich about it. He was at Miss Harding's."

"Where is Miss Harding now?"

"I believe she's in England."

Anderson turned to Judge Knight. "I'd like to have Miss Harding here."

Woolley stood. "Do you want to subpoena her?"

"Certainly."

It was a bewildered Judge Knight who spoke the obvious. "That would be impossible. If Miss Harding is in England she is out of the jurisdiction of this court."

Woolley smiled. "Yes, he would like to subpoena everybody. He would like to subpoena President Roosevelt and Governor Landon."

Being ridiculed, Anderson explained himself.

"I want to show that Miss Astor went to New York the time she said Dr. Thorpe was treating the child brutally. I want the court to learn if she had complained to anyone else about the treatment. If so, why did she go to New York?"

Judge Knight nodded. "Please go on."

LOS ANGELES EVENING
HERALD ☆ Express   THREE CENTS

The Evening Herald and Express Grows Just Like Los Angeles

VOL. LXVI   Hotels and Trains Five Cents   TUESDAY, AUGUST 11, 1936   ★ ★ ★   NO. 118

These photos show the real life emotions of Miss Astor on the stand—not the emotions of a film star, but the emotions of a mother risking everything in her frantic desire to gain the daughter she bore. Opposing her is her former husband, Dr. Franklyn Thorpe, father of little Marylyn, who is equally determined to gain the child's custody. Miss Astor's witnesses have made telling statements against him. Now his attorneys are grilling her on her own private life. It is a tense drama of a "perfect" filmdom romance that faded.

"Now, after you returned from New York, did you ever discipline your child?"

"Yes."

"Twenty times?"

Astor paused. "I don't know. Many times?"

"Did the doctor ever discipline the child?"

"Yes."

"In what manner?"

"In the same manner as I described."

"Did you ever see any marks on the child?"

"Yes."

"Were they extensive?"

"There were bruises on Marylyn's back in the shape of his hand."

"Were they as large as your hand?"

"Doctor Thorpe's hand, after he had let his vile temper get the best of him. It left the baby tearful."

"Were they all over her body?"

"All over her back."

Once again Mary Astor did not give Anderson what he wanted. So he moved on.

"Did you buy Marylyn any clothes while you were in New York?"

"Yes."

Anderson showed Astor a picture of Marylyn in a white coat and bonnet.

"Did you buy Marylyn that outfit?"

"No."

"Who did?"

"Dr. Thorpe. But he put it on my charge account."

Another question backfired. So, Anderson tried a different approach. He became incredulous.

"Was he *ever* kind to her?"

"I wouldn't call it kindness."

"Did he ever show *any* affection for the child?"

"No, but he often insisted that the child show affection to him."

The entire time Astor spoke about him and Marylyn she looked directly at Thorpe, and Thorpe glared back, doing his best to refrain from showing his temper.

Because of her insistence on this point, Anderson had finally found an opening.

"Do you mean to say, that Marylyn has no affection for her daddy?"

"No, I wouldn't call it that. He required her to show affection for him. Dr. Thorpe would come home in the evening when the child was there playing and say, 'Marylyn, come here put your arms around Daddy's neck; now give him a big kiss and say you are glad to see me. Tell Daddy you love him.' And if she didn't do it, he would chastise her."

"With what?"

"His hands."

"Were you present on the Saturday morning when Dr. Thorpe saw the baby at the same time that Judge Knight visited the baby at the Toluca Lake home?"

"Yes."

"Did you see the child playing with her father in the front yard?"

"Yes."

"Did the child appear to be afraid of the doctor?"

"Yes. She did to me. She was acting as she was told to act on many occasions."

Anderson had finally scored a point. Everyone at Toluca Lake had seen how affectionate the child was with her father. In truth, Marylyn adored him. Earlier, in Astor's "baby diary," she had written, "Franklyn is simply crazy about her. When Franklyn comes home at night he starts blowing the automobile horn about six blocks away. She recognizes it instantly. Her face lights up and she cheers."

Astor had taken a tactical position. Now, unable to retreat from it, it had backfired on her. So, having made his point, Anderson attempted to show that Marylyn's mother had neglected the baby by bringing up a cold the child had while Astor was in Palm Springs with Kaufman. But this questioning dead-ended, as Marylyn wasn't seriously ill and had recovered by the time her mother returned home. So, Anderson now tried to show that Astor had given up custody to protect Kaufman.

"Do you remember having a conversation with Ethel M. Pepin and Dr. Thorpe in March 1935?"

"Yes."

"What was the substance of that conversation?"

"The fact that Dr. Thorpe wanted a divorce, the custody of the child, and one half of the property."

"What did Miss Pepin say to you on this occasion?"

"She said, 'I don't think you are getting a fair deal, Mary, but you're stuck with this marriage.' The doctor said he would get the divorce, custody of Marylyn, and half of the property. He warned Ethel not to go over to my side."

"Did you say, 'I want my freedom at any price?'"

"I don't remember."

"Do you remember saying, 'I hate this goddamn town. The further I get away the better?'"

"I don't remember."

"Did you say, 'It's just one tragedy after another?'"

"Possibly."

"Did you say, 'I'm going to New York to try my luck on the stage?'"

"Possibly."

"Did you discuss with Dr. Thorpe plans to take part in *Merrily We Roll Along*?"

"Maybe I did say I wanted to get on the New York stage. All actresses have that ambition."

As Astor had written about this in the diary extracts handed out to the press, Anderson was trying to get her to contradict what she had written, but Astor was being evasive and parsing her words, as she hadn't said these things. She'd written them.

"Did you tell Dr. Thorpe that your next step would be London, and wonder where he would be with a Los Angeles practice?"

"I do not recall saying that."

"Do you recall Dr. Thorpe saying that Marylyn is going to know her father?"

"I do not recall."

"Did you ever say that you planned to educate Marylyn in Switzerland?"

"I do not recall."

"Do you remember that this was the reason that Dr. Thorpe brought his attorney, Ethel Pepin?"

"No. He may have said, 'I love you Mary, but I can't hold you against your wishes—but I will fight to keep my baby.'"

"Do you recall Pepin advising you to get an attorney, and telling you that the doctor had told her to go ahead with the divorce?"

"I do not recall."

As this was getting Anderson nowhere, he was forced to move on.

"Didn't you send Kaufman a telegram on April 12, 1935?"

"Yes."

"How did you sign them?"

"Simply, 'Mary'"

Woolley was on his feet objecting, and Anderson told the judge that he was endeavoring to "explain why she went on the trip." The judge suggested the telegrams be subpoenaed as exhibits, and Anderson continued.

"Did he send you a telegram?"

"Yes, two or three."

"On April 5, 1935, didn't you say you were perfectly fine with the divorce settlement at a conference with Dr. Thorpe and his attorney?"

"Yes."

"Did Dr. Thorpe say to you, 'I want you to realize what you are doing before it's too late?'"

"No."

"Do you remember the doctor saying, 'I love you, Mary, and I don't want a divorce.'"

"I don't remember. He said similar things at various times."

"Do you remember saying you wanted the doctor to get the divorce and the custody of the child?"

"I don't remember exactly."

This was also going nowhere, as the cross-examination was degenerating into Anderson asking Astor if she had done this or that, and her saying she hadn't, with Anderson believing that this would imply that it was true.

"When did the doctor tell you for the first time that if you displeased him he would take the child?"

"I don't remember exactly. It was shortly after the divorce."

"Do you remember the last time?"

"It was on July 5."

"Were you sober at the time?"

"I most certainly was."

"Was Miss Evelyn Laye there?"

"Yes."

"Do you remember what time the doctor arrived to take the child?"

"Sometime in the afternoon."

"Were you or Miss Laye drinking intoxicating liquor at the time?"

"No. We were drinking Coca-Cola."

"Isn't it true that when you are drinking intoxicating liquor, your temper grows very mean?"

Woolley leapt to his feet objected and was sustained. Astor was handed a glass containing Coca-Cola, which she sipped through a straw.

"What did the doctor say to you that night about your drinking?"

"The doctor demanded to know if we had been drinking. I told him I had a highball before dinner." She nodded at the Coca-Cola in her hand. "And that I also had several soft drinks."

"Did you offer Dr. Thorpe a drink?"

Unable to stifle a smile, she shook her head. "No."

The audience laughed.

"Were you intoxicated?"

"Certainly not. We had a cocktail each before dinner, and Miss Laye had a glass of wine with her dinner."

"Well, was Miss Laye intoxicated, then?"

"Certainly not."

"What was the quarrel about?"

"Because I let the baby stay up until after 8:00, way after her bed time."

Judge Knight reminded Anderson it had been the Fourth of July and "a child in good health could be kept up late." So Anderson moved on.

"Were you not afraid of letting your husband treat the child medically when she was ill last February?"

Astor grew angry. "I was not afraid of Dr. Thorpe except when he got in a vile temper about some little thing, and then I was afraid of him, plenty, and it wasn't pleasant to be around."

This drew a round of laughter from spectators. Astor had again succeeded in turning the questions around on Anderson. So, in desperation, Anderson once again brought up Kaufman, trying to establish that they had been in contact recently and by implication that the affair was still on. None of his questions got him anywhere until he brought up the Trocadero.

"When did you last see Kaufman?"

"At a dinner party at the Ernst Lubitsch's home about two months ago?"

"Weren't you with him at the Trocadero on the night of July 8? About a week before this trial began?"

"I don't believe so."

Woolley stood up and objected. "This is a vile and contemptible attempt on the part of the attorney to drag in innocent people and I protest."

Judge Knight looked at Anderson. "Is there any purpose to this?"

Anderson nodded. "Yes, she was there with Kaufman and I saw her there."

Surprised and curious, Knight let Anderson continue.

"You deny you were at the Trocadero during July and that you left with George S. Kaufman?"

"To the best of my recollection, I was not there in July. I was there in June."

"Don't you remember being at the Trocadero the night Irving Thalberg and Norma Shearer were there?"

"I don't remember it."

"Well, that's funny, because I was practically sitting right next to you and Mr. Kaufman at the club that night. Don't you remember seeing me there, Miss Astor?"

"No, I don't." Her tone became patronizing. "I'm sorry Mr. Anderson, but I didn't see you there."

"My goodness! Don't you remember standing beside me while you were waiting for your car to be brought around to the front of the café?"

Astor smiled. "No."

One of the spectators shouted something about Anderson wearing the perfect disguise and the courtroom erupted into uproarious laughter. Joseph Anderson's cross-examination had sunk to the level of comic opera. The bailiff rapped for order and Woolley was on his feet.

"Objection! The witness has already answered the question numerous times. I request and demand that this line of questioning cease unless Mr. Anderson discloses his purpose."

Anderson turned and, losing his temper, barked at Woolley, "She was there and I saw her. Furthermore I'll bring witnesses in to prove it."

Woolley turned to Judge Knight. "Counsel's conduct is contemptuous. He is only trying to drag in the names of a lot of innocent people."

Anderson looked at Knight. "I want to prove, Your Honor, that she was at the Trocadero on the night of July 8th with George Kaufman, because I saw them there."

A reluctant Judge Knight nodded for Anderson to continue.

"Were you there with Kaufman in July?

"Yes, but it was June."

"Were you sober?"

"Entirely. I think I had a Daiquiri cocktail."

Woolley leaped to his feet shouting, "It would seem that counsel now appears in the role of snoop."

The entire courtroom again burst into uproarious laughter as Judge Knight patiently calmed down both Anderson and Woolley. He then asked Anderson to continue. Having made a mistake earlier, confusing gallon and quart, Anderson wanted to correct his gaff.

"Isn't it a fact that on numerous occasions, Mrs. Thorpe, you have consumed as much as a fifth of a quart of Scotch whiskey in a single day since your divorce."

Astor did her best to control her temper.

"No. Certainly not!"

It was a weary Judge Knight who stopped the cross-examination and adjourned the court until the next morning.

• • •

Mary Astor following an exhausting day on the witness stand.

Asked what he would do when he got Kaufman on the stand, Anderson told a reporter, "It will be a tougher session than this one." Joseph Anderson believed that his pounding had gotten the better of Mary Astor. The man was unable to allow himself to see otherwise.

As for George S. Kaufman, while a dozen deputy sheriffs carrying a bench warrant were searching Los Angeles for him, Mr. Kaufman was still comfortably ensconced in his compartment on the Santa Fe Special heading for Chicago.

Regarding the other men mentioned in court, Bennett Cerf was found at his home at 112 West Fifty-Eighth Street in New York.

"I went out with her several times. Our meetings were the most casual possible. And we were always with other people. I daresay she knows a hundred people in New York much better than she knows me."

Dr. Mortimer W. Rodgers, older brother of Broadway composer Richard Rogers, told reporters, "Miss Astor was referred to this office on October 15, 1935, by Dr. Thorpe and was treated in a routine way by me in accordance with his written suggestions for a brief period."

From writer George Oppenheimer: "Miss Astor is just a friend of mine. She is a lovely lady and I wish her well."

Daniel Silberberg, a partner in the brokerage Firm of D.H. Silberberg & Co., wasn't around to comment. Silberberg was on vacation, or at least that was what he told his secretary to say.

As for Mary Astor, she would later recall that for the rest of the hearing "every afternoon I went home under police escort, and Nellie fixed me something to eat, and I had a good masseuse come in to undo the kinks and stroke my back monotonously until finally I fell asleep. The next morning it would start all over again."

29

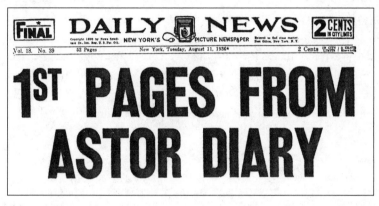

The publication of the diary excerpts created a sensation the likes of which had never been seen before. For today's reader, accustomed to an unbridled press exposing a Hollywood celebrity's most intimate secrets, the degree of this sensation would be impossible to fathom. But in 1936, nothing like those diary excerpts had ever before been disseminated to the public, and it was like a blast of TNT. Although the real diary wasn't anything remotely like the lurid and pornographic forgeries that Mary Astor remembered helped her "achieve the reputation of being the greatest nympho-courtesan since Pompadour," they were sensational nonetheless.

It wasn't the contents as much as it was the frankness of Mary Astor's writing that made this material such a sensation. For the first time, America was taken into the mind of a screen celebrity and read the personal and intimate thoughts of a star unfiltered by a studio publicity department. Mary Astor wrote frankly about her feelings for George Kaufman, for Franklyn Thorpe, and her marriage. This writing contained a candor and honesty unseen before and was, within Hollywood itself, nothing short of harrowing to those who believed that what the public thought true of Mary Astor, they would also think true of the entire film colony.

Although the writing, especially when discussing her affair with George Kaufman, was, as Astor would later describe, "an overemotional account of a romantic interlude," never had so frank a document concerning a Hollywood personality's amorous adventures been made public. Astor spoke off-handedly about open marriages and extra-martial affairs, presenting a woman who lived far outside the social norms of American morality. Thus, those diary extracts made for extremely "steamy" reading, and the fear in Hollywood was that more of the diary would find its way into print. And if Astor spoke so frankly about herself, it could only be imagined what she might have written about others.

• • •

Meanwhile, bench warrant in hand, deputy sheriffs searched both Moss Hart's home and producer Irving Thalberg's yacht, but to no avail. Tipped off that the playwright might be out nightclubbing, deputy sheriffs began checking nightclubs all over Hollywood, but Kaufman was nowhere to be found.

George Kaufman, having disembarked the Santa Fe Special in Chicago on Tuesday morning, was between trains for two hours waiting to board the Fifth Avenue Special. Relieved that no one recognized him, after boarding his train Kaufman locked himself in his train compartment, and prepared to continue incognito back to New York City.

• • •

Just as Tuesday's court session was about to begin, A.P. Michael Narlain informed reporters that a representative of District Attorney Buron Fitt's office was "now in the courtroom" and would be watching Astor on the stand to determine if she was

Mary Astor, Roland Rich Woolley, and Florence Eldridge.

committing perjury and, if she was, that Astor might face "possible criminal prosecution."

Because Joseph Anderson's cross-examination had failed so dismally, his backup plan was now being implemented. Mary Astor was being threatened with possible imprisonment.

• • •

By the time Mary Astor arrived, every inch of available space in that courtroom was filled with sweating, anxious spectators. In addition to Ruth Chatterton, with Astor today were Astor's mother and Nellie Richardson, as well as Florence Eldridge, actor Fredric March's wife. Astor had acted with Eldridge on the stage and with March on film, and when she was married to Ken Hawks the two were among Astor's closest friends, and had always remained loyal, as the day would prove.

Both Eldridge and Chatterton sat with Astor at the counsel table, and were immediately surrounded by reporters. Astor wore the same black suit she had worn on Monday, Chatterton also wore black, while Eldridge had on a purple afternoon dress. When asked if her brother was the same John Eldredge mentioned in court,

Florence told the reporter that her brother was Cromwell McKechnie and that he had absolutely nothing to do with the custody hearing.

Astor told reporters that she had received "several hundred fan letters and most of them were encouraging." Regarding the publication of her diary excerpts, she wasn't particularly enamored. "I wish the judge would either burn the books or lock them up in a safety deposit box and throw away the key." Truth was, when she finally did read these extracts in the *Los Angeles Examiner*, she found it one of the most humiliating experiences of her life.

At the other end of the counsel table, occasionally glancing over at his former wife, Franklyn Thorpe looked glum. Obviously nervous, his hand actually shook when he lit a cigarette, and for good reason. That morning Walter Winchell had taken a swipe at Thorpe in Winchell's syndicated column.

"Dr. Thorpe is supposed to have replied, 'Isn't it terrible that columnists are allowed to put people's names in the papers like that? Look who's talking! The big diary exposer!'"

• • •

When Judge Knight brought court into session, the sheriffs informed him that George Kaufman was nowhere to be found and that rumor put him out of state. Knight wasn't pleased.

"I give you my word that if Kaufman comes within the jurisdiction of this court I will see that he is put in jail and kept there long enough to cool his heels."

Since the courtroom was sweltering, with Judge Knight's permission the four lawyers, as well as the judge, removed their coats to reveal shirts drenched in sweat. Woolley then stood and officially subpoenaed the entire diary, forcing Anderson to bring the two volumes into court tomorrow.

Truth be told, Judge Knight had about had it with Joseph Anderson, the press, the diary, and, in fact, the entire custody hearing. He wasn't happy that Anderson had handed out parts of the diary to the press, despite Knight having made it clear that he would protect the names of innocent parties mentioned in it. He wasn't happy that someone from the prosecutor's office was in his courtroom preparing to charge Mary Astor with perjury. Finally, he wasn't happy that his courtroom had been transformed into a circus for the benefit of the newspapers.

Before him sat two intransigent parents who had lost sight of what was best for their child. Judge Knight simply could not fathom why Marylyn's parents had let things reach this point. Since it was his decision as to which parent had custody of Marylyn Thorpe, he was going to use that authority to put this custody hearing back on track.

He spoke to the two attorneys.

"I am asking you gentlemen, if you would make a great effort to shorten this proceeding as much as possible. I shall expect you, Mr. Anderson, to terminate your cross-examination of Miss Astor within a very few minutes and you, Mr. Woolley, should be able to rest your case within half an hour."

Knight then asked Woolley how many more witnesses he planned to call. Woolley, who had heard the judge, said "only two or three" and that he "would finish with them in about an hour I think depending on what comes up here later."

Judge Knight then turned to Joseph Anderson. Anderson had become so entrenched that, despite what Knight had just ordered, announced that he planned to cross-examine Mary Astor for a minimum of two days, and that even then he still might not get to a cross-examination on the contents of the diary.

An increasingly annoyed Judge Knight asked, "And then?"

Anderson had a list of two hundred questions "largely based on revelations in the diary."

A deep frown appeared on Knight's forehead. His patience was at an end. He immediately recessed court, ordered Anderson, Woolley and their co-counsels into chambers. In chambers Judge Knight made it clear that the proceeding had gotten completely out of hand and that he had heard enough to render a decision. Nevertheless, he much preferred that the parents made the determination and asked the attorneys to press this upon their clients. Anderson, finally realizing that he needed to make the best of this, told the judge that he could bring his client around to a settlement. Woolley thought that it would be much harder but, if the terms were agreeable to Astor, she might settle. However, this would be contingent on Franklyn Thorpe returning the diary.

Joseph Anderson made it clear that under no circumstances would his client return the ledger books. When Knight asked Anderson why, Anderson asked if Woolley could be excused since, in telling Knight, he would be giving away his courtroom strategy. So, Knight requested Woolley leave, and while Anderson took out the diary and showed Knight the "pertinent passages," Woolley and Rank took their seats at the counsel table.

Woolley quietly explained to Astor what had just happened, and that they needed to settle or Knight might make a decision not beneficial to her. Woolley felt that Astor had the upper hand in a negotiation because the court had seen how well she had cared for the baby. As the two had discussed this possibility earlier, Astor let him know that she was open to a settlement. Nevertheless, about the diary the actress was adamant. She wanted it back.

When Anderson was finished, Judge Knight sent him and Narlain out, and Woolley and Rank walked back in. While Woolley was in chambers, a nervous Mary Astor told Ruth Chatterton and Florence Eldridge what Woolley had just told her. Chatterton pattered her on the back.

"Don't feel so bad. It won't be so long until you'll forget it all. Twelve years ago I was in an unpleasant court case myself but it's all gone, and you'll forget it just as I have."

In chambers, Woolley reiterated Astor's position on the diary and explained the reason for it—she wanted to protect her friends from scandal. Knight, realizing that things were at a stalemate, sent Woolley and Rank back out. Moments later the judge was in the courtroom and, still in shirtsleeves, wiped the sweat off his face, put on his judge's robes, and brought the court back into session.

"I am about ready to give a decision on the evidence already heard. My supreme interest in this matter is to save the child, Marylyn, from possible repercussions later in life from lurid testimony painting her mother as a scarlet woman. What we are doing here is retrying the Astor-Thorpe divorce case. All these extraneous matters have no direct bearing on how the conduct of the principals in this case has affected the welfare of Marylyn who, after all, is more important than either of the principals."

Knight looked at both Woolley and Anderson.

"Go back to your offices and prepare this case as a child custody case so the matter can be cleaned up in a day and a half. My God, during all of yesterday's testimony only three or four small points of actual evidence were pertinent. This trial is costing the tax payers $175 a day, and the proceeding already has gone on longer than any such case ever tried in this county. From now on this case is going to be streamlined."

He then asked Joseph Anderson to request a continuance and told Woolley not to object. Both lawyers did as requested and, at 10:00 a.m., Judge Knight announced that the court would reconvene at 2:00 p.m. That said, Knight went back into chambers and closed the door behind him.

30

The court was pandemonium. It was evident that Mary Astor wouldn't be taking the stand and that the diary wouldn't be entered into evidence. Disappointment was rampant.

Since Woolley needed to be in touch with Astor during the negotiation, she had to go somewhere where he could reach her by telephone. Relieved to be leaving that crowded, sweltering courtroom, Astor, her mother, Nellie Richardson, Chatterton, and Eldridge all left together.

Lillian Miles was outraged—or at least pretended to be. Although her Florida relationship with Thorpe wouldn't be coming out, still left on the table was her sleeping with Thorpe at the Toluca Lake house.

"I'm so furious I can hardly speak. This can't be stopped now. We haven't had our day in court. My own reputation has been slandered and blackened. If the case is settled now, I can tell you that if that happens I'm going to take every legal step possible to clear my name."

Franklyn Thorpe was also angry. He made it plain to reporters that he had absolutely no intention of giving Mary Astor back her diary. One reporter mentioned rumors that the diary was "being offered for sale on the open market."

"I want no money. But what I do want, and will keep fighting for, is the assurance that Marylyn's best interests are safeguarded."

• • •

Anderson and Woolley immediately booked a room at the nearby Biltmore Hotel. For Anderson it was a victory. His intractability had succeeded in getting Mary Astor to the bargaining table. For Woolley, his job was now to get his client the best possible settlement. During a brief period, MGM attorney Mendel Silberberg was also in the hotel room. Considered one of the most powerful attorneys in LA, Silberberg wanted a look at the diary to confirm what Mary Astor had said about a forgery and determine whether Irving Thalberg or other MGM employees were mentioned. Satisfied that his client wasn't at risk, Silberberg pretty much reiterated what Thalberg had said on Saturday—a settlement was the best thing for everyone, including the industry. That out of the way, the attorney left the conference and met with reporters, where he pretty much restated the movie industry's take on this.

"There is tremendous pressure being brought to bear in Hollywood to settle the case at once."

Back at the meeting, Woolley made it clear that Astor wanted Marylyn for the school year and didn't mind Marylyn spending her summer and vacations with her father. Joseph Anderson proposed six months shared custody. Woolley reasoned that nine months of exclusive weekends was the equivalent of six months in actual time. After an agreement was reached on that issue, next up was the question of Marylyn's nurse and general care. Franklyn Thorpe wanted Nellie Richardson fired on the spot. Woolley discussed this with his client and Astor agreed that she and Thorpe would both need to agree on the hiring or firing of Marylyn's nurse. Since it would take two votes to fire her, Nellie Richardson kept her job.

Nevertheless, in the future Thorpe would have a say in who took care of Marylyn.

Then there was the diary. Astor wanted it returned intact, but Thorpe felt that if he lost possession Astor would have no reason to drop the Florida bigamy suit.

When the attorneys had been at it for over three hours, the diary issue still unresolved, Woolley called Knight just before 2:00 p.m., asking for an additional hour. Knight gave them the hour and, when it was up, two more. Then, shortly before 5:00 p.m. Astor, Thorpe, and their attorneys fought their way through the crowds into the courtroom. Mary Astor had Ruth Chatterton on one side and Florence Eldridge on the other with her mother and Nellie Richardson bringing up the rear.

When everyone was in their seats, Knight requested the attorneys join him in chambers. Because Astor had wanted full custody, and this compromise wasn't what she had hoped for, Chatterton and Florence Eldridge assured her that it was a "moral victory" to accept the shared custody. Nonetheless, Mary Astor appeared relieved that it was nearly over. At the other end of the counsel table, Thorpe was just as relieved. Although he had looked glum in the morning, he was now smiling and chatting with family and friends, including his sister Clara.

In chambers, both attorneys made it clear to Knight that they were pretty much in agreement on everything except the diary. So, the judge told them to return to the courtroom. Bringing the court into session, Judge Knight didn't look or sound happy.

"I warn you gentlemen, I am growing impatient. If there is any more trouble over this diary, I intend to take it into the custody of the court and lock it up. You must either reach an agreement or proceed with the case without further loss of time and confine your examination to the point at issue—the custody of the child. I will do everything within the province of the court to prevent dirt being thrown into this case and casting its blight on the future of the child." Knight glared at the two, making his message absolutely clear. "Gentlemen, is the status the same as it was?"

They both nodded, but it was Joseph Anderson who spoke.

"Your Honor, may this matter be continued until tomorrow morning, as I ask the court for additional time to settle this matter?"

Knight nodded. "That being the case, we will set it over until tomorrow morning at ten o'clock. Not only is the baby's present life involved, but so is her future. The issue before the court is solely one of her custody and welfare. I wish you gentlemen Godspeed."

Judge Knight then adjourned the court until Wednesday morning.

• • •

Mary Astor, Ruth Chatterton, Florence Eldridge, Astor's mother, and Nellie Richardson practically ran out of courtroom, struggling through a noisy mob. Their way blocked to the elevators, Roland Woolley needed to push a path through the crowds for them. Then, as Astor had done every day that week, she went home with a police escort, and Nellie made her dinner.

Meeting together again, the attorneys discussed the diary. Thorpe was adamant about keeping it. He had spoken about this earlier. "Look at what happened to Harry Bannister. He settled his custody suit with Ann Harding. Then she waited until the sensation grew cold, went to court, got more and more her way, and finally got the child entirely."

So the discussions continued through the night, with Woolley traveling to Astor's Toluca Lake home to discuss the situation while he and Anderson used the telephone to make proposals and counterproposals. By evening's end both attorneys realized they had a problem. Astor and Thorpe had dug in their heels and refused to budge.

31

Before court resumed on Wednesday morning, an outraged Lillian Miles was once again pleading innocence. "This thing just can't be stopped. I do so want to get into that chair and deny the dastardly things that have been said about me and Dr. Thorpe." She was referring to the Toluca Lake sleepovers and told reporters that she was prepared to take legal steps to clear her name.

At 6:42 a.m. that morning, Kaufman had disembarked from the Fifth Avenue Special just outside New York City in the town of Harmon, where his sister, Ruth, was waiting. From Harmon she drove her brother to New York, where he planned to temporarily stay with Moss Hart's parents in Manhattan. After that, the playwright wasn't quite sure what he would do.

In Los Angeles, Woolley, Anderson, and Thorpe met with reporters, and Woolley announced that a tentative agreement had been reached and only needed the judge's approval.

When asked how he felt, Thorpe spoke frankly. "I'll be a happy man again when this is over. This whole thing has been shocking—awful. I didn't bring the action in the first place, but after it was started, I was determined to fight it through."

In other words, it was Mary Astor's fault that he had stolen her diary, threatened her with it, and then quoted it in court while his attorney handed out pages to the press. Franklyn Thorpe had been playing that same record for the past month. Unfortunately, no one was buying it anymore.

· · ·

Inside the courtroom Mary Astor wore the same blue taffeta dress and mushroom hat that she had worn her first day on the stand. Sitting on either side of her was Ruth Chatterton, still chewing gum, and Florence Eldridge smoking a cigarette. Nellie Richardson, Astor's mother, and Ardys Clark—Marylyn's former Tower Road nurse—were also in the courtroom.

In the weeks to come, Ruth Chatterton and Florence Eldridge would be lauded for standing by their friend. Even Walter Winchell would write, "let a harvest of orchids be draped on Ruth Chatterton and Florence Eldridge, who risked public damnation by sitting through the trial with Mary Astor. That's 'moxie' in the movie colony, where the biggies have storm cellars to hide in when a pal needs consolation, comforting, and help." Ruth Chatterton later admitted that it may not have been the wisest decision for Mary Astor to keep a diary, but "she shouldn't be pilloried for that."

At 10:00 Judge Knight escorted the lawyers into chambers, where the issues holding up a settlement were finally hammered out. Mary Astor didn't want Franklyn Thorpe to have Marylyn on Sundays since Sunday was her only day off. Consequently, Judge Knight ruled in Astor's favor on the grounds that to "shunt the child from one parent to the other would be injurious to her."

This resolved, Woolley left chambers again and whispered Knight's decision to Ruth Chatterton who, still chewing gum, listened and then told Woolley that it was "marvelous."

From that point on the main stumbling block was the diaries. After some discussion with his client, Woolley persuaded Astor to agree that she would allow the ledger books to be impounded by the court and sealed in the hall of records. This became a no-go with Thorpe, who still wanted possession as insurance that Astor would live up to the agreement they had just reached.

Joseph Anderson went out to consult with his client and then, when asked how the conference was proceeding, spoke to the press.

"We have made every concession. But I must protect my client from future actions. If this case is not settled on our terms I'll spread every word in the diary over the record even if we have to keep Miss Astor on the stand for a week."

There was only one problem. Judge Knight and not Joseph Anderson had control of what parts of the diary would and would not be admitted in court and it was Judge Knight who finally came up with a compromise. The diary would remain under lock and key to be used as evidence only if the custody case was reopened.

Mary Astor was relieved, if not entirely pleased, at the diary being impounded, with both Chatterton and Eldridge telling her that it was the best thing for everyone.

Then Thorpe was reminded that a deputy county clerk—now serving time in San Quentin—had stolen $75,000 that had supposedly been held under seal in the county vaults as evidence. So, Thorpe became dead set against having the diary sit in the archives of Los Angeles County, and they were back to square one.

During the long recess, the stifling courtroom all but emptied of spectators. While Astor waited at the counsel table—drumming her fingernails and swinging her legs—she talked with Chatterton and Eldridge. After drinking some ice tea, she posed for a photographer with Chatterton, and then killed time by reading fan mail and telegrams sent to her by way of the courthouse.

In chambers Judge Knight spoke individually to Anderson and Narlain and then individually to Woolley and Rank, suggesting "a neutral custodian" be appointed. Narlain left chambers and whispered this to Thorpe. Thorpe listened carefully, eyes half closed, and then shook his head and said, "No." Getting up, Narlain headed for chambers, but Thorpe called him back, and the two spoke quietly for a few more minutes.

Eventually Knight's suggestion was agreed to by both sides. After the attorneys returned to the courtroom to inform their clients, Judge Knight walked out. Sweat pouring down his face, he didn't bother putting on his robes when he adjourned the court for a lunch break.

• • •

The net paid circulation for Jeans exceeded
Daily---1,600,000
Sunday-2,700,000

DAILY NEWS FINAL

Copyright 1936 by News Syndicate Co. Inc. Reg. U. S. Pat. Off.

NEW YORK'S PICTURE NEWSPAPER   Entered as 2nd class matter Post Office New York, N. Y.

Vol. 18. No. 41   60 Pages   New York, Thursday, August 13, 1936*   2 Cents IN CITY / 3 CENTS Elsewhere

MARY GETS BABY; DIARY TO COURT

Woolley spoke to the press. "The essentials have been arrived at. We are now concerned with ironing out the details. I can safely say that the diary is no longer an issue."

At 2:00 p.m., Judge Knight brought the court back into session, then called a recess while he and the attorneys marched back into chambers, where it was finally decided that the diary would be kept under lock and key, its location known only to the judge. Thorpe was then called into chambers so it could be explained to him the precise meaning of "custodianship." Thorpe then spoke with reporters.

"I think we will reach an agreement, but things have been so hectic we really haven't had time to sit down and go over it all calmly. All I want to do is protect my daughter."

"Are you happy?"

"No. I am not happy. How could I be happy? I am glad though that this litigation has been stopped. The main concern I have at this time is that several of my friends whose names were mentioned in the testimony will not be vindicated."

He was, of course, referring to Lillian Miles. As Norma Taylor had all but disappeared, her "innocence" was no longer his or anyone else's concern. In fact, at this point, it probably wasn't even Norma's.

A few minutes later everyone left chambers, and Judge Knight took the bench to make a statement.

"I am going to appoint a neutral custodian to take charge of the diary, so that neither faction will be favored. In case of further legal troubles between Miss Astor and Dr. Thorpe, either side may subpoena the diary. This agreement was reached in the interest of the child and the mother."

That said, he adjourned the court until 10:00 tomorrow morning.

• • •

Astor left the courtroom and, after meeting with Woolley in his office, went straight home under police escort so she could be with her daughter.

Shortly afterwards, Judge Knight held a brief press conference.

"The settlement fully protects the interests of little Marylyn, Mary Astor, Dr. Thorpe, and everyone else connected with the case. And contrary to rumors, there has been no pressure exerted upon me by motion picture interests. Any pressure was placed upon the principals involved, not the court. I am only thinking of the baby. She is too young now to know what this is all about but, when she grows to womanhood, I would hate to have her feel that in this court, when she was only four years of age, she didn't have a friend."

• • •

After seeing Astor off, Woolley returned to his office with Joseph Anderson, where the two worked on a joint public statement.

"As a result of a conference today, it would appear that a basic understanding has been arrived at. Details concerning the same were discussed and the entire matter of a settlement will be submitted to Judge Knight for his consideration and approval in the morning."

It was signed Roland Rich Woolley and Joseph Anderson.

32

Thursday's session was held in a courtroom on the twenty-first floor of the City Hall tower. Even though it was sweltering, the room was packed. Paul Schofield, the screenwriter who had shared the Toluca Lake house with Thorpe, was also in court. Nellie Richardson's testimony had implied that his former wife had slept with Thorpe.

"Depend on it—I'm going to take legal steps to refute that slanderous testimony. Thorpe is my friend. It was an outrageous slander against an innocent woman and a decent, honorable man."

The innocent woman, Schofield's former wife, had "sent him several sizzling telegrams" demanding that her name be cleared; ergo his reason for being in court.

As for Lillian Miles, she told reporters that she wouldn't leave that courtroom until she had "at least a semblance of her day in court." Affidavits would be handed to Judge Knight proving neither she nor Mrs. Paul Schofield had ever spent the night in Dr. Thorpe's bedroom. The affidavits were from Miles's brother, her mother, and Paul Schofield—not particularly unbiased participants.

• • •

Franklyn Thorpe's mother wasn't in court and neither were Chatterton, Eldridge, Astor's mother, or Nellie Richardson. Hence, Mary Astor sat alone. Wearing her familiar black suit, she was so exhausted that when photographers attempted to take photographs, she waved them off.

"No. You've had enough."

But when Astor learned that Alfred Hofer, an elderly spectator, had traveled all the way from New Jersey to wish her well, she walked over and the two spoke for a bit.

When court was brought to session the judge granted a black woman a divorce by default, giving the mother full custody of her child. The elated woman thanked the judge.

Standing, Judge Knight then signaled Mary Astor, Franklyn Thorpe, and their attorneys to follow him into chambers. During the hearing Knight had tried his best to remain impartial, but during the next hour, the judge spoke frankly. He told them that his main concern was the damage the two had caused their child because they had lost sight of the child's needs. Thorpe should never have used the diary to threaten to deprive a mother of her child and Mary Astor, instead of accepting a reasonable settlement, had prolonged the proceedings, precipitating a national scandal that had engulfed their daughter, a little girl who would live under its shadow for the rest of her life. Nevertheless, now that it was over, both parents needed to put it behind them and make it their job to raise their little girl to the best of their abilities. Tears flooded Mary Astor's eyes.

Finally, the judge told both parents that if further difficulty arose between the two over Marylyn's custody, it would be the court that would make the final decision, which might include taking the baby away from them. Turning to Thorpe, Knight warned him that the court would not tolerate interference from him as the baby's doctor to undermine Marylyn's relationship with her mother.

the child is with either the father or the mother, as provided by the order of the Court, said father or mother will at each and all said times provide a suitable home with competent help to care for and look after the welfare of the child; that said child will not be placed by either said father or mother at any time in the home of any third person.

Dated: August 13th, 1936.

That said, Mary Astor, Franklyn Thorpe, Roland Rich Woolley, and Joseph Anderson all signed the settlement agreement.

When the chamber door opened, Ethel Pepin walked out and announced that Knight had officially approved the settlement. Then Knight and Roland Rich Woolley—Astor on his arm—appeared. The others followed. Wiping the tears from her eyes, Astor was confronted by a barrage of flashbulbs and lowered her head to avoid the blinding light.

"I'm too tired to say anything. But I'll be glad when this is all over."

Knight took his seat on the bench and announced that he would render his final decision after lunch. Until then he planned to study the settlement. He also asked attorneys to appear fifteen minutes early for a "last-minute meeting."

Finally, he ordered Joseph Anderson to hand him the diaries and was given the two ledger books. Court would recess until 2:00 p.m., during which time Knight would ensure that he had just been handed the *entire* diary. "But I have no desire or intention of reading the entire contents."

That said, court was adjourned.

• • •

Astor, led by Woolley and Rank, left a courtroom that had erupted into a bedlam. Everyone was shouting at once. Although Woolley advised her not to say anything, reaching the courtroom doors, Astor turned to the reporters.

"I am happier than I have been for a long time."

Elsewhere, Anderson told press, "Everybody's happy—well fairly happy, anyway."

He was referring to Thorpe, who was also talking to reporters.

"While I admit I am not entirely happy over this new arrangement, I feel that with the aid of Judge Knight my attorney reached the best solution possible. In disposing of this custody suit they will dismiss the annulment, property settlement, and trust fund actions."

As it would be dismissed "with prejudice," the bigamy suit could never be brought up again, and that part of Franklyn Thorpe's past would remain buried. A reporter then asked if Thorpe thought whether he and Mary Astor might ever get back together. Thorpe grinned.

"Do you mean that Mary and I might remarry? It's unthinkable."

"When the baby is in your care will she have the same nursemaid?"

"You mean Nellie Richardson." Thorpe's smile disappeared. "I should say not. You know my opinion of that woman."

"What about Kaufman?"

"No, I don't plan any legal action. I just want to forget the whole thing."

• • •

Before the afternoon session Knight spoke with Woolley and Anderson. He requested that neither side issue statements declaring a victory. He felt this would give impression of a contest rather than an effort to work out what was best for the child.

Fifteen minutes later, when court resumed, Judge Knight read his prepared decision. In part he said:

"The proceeding has from the very first been obscured by morbid sensationalism and by a furor of publicity. The chief victim, however, is a little child, whose inherent rights and welfare have seemed to escape adequate attention. It is the duty of the court to protect those rights. Let neither parent feel that either has gained an advantage over the other, for if there is any victory it is that an innocent child has been spared the further likelihood of future grief and humiliation.

"Much has been said here and in the press concerning a diary written by the mother and held in the possession of the father. In fact, the court feels that altogether too much had been said about the diary and far too little about the child and her fundamental right to a wholesome and happy existence.

"It is obvious that any hurt suffered by the mother as a result of publication of the diary will fall eventually with greater force upon her child. Further, the court feels that such publication by consent and direction of the father not only would work pernicious mischief but establish between father and child a condition which, as she reached maturity, would cause her to look upon such a course with abhorrence.

"Doctor Thorpe has agreed to surrender the said diary to the custody of the court and it is therefore an order of the court that the diary be sealed and placed in a depository for safekeeping. This depository cannot release the diary without an order of the court. The court closes that phase of the case with an earnest hope that it will quickly be forgotten and that the life of this four-year-old baby shall be permitted to proceed free from the baneful effects of embittered parental strife.

"The minor child of the plaintiff and defendant will remain with the mother for nine months commencing September 1 and ending May 31 of each year. Franklyn Thorpe shall have custody of the minor child during the vacation period commencing in June and ending in August. Each party shall have the right of reasonable visitation. It is further ordered that the said minor child shall not be removed from Southern California without an order of the court or the consent in writing of both parents. The court may, according to its judgment, set aside the agreement at any time."

While Judge Knight spoke, Thorpe didn't take his eyes off him, while Astor kept her eyes downcast, adjusting her glove as she listened.

Just before Judge Knight left the bench, Narlain hurried over with the three affidavits announcing that they would "clear the names" of two women wrongfully accused during testimony.

"These women have no other recourse in clearing their names of false and malicious accusations."

Woolley immediately objected at this effort to refute "testimony that was entered formally." As the case was settled, Woolley couldn't care less about these affidavits, which were designed to help two women maintain their respectability. His objection was pro forma. If, in the event the case should be reopened, he wanted to ensure that these affidavits would have absolutely no merit when attempting to refute testimony given under oath.

The judge overruled and agreed to admit the affidavits if they were merely denials and not counterclaims. Judge Knight saw no reason to prevent the two women from doing a little face saving and, with it, finally put an end to the Astor-Thorpe custody hearing.

This done, the court was adjourned.

• • •

Lillian Miles, believing her name finally "cleared," was asked whether she and Thorpe might marry. Miles, in her "Dixieland accent," smiled.

"He hasn't asked me, and if he did, I wouldn't tell you. I'm a woman who can keep a secret."

No one listening doubted that.

Astor, Woolley beside her, left the courtroom in pandemonium. Pushing through the crush, Astor kept repeating to reporters shouting questions at her, "Please. Not now."

The two went straight to Woolley's office, where reporters were waiting. Astor, looking exhausted, absent-mindedly picked at the stock certificates Thorpe had returned. They were the securities he had planned to use to pay attorneys if Astor ever refused to return the baby.

"I'm tired, awfully tired. Mr. Woolley will not permit me to discuss the case. But I am of course thankful that this dreadful ordeal need not continue further."

"What are your professional plans?"

"I am under contract to Columbia. My agent told me of an offer from one of the British companies several days ago, but my producers will decide that, of course."

"And your plans for the baby?"

"Bring up my daughter in the finest way I know how."

Woolley then handed out a statement he had prepared for Astor.

> A month ago I reached a decision that the condition under which Marylyn and I were forced to live was intolerable. I decided to fight for the custody of my baby, to make any sacrifice necessary to insure her future welfare and happiness, which is the God given right of every mother. Naturally I was aware that I would have to face unpleasant notoriety, which might jeopardize my screen career. I merely acted as any other conscientious mother who loves her baby would have acted. I fought for Marylyn. I feel that I have won and this feeling makes everything worthwhile.

Following this, Mary Astor went home in a taxicab. She planned to celebrate that evening by having dinner with Ruth Chatterton and Fritz Lang.

• • •

Roland Rich Woolley had also prepared a statement, which he had given to the press while still in the courtroom.

> Thirty days ago, when we were forced to start this fight, Doctor Thorpe had legal custody of Miss Astor's little daughter, Marylyn. In order to liberate Miss Astor and her daughter from being at the mercy of Doctor Thorpe and be placed with the mother where she rightfully belonged, this fight was instituted. A few days ago for the sake of the child I proposed to the opposition that, if Miss Astor had complete control and supervision of the child and it would live with her during each school year, Miss Astor would be willing to have the child visit with the father during the summer vacation period. This proposal was finally accepted. We also demanded that Miss Astor's

diaries the contents of which have been so maliciously and so scandalously used outside of the court be turned over to the court and impounded and sealed. This demand was acceded to. Dr. Thorpe is returning to Miss Astor $5,000 in negotiable securities. Miss Astor gallantly conceded to dismiss the annulment proceedings on the urgent insistence of the opposition. On behalf of Miss Astor as well as myself, I wish to state that we are gratefully indebted to Judge Goodwin Knight for his fairness and his wonderful cooperation supervising and approving the conclusion of these matters.

Still in court, Franklyn Thorpe read Woolley's statement, and his eyes bulged out of his head while Joseph Anderson shouted at Woolley's assistant counsel.

"We agreed not to comment on this settlement. We demand that this whole thing be reopened." Anderson rushed to Judge Knight's chambers "to see what the court had to say about this." In chambers, Knight agreed to take Anderson's protest under consideration.

Leaving the judge's chambers, Anderson headed straight for the press.

"There was an agreement that no statements were to be issued. He can't get away with this. My inclination is to reopen the whole case and put every word of the diary into the record."

Thorpe realized that he needed to immediately rein in his attorney. The last thing that Franklyn Thorpe wanted was to reopen the case. Therefore, he took Anderson aside and reiterated what the judge said could happen if they reopened the case—Marylyn might be taken away from them. Anderson finally turned back to the reporters.

"For the best interest of the child, Dr. Thorpe does not want to take further official action and he would leave it to the public to decide who was the best sport in this litigation."

Lingering in the courtroom and puffing on a cigarette, Thorpe claimed that he had gotten a "raw deal."

"I capitulated because I didn't want my daughter's name dragged through the courts for years. Am I happy? I'd rather say not. The whole thing has been a strain on everybody and I'm deeply sorry that the case was ever started. I will of course make every effort to see that the terms of the court's joint custody order be carried out. Although, I still can't see why she felt it necessary to bring this into court."

He was asked if he thought that the settlement would work.

"I'm no prophet. It is a comforting thought that the court would have the final say if any argument arose. I have definite plans for her education, for her cultural and social future. I am building a beautiful new house out in the Toluca Lake District with a nursery for Marylyn."

"And regarding Woolley's statement?"

"It was grossly unfair. But Mr. Anderson is the man to comment on that."

Later, Anderson again announced that he would move to open the case and issued a statement to that effect. When Woolley heard this he said, "Anderson is talking up his sleeve. I had made no agreement with anyone not to issue a statement."

While almost everyone announced that they were planning a vacation, all Mary Astor wanted to do was be with her daughter.

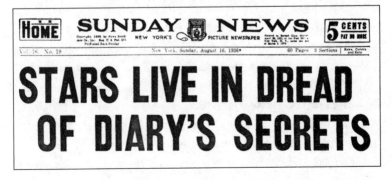

KAUFMAN TALKS

33

On Friday an exhausted Mary Astor remained in seclusion at Toluca Lake with little Marylyn. Whenever reporters appeared, security guards were ordered to refer them to Astor's attorney. Meanwhile, Deputy Sheriff Ray Bogie was dispatched to Moss Hart's home, where he searched it "top to bottom behind every door and in every closet." Other deputies were at Union Air Terminal. When these deputies returned empty-handed, Knight issued a permanent bench warrant.

"I'll put this man, Kaufman, in jail all summer if we can ever find him."

As for Joseph Anderson, he was still talking about reopening the case. "Our first move will be to file a petition in Judge Knight's court asking whether Woolley's statement is not in contempt and whether it shows an unwillingness to abide by the terms of the agreement."

When Judge Knight heard this, he immediately stopped what he was doing and spoke to the press.

"My patience is practically exhausted. If this case is reopened it will be reopened by the court solely for the purpose of protecting the interests and welfare of the child. Let there be an end to the agitation of this private quarrel in public places."

Apparently the message got through, because Anderson announced that the case would remain closed.

"I believe that Judge Knight's statement, which I interpreted as a reprimand to Woolley, is sufficient to clear my client's name. Dr. Thorpe and myself are satisfied with the judge's ruling and do not believe it is necessary for further recourse to law."

Roland Rich Woolley, about to board a plane, was asked to comment.

"The reference that Judge Knight's warning against reopening the case was directed against me is silly."

And that was pretty much Woolley's opinion of Joseph Anderson. Woolley's client now had virtual custody of the baby and Franklyn Thorpe could no longer threaten Mary Astor with taking the baby away or using the diary against her. Woolley had done everything that he had promised to do. Not only was Joseph Anderson a sore loser, but he was hopelessly thin skinned to boot.

• • •

Friday morning, chapter one of Franklyn Thorpe's serialized autobiography entitled "I Married an Actress" appeared in the *New York Daily News*. It would run for the next seven days. Basically a self-serving account of his marriage in which Thorpe—quoting the Bible and even Jesus Christ—detailed his former wife's peccadilloes while failing to mention a single one of his own. Calling the diaries "a distinguished document of the human soul" he went on to compare Mary Astor to Mary Magdalene, kindly requesting that the public not throw the first stone.

• • •

But the big news came on Saturday, when George S. Kaufman finally surfaced in New York City and conducted a press conference at his East Ninety-Fourth Street home. With the case over, Kaufman had concluded that coming out of hiding was his only option.

Sitting on a sofa in his drawing room, legs crossed, wearing wire-rimmed glasses, Kaufman had on gray flannel slacks, an open-collar blue shirt, tie, and leather house slippers. Since New York

City was enjoying one of the hottest summers on record, Kaufman, like everyone else, was bathed in sweat. He chain-smoked while he spoke.

"I decided to call the press because I wanted to prevent you from hounding me."

Kaufman then removed an envelope from his hip pocket.

"Being a little nervous and unaccustomed to extemporaneous speaking, I've made a few notes. First, I think there must be more important things in the world than anything I could possibly say. I suppose I owe some explanation and a certain amount of apology goes with that. Any interview would have been incoherent and foolish. I was made miserably unhappy by the case and am correspondingly happy now that it is over. I am sure Dr. Thorpe will be glad to know that I haven't slept very well for the last couple of weeks. The only thing that I resent is that some newspaper writer referred to me as a middle-aged playwright. It was a nasty blow. Dr. Thorpe may also be pleased to know that I didn't sleep very well in prospect of this interview. I was very nervous and unfortunately this state endured while the trial lasted. I have one piece of news for the great American public. You may say that I did not keep a diary."

Kaufman opened the floor to questions but told reporters that he was under advice of counsel. When asked how he had eluded the sheriffs, Kaufman gave a detailed account of his drive to San Bernardino and the train ride east. He then posed for photographers.

"Shall I comb my hair? Oh hell with it," he said, and then let them photograph him just as he was.

"Are the fears of movie executives justified as to the damaging effects of the Astor case on the box office?"

"I really don't know whether they are worried or not. Motion picture popularity always hangs on very thin threads anyway."

"What did you mean when you said that you were being crucified?"

"I understand I am in contempt of court—but I'm not supposed to talk about that."

"Have any of your friends suggested that you might have run out on the actress?"

"I'm not sure I have any friends left."

"Do you know Knight announced he would have you arrested as soon as you set foot in California?"

"Yes, I'm aware of what he said."

"Have you read the settlement?"

"The disposition of the Astor case has nothing to do with me and I would like to have the whole thing forgotten so I can return to work."

"What are you working on now?"

"*Stage Door,* which is scheduled to open at the Music Box on October 10. Following that, I plan to begin production on the play that I wrote with Moss Hart."

"When do you intend to go to California again?"

"I have no reason for returning to California."

"But won't you have to go back to California to fulfill your MGM contract?"

"I am under contract to MGM, but there is no call on my services."

"Did you read Mrs. Kaufman saying that you were both adults living adult lives?"

"Yes, I heard about the remark. You can't always live your life to please everybody."

"In view of the circumstances, do you think Mrs. Kaufman is an unusual wife?"

"There's no question about it. We have been in constant touch with each other. I think she's in Holland right now, and was in France. I will meet with Mrs. Kaufman when she arrives from Europe in a few days. Say, I wonder if I'll go through this on the dock when she comes in?"

"Been in touch with her?"

"Constantly. At great expense, too, on the trans-Atlantic telephone."

"Any trouble?"

"Not in the least. She's been not only sympathetic but comforting."

"How do you think this case will affect Miss Astor's career?"

"I don't know why it ever got such publicity anyway. Nobody cares about writers and Miss Astor is not such a big star—although she used to be a very big star in silent pictures."

"Dr. Thorpe is writing a history of the whole thing, a sort of biography. It's running in the papers."

"I'll wait till it comes out in book form."

"Have you been contacted by Dr. Thorpe?"

Kaufman wiped the sweat off his face. "I have heard nothing from him. But I've lost seven pounds since this thing began and if Dr. Thorpe can see his way clear, I hope to get it back."

"Did you know beforehand that Miss Astor was keeping a diary?"

"I don't think I ought to answer that. I would like to say though that the diary does give a few false impressions. I am amused by the picture people seemed to get of us staggering from one joint to another drinking brandy and cocktails. I take a cocktail about once every four years. If I take a second one I become violently ill."

"How do you feel about deputies searching Hart's home?"

"I honestly regret that Moss has been bothered by the police turning his home upside down looking for me when I wasn't even there."

"Did you see Miss Astor?"

"Once, we had dinner at friend's house about ten days before this thing started and I didn't know anything about it then."

"Would you object to seeing her again?"

"No. I have no bitterness toward Miss Astor. I can understand her solicitude for her child. Unfortunately it started a juggernaut, and it so happens that this juggernaut ran over me and I was miserable while it was on. I hope some big newspaper story breaks to divert public attention from me so the public and I can forget it."

Judge Knight, informed about George Kaufman's New York press conference, didn't mince words. "As long as Kaufman is outside the jurisdiction of California, there is nothing that can be done. But Mr. George Kaufman had better have had a very good excuse for leaving the state. This court would be lacking in self respect if it did not enforce its orders."

Kaufman's press conference accomplished exactly what he had intended. From that point on the press pretty much left George Kaufman alone. The only question left was how Beatrice Kaufman would respond, and that would be answered when she finally returned from Europe.

• • •

Mrs. Kaufman arrived in New York on board the Ile De France on August 27. Before the woman had even had time to leave her stateroom, the press raced aboard and crowded around her. Although Beatrice hadn't slept she was polite, but steadfastly refused to answer questions.

"I tell you, I have nothing to say!"

"In London you told the press that your husband and Miss Astor just had a 'flirtation.' After all that's come out, do you still feel that way about it?"

"I have nothing to say."

When she was informed about Kaufman's press conference in which he talked about the Astor case, Beatrice was surprised, as Kaufman hadn't told her about it.

"I don't believe it. Well, even if he did, there's nothing I can say. The story is dead."

"Are you thinking of divorcing your husband?"

"I have nothing to say."

In the corridor Beatrice met songwriter Irving Berlin. He and his wife had returned from Europe aboard the ship with her.

"How am I doing?"

Berlin nodded. "You're doing all right. Just *don't* say anything."

Berlin knew it best to say nothing to reporters in a "feeding frenzy." Later, in the quarantine, Beatrice was asked about her comments in London.

"What I said in London still stands. We should be allowed to go back to obscurity. The story is dead."

Then on the pier, handing luggage keys and customs declaration to a maid, she looked for Kaufman. He was hiding behind a car and, as soon as he saw her, edged over. Dressed in a brown sports coat and gray flannel slacks with his hair uncombed, he looked disheveled. Greeting each other with flashbulbs popping, they looked uncomfortable. Kaufman spoke first.

"How are you?"

Beatrice shook his hand. "I'm fine, and you?"

Kaufman shrugged, and a reporter asked Beatrice if she had any comment to make on the Astor case.

"I said all I have to say in London. The story is completely dead. Why can't you leave it there?"

Reporters hammered Kaufman with questions. He answered none of them, while Beatrice was again asked about the possibilities of a divorce.

"I still have nothing to say."

After whispering to each other, Kaufman took hold of Beatrice's elbow and led his wife towards the pier elevator. Reporters and photographers crowded in with them.

"Would you like to say anything, Mr. Kaufman?"

"No!"

On the street, followed by reporters and photographers, the two met with Howard Reinheimer, the Kaufman's attorney. Then, after a brief chat, Kaufman took Beatrice by the arm and guided her to the nearest taxicab. After helping her in, he and Reinheimer followed. Kaufman spoke to the cabbie.

"Drive on. Just drive."

Kaufman didn't want reporters hearing where they were going, but it didn't matter. They just piled into taxis and sped after them.

Inside the cab Kaufman turned to Beatrice.

"I'd rather not go to the house. There'll be newsmen there."

Reinheimer spoke up. "Come to my office."

Beatrice looked at her husband. "George, one of the reporters told me you held a news conference."

"I had to. They would have hounded me."

"I thought at least you'd wait for me. We could have done it together."

"I'm too nervous to know what I'm doing."

"George, you look terrible."

"I feel rotten about this, Bea."

She smiled and took his hand. She was telling him everything was all right. Arriving at the attorney's building, they realized that there was no way of escaping reporters. So, Reinheimer got out, and the Kaufmans decided to head on home. Several reporters remained and, in machine-gun fashion, shot questions at Reinheimer.

"Why didn't Mr. Kaufman kiss his wife on the pier?"

"Why did they look so solemn?"

"Why no smiles?"

"What's it all mean?"

Reinheimer finally answered. "It didn't mean a thing. They are just a normal couple and it was just a normal greeting."

"Will there be legal action?"

Reinheimer was categorical. "There certainly will not. Not a separation and not a divorce."

When the Kaufmans arrived home reporters were waiting, and before the two had even gotten out of the cab the questions started.

"Were you with your lawyer because you're thinking of a divorce?"

Beatrice shook her head. "Not at all." She looked at Kaufman. "Shall we say Mr. Reinheimer is a mutual friend, or a good friend?"

Kaufman nodded. "Yes—that's all right."

Kaufman turned away and carried Beatrice's luggage into the house.

Later that day the Kaufmans sent a brief note out to the reporters camped on their doorstep.

"We have only one thing to say and that is we have nothing to say about the Astor case."

The following morning, through attorney Reinheimer, Beatrice Kaufman issued a formal statement.

"Mr. Kaufman and I are pursuing the usual routine of our lives. We have no intention of changing its order. Naturally, we both regret that an incident which must have occurred in the lives of many adults was made the focus of public interest. We earnestly wish to be permitted again the peace and privacy of ordinary individuals."

With Beatrice once again in charge, the two never discussed the subject in public again.

34

Mary Astor had taken to heart what Judge Knight had said regarding the damage the scandal might cause little Marylyn as the girl grew older. Consequently, Mary Astor and Franklyn Thorpe did their best to assure the public that the two were perfectly happy with the new custody arrangement.

On the Sunday following the settlement, Thorpe took a few hours off from hunting big game at Tehachapi Ranch with Clark Gable to drive down to Toluca Lake. News photographers and reporters watched Marylyn run into her father's arms and a short time later they watched Thorpe drive her to his apartment on North Whitley Drive, where Paul Schofield and Thorpe's parents were waiting. Then, the baby sitting beside him, Thorpe read Marylyn the funny papers. Because Thorpe and Astor had permitted press in, the resulting story—fully illustrated—was of a happy child spending time with a loving parent. After bringing Marylyn home, Thorpe rejoined Clark Gable for a final day of shooting.

• • •

On September 1, Marylyn began a one-month stay at Thorpe's, with Thorpe assuring the press, "We are making arrangements for a comfortable and beautiful place for Marylyn." Few if any of the news stories mentioned the rancor of the court battle, and there was

ABOVE: Marylyn during her month long stay with her father. Her middle name, Hauoli, is spelled out in the toy letters.

RIGHT: Marylyn with her mother following the baby's month with her father.

BELOW: Astor arriving at *Dodsworth* preview with Marcus Goodrich.

no mention of the diary but, instead, the "friendly terms" that now existed between Thorpe and Mary Astor.

As for the "purple diaries," on September 8 it was reported that the two ledger volumes had been placed by the county treasurer under official court seal in the vaults of the Los Angeles treasury. All copies would remain sealed until Marylyn Thorpe turned twenty-one, when any custody issue would be moot.

Then, as fortune would have it, a newspaper story that "diverted public attention" did break. That summer, Edward VIII, King of England, went on a cruise with his paramour, the still-married American divorcee Wallace Simpson. Their relationship made the headlines and stayed there until October, when it was rumored that the two planned to marry. By the end of the month Simpson had filed for divorce, and in November the king informed the British government that the two would marry. Finding the marriage of an English monarch to a twice-divorced woman unacceptable, the government threatened to resign. So, unable to give up Simpson, and wanting to avoid bringing down the governing party, in December King Edward VIII abdicated "for the woman he loved." It was the first time in history that an English monarch had done so. In comparison, the Astor-Thorpe custody battle was small potatoes and, as such, rapidly receded from the public consciousness.

• • •

The only question that remained was whether Mary Astor still had a film career. Because film exchanges were besieged with requests from theatre owners for "anything with Astor in it," Samuel Goldwyn ordered *Dodsworth* rushed into release a month ahead of schedule. The success or failure of the film would tell the tale.

Hence, the September 15 preview of *Dodsworth* at the Hollywood Warner Theatre was more like a Hollywood premiere than a preview, and the most anticipated film event of the year. When Mary Astor appeared with Marcus Goodrich, hundreds of fans outside the theatre mobbed and cheered, making it difficult for the police to hold back the admiring crowds and forcing police to push their way through.

Walter Huston and his wife were there, as well as most of the other cast members. In the case of Ruth Chatterton, it would have taken a team of horses to keep her away. When the theatre went dark and the credits appeared, Mary Astor's name on the screen was given a two-minute ovation.

Regarding the audience's response, Mary Astor would recall, "The character I played was a charming and gracious woman. The public could not match her with the luridly immoral woman the tabloids had painted. My first line was spoken offscreen, but the moment they heard it the audience burst into spontaneous applause. Nothing has ever warmed me so much that I burst into tears. I was told that it happened at every performance at that theatre, and that it happened in many cities."

Following the film's famous final close-up, Mary Astor left the theatre, where hundreds of fans shouted "Great work, Mary!" Overcome by their show of support for her as an actress and a mother, Mary Astor openly wept, telling reporters how much she appreciated the "kindness" all these people had shown her. To Hollywood the message was loud and clear; Mary Astor had passed the "acid test." The scandal, the diary, the week after week of headlines had not hurt Mary Astor in the public's view; on the contrary, it had made her even more popular.

A few days later the New York reviews came in.

For Archer Winsten at the *New York Post*, "In view of the recent Mary Astor scandals a spectator might foresee considerable distraction in her appearance on the screen. Her film presence is so charmingly simple, and her acting so good, that you have forgotten before you have time to brood upon the fact that this is indeed the one whose name graced the headlines so recently. Miss Astor is that appealing."

Kate Cameron wrote in the *New York Daily News*; "On the screen Mary Astor's presence in the role of the other woman fails to distract one's attention from the screen drama. As the sympathetic Edith

Mary Astor in her first scene in *Dodsworth*.

Cortright, who helps Sam Dodsworth over the trying period of his wife's gradual desertion of him, Miss Astor fulfills her assignment."

B. Johaneson of the *New York Mirror* was succinct. "Mary Astor gives the finest performance of her career."

The *Time Magazine* piece was both a laudatory review and a news story. "'Why don't you try stout, Mr. Dodsworth?' drawls a woman's voice from the shadowy corner of a steamship deck. Sam Dodsworth, who has just asked the steward for a drink, whirls around, surprised. Mr. Dodsworth's surprise was nothing to that of producer Sam Goldwyn and his staff when, at this line, the audience at a Hollywood preview last week burst into applause. The applauders were not partisans of stout but of Mary Astor, whose first line they recognized even before the camera moved over to her. Throughout the picture they kept applauding frequently and, as she was coming out of the theatre in the flesh with screenwriter Marcus Goodrich and her mother, they mobbed her, cheered her, shouting, 'You're all right, Mary,' and begging her for her autograph. Thus did the public affirm its recognition of a fine performance and its sympathy for Mary Astor's position in her recent suit to get custody of her daughter. Meanwhile, fate brought Mary Astor the greatest picture and the most human-sympathy-winning role of her life, just when she needs it most."

About all this Astor would later recount, "For a long time after the trial I was shy of people. I was afraid of what the notoriety might do to my work; others, I knew, had gone under as a result of scandal. At the time I had to appear at the preview of *Dodsworth*—when my name had been splashed all over the papers—I winced at the thought and shrank at what the audience's reaction would be when I appeared on the screen. But the effect was almost the opposite from what I had feared. I have always been amazed that I was able to continue my career after what happened to me. When I had my problem I told myself, 'Okay, kid, I've had it and I'm ready to call it quits,' but it didn't turn out that way. That convinced me, as nothing else ever could, that the public is understanding. I had thought I was through in pictures, but my career has never stopped."

In short, as Samuel Goldwyn wisely put it, "A woman fighting for her child? This is good." What America had really witnessed during those weeks of scandal were not the exploits of a promiscuous woman but, instead, a mother willing to sacrifice both her career and suffer public humiliation for the sake of her child. Years earlier films like *Madam X*, *The Sin Of Madelon Claudet*, and scores of others dealing with mother-love sacrifice had been big hits. Now, in 1936, during four weeks that summer, newspapers all over America had been filled with the real thing. Not only did the mothers of America relate to this mother, but also, seeing themselves in her plight, were actually cheering the woman on.

As a result, Mary Astor—against all odds—had transcended a national scandal that could have destroyed both her and her career and not only came out of it unscathed but also a bigger star than when it had begun. Thanks to Franklyn Thorpe and those infamous "purple diaries," Mary Astor was once again a big box office draw. Consequently, during the next eight years, as her film career moved into its third phase, working freelance sans a studio contract, Mary Astor would come into her own as an actress and do some of her finest work.

AND THEN

35

Norma Taylor finally returned to Hollywood, but it wasn't to storm into Judge Knight's courtroom. Norma came back two years later to make a B movie aptly titled, *I Demand Payment*. She was twelfth in the cast list. Moment in the sun over, Miss Taylor quickly faded into obscurity. It is noteworthy that nowhere in Tommy Manville's biography is the name Norma Taylor even mentioned.

Actress Evelyn Laye and her husband Frank Lawton never worked in Hollywood again. In 2009, ten years after Laye's death, it was finally revealed that King George VI—sixteen years prior to his ascension to the throne—had a brief affair with Miss Laye. In fact, it was Laye who had recommended the speech therapist whose work with the King's stammer served as the basis for the Academy Award-winning film, *The King's Speech*.

Nellie Richardson—labeled by *Time Magazine* as "the Tattling Nurse"—took care of Marylyn until she was nine. Richardson, like her employer, was an unbendable disciplinarian. Consequently, by her own admission, Marylyn was something of a "brat" with her nanny. Truth was, Marylyn considered Richardson too bossy, and wasn't sorry when the woman finally left Mary Astor's employ. A number of years later, Richardson took Marylyn out to lunch and they had a pleasant afternoon together. The trial—and Nellie's role in it—was never mentioned.

Following the trial Lillian Miles remained in Franklyn Thorpe's life for a number of years. In fact, when Franklyn Thorpe married his third wife, she and Lillian got along "famously." With near-flawless skin, Miles took care to dress well and keep her figure. Consequently, with her son grown, her mother gone, and her "reputation" intact, she finally remarried and, after officially becoming Lillian Lawton Miles Williams, moved to Arizona. At Franklyn Thorpe's funeral—looking thirty years younger than her seventy-five years—Miles spoke confidentially to Marylyn, asking if she "had known"—meaning did Marylyn know how much Lillian had loved her father. Marylyn replied that she had, understanding that her father had been the great love of this woman's life.

In February 1937 Ruth Chatterton left Hollywood. With no control over the quality of her film work and her advancing age limiting her choice of roles, Chatterton had no intention of being typecast as mothers or relegated to character parts. Ruth Chatterton was a star and she intended to remain so.

So, after giving her finest screen performance in *Dodsworth*, Chatterton made only two more films, both shot in England. Then, for the next twenty-four years, she divided her time between the stage, radio, television, and a second career as a successful novelist. Among other roles, she appeared in *The Little Foxes* as Regina Giddens. It was a performance the playwright, Lillian Hellman, believed to be the finest interpretation of the character ever presented onstage. In 1953, Chatterton even tried her hand at Shakespeare, playing Gertrude in a TV production of *Hamlet* opposite Maurice Evans.

In the late 1940s, Chatterton lent her support to the plight of Jewish Holocaust victims fleeing Europe for Palestine, efforts that eventually lead to the formation of the State of Israel. In 1950, her first novel *Homeward Bourne* hit the *New York Times* Best Seller List, where it remained for the next twenty-three weeks. At last Chatterton had found a medium in which she was her "own master." On November 17, 1961, sitting at a typewriter in her Connecticut home polishing her fifth novel, Chatterton suffered a cerebral hemorrhage and died seven days later.

Florence Eldridge encouraged her husband, Fredric March, to return to Broadway, and the two worked almost exclusively together. On stage opposite her husband, Eldridge played the role of Mary Tyrone in the premiere production of Eugene O'Neil's *Long Day's*

Journey Into Night, generally considered the greatest American play of the twentieth century.

. . .

In 1946 Goodwin Knight ran successfully for lieutenant governor of California. It was a position he would hold until Governor Earl Warren was appointed Chief Justice of the Supreme Court. Knight succeeded Warren and, on October 5, 1953, became the Governor of California, easily winning reelection the following year.

In 1936 Roland Rich Woolley built a home in Toluca Lake not far from Mary Astor where he, his wife, and his daughter would spend the rest of their lives. At the time of his death Woolley was a multi-millionaire. He remained a staunch Mormon and, as his sole heir, Woolley's only child, Mary Alice, left the entire Woolley estate, including the house in Toluca Lake, to the Church Of Latter Day Saints.

Only five years after the custody battle, Joseph Anderson was killed in a head-on collision near King City, California. Although he had been a lead attorney in the most sensational trial of the period, it was only a search through the man's wallet that enabled the police to identify him.

. . .

And what of the men whose names Joseph Anderson brought up in court?

Publisher Bennett Cerf continued publishing notable books. In the mid 1940s, he became an author of humor books and a household name in the 1950s, when he appeared as a panelist on the popular television game show *What's My Line*. He was a regular on the show until his death.

Writer George Oppenheimer—one-time publisher, friend, and coauthor with George Kaufman—continued his successful screen-writing career, earning himself an Oscar nomination. During World

War II he produced and directed training films, and in 1950 began writing for television. Switching careers in 1955, he became the drama critic for the Long Island-based newspaper, *Newsday*.

In 1941 Marcus Goodrich finally published his long-gestating novel, *Delilah*. A bestseller, the *New York Times* called it "the best sea story since Captain Horatio Hornblower" and the *New Yorker* considered it "a remarkable work of art." In 1946, Goodrich married actress Olivia DeHavilland, a marriage that lasted seven years. The writer eventually retired to Richmond, Virginia, where he lived modestly until his death.

Dr. Mortimer W. Rodgers, elder brother of Broadway composer Richard Rodgers, rose to the top of the medical profession and never felt eclipsed by his famous younger brother.

Stock broker Daniel Silberberg, a man who fought a successful battle to keep his private life private, was financial advisor to the *New Yorker Magazine*. He counted among his closest friends *New Yorker* founder Harold Ross, Alexander Woollcott, George Gershwin, Robert Benchley, and Peter Arno. Until his death, Silberberg signed notes to friends Daniel Silberberg, F.K.C.B. It was not an English title; it meant "Former Kansas City Boy."

Count Alfredo Carpegna, Spanish sportsman, playboy, and "heel-clicking nobleman" had, ostensibly, come to Hollywood in the early 1930s to produce movies. He coproduced one film and, with that lark out of the way, Carpegna was free to pursue his real career as a Hollywood playboy. He regularly appeared in the columns as "companion" to some of the town's most beautiful women.

Over a long career, character actor John Eldredge amassed over two hundred movie and TV credits. Of interest is that this lifelong bachelor and son of a clergyman never had a hint of scandal attached to his name except, that is, for being mentioned in the Astor-Thorpe custody trial.

36

John Barrymore and notoriety became synonymous with one another in the years following the custody battle. On November 8, 1936, Mr. Barrymore and Miss Elaine Barrie finally married. Their fights, arguments, threats, numerous breakups, and reconciliations made great fodder for the newspapers. By New Year's Eve, a jealous fight ensued at the Trocadero, and Barrie sued for divorce.

Barrymore hired attorney Harry Huntington to put his financial affairs in order. Barrymore, who during his acting career had earned over $3 million, was now $162,000 in debt. So the actor put everything he owned on the block, but it wasn't enough. Desperate for money, Barrymore was forced to accept any film role offered, and his days as a leading man came to an end. Playing character roles, he was often the best thing in these films. When Mary Astor worked with Barrymore in one of his better movies during this period—oddly enough playing his wife—she recalled, "even with cue cards and only a faint idea of what the picture was all about, he had enough years of experience behind him to be able to act rings around anyone else."

During production, well aware of how his life had turned out, Barrymore confided to Astor, "It's a good thing I couldn't get you away from your family. I would have married you, and you would have had a miserable life."

Not long before Barrymore's death, Mary Astor was appearing on a radio program and Barrymore was scheduled that day on another show. She would remember, "I was on the second floor of the building where the dressing rooms were. A long bleak fluorescent-lighted hall—there was no one else around, and I saw him walking down the hall ahead of me. I wanted to catch up and say hello, but I didn't. He stopped like someone who just couldn't walk another step. He leaned against the wall in sheer fatigue; his body sagged. It was no time to intrude, so I retraced my steps. In that long bleak hall, I saw a man who was catching his breath before doing battle, and quite a battle it was, with death."

It would be the last time Mary Astor ever saw John Barrymore.

• • •

In early September 1936, Irving Thalberg caught a cold that quickly developed into strep throat. The illness was eventually diagnosed as pneumonia, and Thalberg died twenty-four hours later. He was only thirty-seven years old. Thalberg's death not only ended plans for his independent production company, but also abruptly terminated George Kaufman's plans to write and direct films. Nonetheless, Kaufman did return to Los Angeles six months later. Franklyn Thorpe withdrew the subpoena, permitting Kaufman to come west in mid-March 1937, and a month later the arrest warrant was dismissed as well. On this trip, Kaufman made a conscious effort to avoid Mary Astor, telling friends, "When a building falls on you, you don't take a chance of it falling again."

Stage Door and the unnamed play Kaufman and Moss Hart had completed in the midst of the custody battle opened on Broadway, and both were smash hits. In fact, the unnamed play, now titled *You Can't Take It With You*, actually won Kaufman his second Pulitzer Prize. Both plays were made into films, with the film version of *You Can't Take It With You*, directed by Frank Capra, winning the 1938 Oscar for best picture.

In the early 1940s, after Moss Hart had struck out on his own, Kaufman found it increasingly difficult to find cowriters and so wrote less, but directed more. As a result, he had far more misses than hits. It didn't help when Beatrice died in 1944 of a cerebral hemorrhage, and left Kaufman emotionally devastated. He would marry again but Beatrice—wife, mother, friend, confessor, advisor—

was irreplaceable. Nevertheless, Kaufman's womanizing remained undiminished until ill health and age finally brought it to a halt.

In 1952, Kaufman suffered a mild stroke, and during the last ten years of his life was in declining health. However, the playwright still managed to write one hit play, *Silk Stockings*, and coauthor and direct another, *The Solid Gold Cadillac*. In the 1950s he became a television personality, appearing as a regular on one program and then as a frequent quest on various New York-based talk shows. Kaufman became so recognizable that perfect strangers would stop to talk with him as if they were friends. Kaufman found this predicament deplorable, but it certainly didn't stop him from appearing on television. In fact, on *The Jack Paar Show* during Kaufman's last television appearance, the man was so ill that Paar was worried George Kaufman might actually die right there on the show.

Today George Kaufman is remembered—if at all—for two principle reasons. *You Can't Take It With You*, his most famous and enduring play, is regularly revived in regional and community theatre settings, and for the affectionate portrait of Kaufman in Moss Hart's brilliant memoir, *Act One*. The book details Hart's entry into the world of theatre, with its second half devoted to an account of the writing and production of Hart's first collaboration with Kaufman. *Act One* is, and probably will always remain, one of the finest books ever written about the American theatre, and for anyone reading it, the book's lovingly detailed portrait of George Kaufman will bring the man to life again.

• • •

Although by early 1937 Franklyn Thorpe's name had pretty much disappeared from the public eye, his divorce, as well as the custody battle, had wreaked havoc on the doctor's finances. It wasn't until July 1937 that he was finally able to pay off his legal bills. As a result, he never did purchase the house he had talked about. Instead, Thorpe continued living in apartments, and that was where Marylyn spent her scheduled visits as well as her summer vacations. Thorpe

Franklyn Thorpe in the 1940s.

would continue his hunting trips with Clark Gable, and the two remained hunting buddies for many years. In fact, Thorpe wore the Hamilton watch Gable had given him for the rest of his life.

As for his professional career, Franklyn Thorpe was a skilled and able MD and, amazing as this may seem, remained Mary Astor's principal physician well into the 1940s. Having progressed from general surgery to obstetrics, then to geriatrics and finally to meta-biology, Thorpe maintained a practice, and his loyal patients stayed with him for many years.

Yet, although he treated some of the biggest names in Hollywood, Thorpe would often provide his services free to those who couldn't afford them. Since Thorpe enjoyed being his own man he steadfastly refused to become partners in a large, potentially lucrative practice. Instead, he kept the same small office he had opened on the sixth floor of the First National Building on Hollywood Blvd. in 1931. He would maintain that office for forty-six years. As he liked to keep things simple, Thorpe did all his own paperwork, with his secretary handling the appointments, accounting, and billing.

Franklyn Thorpe's private life was somewhat more convoluted. As a gynecologist, he came into contact with scores of women—and, since women found him extremely charismatic—Thorpe always had lots of women around him. Lillian Miles and a woman by the name of Olive McGuire were among those who had long-term relationships with the man simultaneously. In fact, both women knew the other, and when Marylyn was eleven, the two sans Thorpe took her on vacation to Lake Tahoe. To this day, Thorpe's daughter believes her father would have made a great polygamist.

Thorpe did marry again. The first marriage was to Virginia Bancroft, a woman half his age. After living together for a while they officially became husband and wife, and remained married for the next seven years. One day, Marylyn showed up at her father's apartment unannounced. Virginia was there, but Thorpe wasn't. Instead there sat Henry Dennison, the Dennison Chili heir, with whom Virginia was having an affair. Virginia was soon off with Dennison but not before she had pocketed the cash Thorpe kept socked away inside a boot hidden in his closet. Thorpe's fourth "official" wife was Maxine Reynolds, a woman closer to Thorpe's age, and that marriage lasted until his death. Maxine was an artist who had been one of Thorpe's patients. An alcoholic, Thorpe helped sober her up. After living together, the two were secretly married in Mexico so that, still using her last name, Maxine could continue receiving alimony from her former husband. Although Thorpe was fairly "prudent" about money he was never very good with investments. This was the reason for the ruse, since it permitted the two to continue living in Maxine's Brentwood home where they maintained a very comfortable lifestyle.

Maxine loved Thorpe deeply and stoically tolerated his temper, which could—as Astor had testified—become quite abusive. Marylyn vividly remembers his shouting and impatience with Maxine and those times, as well as anytime he displayed his temper, were the few times that Marylyn was embarrassed and ashamed of her father.

Thorpe's parents spent their last years in a small house on Ventura Blvd., where they raised champion Chihuahuas. At the time of her death in 1947 Thorpe's mother, Cora, was seventy-eight and his father, Samuel, was eighty-six when he died in 1954.

From the 1950s onward Franklyn Thorpe was a yoga enthusiast, having been taught the discipline by his sister Clara Spring, one of the leading teachers and yoga exponents in America. In fact, Clara's 1959 book on yoga, reprinted well into the 1970s, had an introduction written by Thorpe. Always an exercise enthusiast— when married he and Astor would sometimes jog together—for the rest of his life Franklyn Thorpe faithfully did his daily yoga workout.

Thorpe was proud of the fact that he could still fit into the uniform he had worn as a teenager while in military school.

As for Mary Astor, because Thorpe was Astor's doctor for a period, there was a time when they became close again and actually considered—if briefly—a possible re-marriage. But, with their temperaments, it was more wishful thinking. The last time they saw each other, Thorpe gave her a hug and the two spoke for a bit. Later, when asked how she felt about her former husband, Mary Astor was succinct. "Ah, the old fart!" And those were pretty much her last words on the subject.

On February 10, 1977, Thorpe and Maxine were walking to their car across the street from his office. Suffering from early onset dementia and the beginnings of Parkinson's disease—his arms filled with grocery bags—Thorpe stumbled off the curb, fell, and hit his head, which brought on a cerebral hemorrhage. He immediately lost consciousness and, without regaining it, died two days later. Oddly, only weeks prior to his death he had told his daughter "I've gotta get out of this place," meaning that he was ready to move on and so, when Franklyn Thorpe did move on, he was more than happy to go.

At his funeral—besides friends and family—three generations of patients gathered. Seeing all the women there, it wasn't much of a stretch for Thorpe's daughter, Marylyn, to conclude that many of the women at the funeral had been, like Lillian Miles, much more than just patients.

37

Following the custody battle Mary Astor and Ruth Chatterton grew even closer. Astor became a fixture at Chatterton's home, among a circle of friends that included writers and people involved with the theatre—the sort of individuals to whom Astor had always been attracted. "For the sake of my little girl I had won a tough battle with the odds heavy against me. The sword of Damocles had been lifted. The only truth that I cared to face was that I loved Marylyn and knew that I could be a good mother to her. The rest of the summer I spent a lot of time recuperating at home and at the beach with friends. They were fewer now, but they were those who hadn't panicked at the idea of being associated with me in an unsavory episode. It takes a crisis to find out who one's friends are. I sharpened my wits and became more cautious."

At Chatterton's, Astor met Manuel del Campo. Seven years her junior, he was handsome, well-educated, extremely charming, spoke with an English accent, and had a continental air about him. The two began an affair leading to a quickie Yuma, Arizona marriage that, in February 1937, made the front pages all over the country.

Mary Astor's third husband, unlike her first two, was basically a playboy. Although she found him work as an assistant film editor, he much preferred nightclubbing and partying to pursuing a career. Her husband was also an unrepentant womanizer who had no qualms about making a pass at other women in front of his wife.

The two had a son, Tono, and, although del Campo loved the boy, he loved his freedom more. So, when war began in Europe, he joined the Royal Canadian Air Force, and he and Astor divorced.

During the war Mary Astor kept busy. She "went on innumerable

Astor with del Campo and son Tono.

bond tours through camps and factories," did "spot-announcement records to sell bonds and recruit for civilian defense." In addition, she not only taught occupational therapy to vets in Birmingham Veteran's Hospital but, because she had, at Ruth Chatterton's insistence, learned to fly, also did "duty" with the Civil Air Patrol in Texas.

• • •

Following *Dodsworth,* Astor did two films for Columbia and went freelance. No longer tied to a studio contract, creatively these would be the apex of Mary Astor's film career. In 1941 alone she not only won an academy award for her role in *The Great Lie* but also created an iconic performance in *The Maltese Falcon,* a film that would raise her into the pantheon of great motion picture actors. Her work in the film is so skillfully multi-layered that, with each successive viewing, it becomes richer and more complex. In the years to come this single performance would allow her to eclipse many of her contemporaries. Consequently, *The Maltese Falcon* is the film

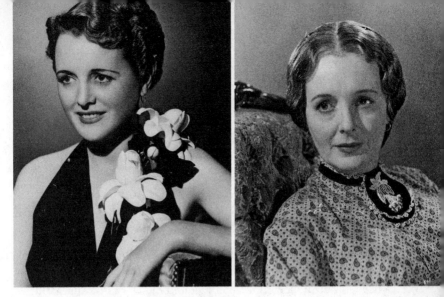

Astor screen image before and after joining MGM.

for which Mary Astor is best remembered, as it gives the clearest indication of the true magnitude of the woman's talent.

Wanting a steady income, in 1943 Astor signed with MGM, where she became one of the "More Stars Then There Are In Heaven," for which Hollywood's preeminent studio was famous. Having previously played femme fatales, MGM now saw Mary Astor as a "mother-of-the-year," her fate sealed with the release of *Meet Me In St. Louis*. Her portrayal of Judy Garland's mother is so genuine in its conveyance of idealized motherhood that it is not only one of Astor's finest performances but also the glue that holds the film together. Since *Meet Me In St. Louis* was one of the highest-grossing films of the 1940s, its immense success pretty much typecast Astor.

About this time her father died, and her mother would die three years later. The two had lived in a tiny house in Lancaster, California with a small barn in which they raised goats—a far cry from their Beverly Hills mansion.

A career turning point should have been Astor's performance in *Desert Fury*, a loan out to Paramount. In this Technicolor melodrama Astor played Lizabeth Scott's mother, Fritzi—a hardnosed businesswoman with a will of iron, a far cry from the idealized mother in *Meet Me In St. Louis*. Nevertheless, her acting in the film consistently rings true, and her performance is about the only thing memorable about the movie. If Mary Astor had been aggressive in seeking such roles as she aged into her forties, she could have used Fritzi to reinvent her screen image. Unfortunately, while at MGM, the few times she was permitted to play something other than a mother, they were inconsequential parts that did absolutely nothing to help redefine her screen image.

In 1948, while playing yet another mother in the lavish Technicolor remake of *Little Women*, Mary Astor, at age forty-three, began to experience a menopausal depression that grew so severe that, unable to deal with what she often called studio drudgery, she begged out of her MGM contract and didn't work again for three years. Those years would prove the most difficult of her life.

During the 1930s and much of the early '40s, Astor was a recreational drinker. Extremely disciplined, she never drank while making a film, nor did she ever drink on the set. But what had started as recreational drinking eventually became drinking to cope. When she couldn't sleep, she drank. When she felt morose or lonely, she drank. When things became difficult, she drank. This was especially true during the late 1940s, as she aged and the roles MGM gave her grew increasingly limited. So the drinking increased dramatically, until she was putting down a fifth of Scotch every night when she wasn't working. Her 1945 marriage to her fourth and final husband, Tom Wheelock, didn't help matters, as he was also a heavy drinker and this only exacerbated the problem.

Now, in the throes of a deep menopausal depression, Mary Astor was not only using alcohol to cope but also to self-medicate. Because she was so listless she needed to use Benzedrine just to get out of bed, and the depression eventually developed into a breakdown. Sleeping in her library on a studio bed, she rarely left the room, and took "large quantities of sleeping pills" after a day of drinking just to get a few hours of sleep. "But alcohol," she reflected later, "will soothe and relax for only a while." The drinking and her withdrawal from everything became so acute that in 1949 she finally went to a sanitarium to detox, shakes and all. Mary Astor would battle alcoholism for the rest of her life, sometimes winning, sometimes losing.

A year later she and her husband separated and then, in May 1951—"blind drunk"—she accidentally took too many sleeping pills, and called for help. When the police arrived it was listed as an attempted suicide, which was how the newspapers reported it.

Because her fourth husband had squandered her money on bad investments, by 1952 Mary Astor was so broke that the local food market refused to make deliveries. Just to make ends meet she was forced to apply to the motion picture relief fund—having paid into the fund out of every paycheck—and they covered her bills for almost a year. Then, while being treated for bronchial pneumonia, fibroids were discovered on her uterus, and she immediately underwent a hysterectomy that saved her life.

When someone reaches their nadir it becomes obvious what they are made of, and the one word that describes Mary Astor during this period is determination. At age forty-six, her career in Hollywood "through," Mary Astor had to start over again. Swallowing her pride, she walked into a bank and obtained a loan to travel east, to find stage work. First it was replacing the star when a Broadway show went on tour. Then it was summer stock, and finally work on Broadway. Not long after, the television offers came. Having worked in Hollywood during its early days, she had come full circle and was now working in live television during TV's early days. Over the next ten years Mary Astor appeared in nearly fifty TV shows, both live TV and filmed anthologies. It was a remarkable achievement.

About live TV she would write, "I was never bored during this time. Of course I'm talking about what they call the 'early days' of television—live, and alive. It was experimental, crazy, and wonderful. The working form was close to theatre inasmuch as we took time for rehearsals—a week to three weeks. No hurry, hurry, let's get the shot before lunch. Every show was as exciting as an opening night in the theatre."

As live television gave way to taped or filmed programs, she appeared in both as well as the occasional film. This wasn't the glamorous Hollywood of the 1920s, '30s, and '40s. There were no hours of tedium posing for publicity shots, as it was no longer her function to be a dream-factory fantasy. It was about acting, and it was work, hard work, something that Mary Astor had never been adverse to, and so she thrived.

• • •

In 1959 Astor published her autobiography, *My Story*. One of the many "tell-all" star autobiographies of the period, this book was quite a bit more because Astor wrote unsparingly and insightfully about herself. The genesis of the book had occurred a few years earlier. Following her breakdown, in an effort to come to grips with the seemingly insurmountable emotional issues that had plagued her all her adult life, Mary Astor entered "a short period of psychotherapy." Her therapist recommended that she write about her problems as a means to sort through her conflicting feelings. Putting down the highs and lows of her life proved beneficial. It was these writings—expanded with the help of editors—that became *My Story*.

While living in her Malibu beach house, she finally completed the book. The sounds of the ocean filling her home, Mary Astor loved it there and called it "Stella Maris," Latin for "Star of the Sea."

With the publication of *My Story*, Mary Astor was hooked. "I'd seen my name on a hardcover book," she explained, "and I had found it a bigger thrill than seeing it in marquee lights." Astor—like Ruth Chatterton before her—had found a medium in which she could finally be her own master. So, using the money coming in from movie and TV work to pay her bills, she wrote full time, and a second book, a novel, appeared in 1963.

In writing *My Story* Mary Astor had been a novice. She merely wrote what she remembered, and editors made it work as a straightforward narrative. Spending almost four years on that second book, Astor taught herself how to create a narrative on her own. "It was a whole new discipline," she recalled. "You work alone,

CLOCKWISE FROM RIGHT:

Roy Schatt photo of Astor and James Dean clowning during a TV rehearsal for the 1955 *United States Steel Hour* episode, "The Thief".

Mary Astor, author.

Astor with her original Oscar plaque and statuette replacement.

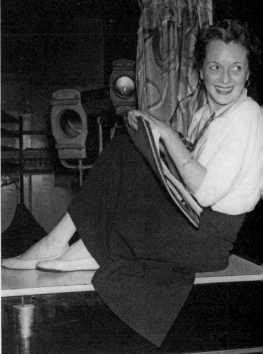

and it takes time, time, time, to write a book." Writing had become a compulsion, and soon she "was beginning to resent the time spent— even if it was only a week of work, in a filmed TV show. When I've got a book in the works, I feel as though I have a lump of something in my stomach and wish I could take something for it. I don't want to be bothered until I get rid of it. Finally words, paragraphs, pages begin to happen and there is relief." As the writing continued she became more and more reclusive, so reclusive that eventually it was just Astor and her Siamese cat, Missy. She would muse, "Writing and walking on the beach and seeing a few people occasionally is the life for me."

In 1964, her agent called. "There's this cameo in a movie with Bette Davis." The film was *Hush, Hush Sweet Charlotte*, and it would be her last. For a time Joan Crawford was in the film—later replaced by Olivia DeHavilland—and when Crawford arrived on location with seventeen pieces of luggage and an entourage, Astor found it a bit much, as her days of Hollywood pretense were long behind her.

"There comes a day," she remembered, "when you have to make up your mind what you must do. I couldn't carry two jobs." So she wrote a friend, "I seem to be wasting spit and high blood pressure tablets" waiting for "a good picture," and then she asked the Motion Picture Country House—an assisted-living facility— to add her name to their long waiting list. In November 1965, she withdrew from the American Federation of Television and Radio Artists, officially ending her acting career.

Eventually Astor moved to Mexico and lived in the American colony at Alamos, Sonora. As she had done with her acting, Astor methodically mastered the craft of writing. Over a five year period she completed three additional books, two novels and, while in Mexico, a second autobiography, *A Life On Film*, which concentrated on her film work. This last book sold extremely well, and a chapter was excerpted in both *TV Guide* and *Reader's Digest*, while a piece on Humphrey Bogart appeared in the *Sunday New York Times*. Not only did Astor enjoy writing the book, but it also remains one of the finest books ever written about the nuts and bolts of movie acting during Hollywood's "golden age." In the book Mary Astor summed up her film career in seven well-chosen sentences.

"There are five stages in the life of an actor: Who's Mary Astor? Get me Mary Astor. Get me a Mary Astor type. Get me a young Mary Astor. Who's Mary Astor?"

In the midst of this writing binge, the damp and extremely hot Mexican climate affected her lungs and, developing COPD, Astor now needed an oxygen machine to breathe. Finally, following a heart attack, she moved back to the States, staying with her son in Fountain Valley until she recovered. Afterwards, Astor moved to an apartment in Huntington Beach so her son and daughter-in-law could look in on her.

In 1973, Astor finally took up residence in the San Fernando Valley at the Motion Picture Country House. Since her retirement, annuities had matured; Astor had a steady income and, paying her own way, could afford a one-room cottage. She had privacy, and it was here that Mary Astor completed her last, unpublished novel as well as several shorter pieces.

In June 1976 she appeared on the *Today Show* promoting the MPCH, and in February 1980 was on the cover of *Life Magazine* in a sexy photo from the '30s. Astor told the interviewer that it was the longest she'd ever lived in a single place. Lamenting that so many of her friends and coworkers had passed on, she informed the interviewer that this was the reason she had consented to have her picture taken. "So, people won't think I'm dead yet." It was said with that sardonic Mary Astor smile.

The loss of her friends weighed heavy on Astor, and she'd write, "As one gets older it seems to be harder to lose" friends. Since Astor had always been particular about her friendships, being surrounded by people with whom—other than making films—she had very little in common wasn't easy. Since Mary Astor was a woman who always lived in the present, talking about her movies was definitely not her "favorite topic of conversation."

So, at the MPCH, she kept pretty much to herself, even eating at her own table in the common dining room because she didn't want to listen to an incessant battery of "organ recitals"—her shorthand for residents discussing malfunctioning kidneys, bladders, and every other organ in their body. Mary Astor had better ways of occupying her time. Complaining, or listening to complaints, simply wasn't one of them.

It was during this period that Astor suffered a series of mild strokes, resulting in her becoming even more reclusive and, often, quite difficult to be around. A chain smoker all her life, she eventually developed emphysema in addition to her COPD and, in 1985, was moved to the MPCH's hospital facility. Two years later on September 25, 1987, at age eighty-one, she died in her sleep with her son, Tono, and his wife at her bedside.

If Mary Astor had an epitaph it would most likely have read, "Sing no sad songs for me. Considering everything, I had a pretty good run."

38

One of Marylyn Thorpe's earliest memories is of sitting on the staircase at the Toluca Lake house and watching her father being chased by none other than Miss Norma Taylor holding what Marylyn thought at the time was a knife. She also remembers Nellie Richardson grabbing her and pulling her out of the way. Quite understandably her father never mentioned this, as both Marylyn's parents made a concerted effort not to tell their daughter anything about the custody battle. In fact, Marylyn didn't even know there had been a custody battle until she was a teenager. For most of her life she thought it a skeleton best left in the family closet.

Mary Astor had paid a very steep price for the right to bring up her "daughter in the finest way" she knew how. And, as with all mothers, her success would depend both on maternal love and good intentions as well as Mary Astor's inner strengths and personal weaknesses.

• • •

Following the custody battle brouhaha, America pretty much lost interest in Marylyn Thorpe. Except for an occasional article about her mother in which Marylyn might be mentioned, Marylyn had a relatively normal childhood and adolescence, but it certainly wasn't the enviable life the press made it appear to be. When Marylyn reflects on her childhood, what she remembers most was her loneliness and isolation, how she was always wishing her mother had more time for her. Sadly, Marylyn remembers spending more time with servants than with her parents.

There were reasons for that, reasons that were, although unfortunate, unavoidable. Astor earned the paycheck, and in Hollywood back then that meant six-day workweeks and twelve-to-fifteen-hour work days. Mary Astor deeply regretted that she "never had enough time with Marylyn because," as she would later recall, "I rarely got home before seven sometimes for weeks at a time before a break came and I had a few days off."

So, like many professional women today, Mary Astor supervised her daughter's upbringing, and under her mother's strict orders, Marylyn was raised with "no undue pampering."

Since Marylyn knew nothing else, she made the best of it. Nevertheless, this didn't make it any less painful or take away her sense of loss.

• • •

Whenever Marylyn is asked which film role her mother played that most resembled Mary Astor in real life, Marylyn answers without hesitation.

"*Desert Fury* was really her, and she played Fritzi tough to the max!"

In the film Fritzi Haller is a smart, no-nonsense businesswoman and mother who expects her daughter to do exactly as she is told. Although she loves her daughter deeply, Fritzi is unable to express it. It's only in Fritzi's determination to protect her daughter by controlling almost every aspect of her life that Fritiz's love can express itself.

Like Fritzi Haller, Mary Astor was a no-nonsense mother who wasn't, by nature, a nurturer. Raised by an inflexible tyrannical father, as a mother, Astor was also inflexible. What Mary Astor could do was give her daughter what physical affection she had to give and provide Marylyn with a strict, disciplined childhood. The strategy eventually produced a secure adult, which was what Mary Astor believed was the best a mother could do for her child.

Mary Astor also believed that, to maintain her child's respect

TOP: Marylyn Thorpe, age ten.

MIDDLE: Astor, Marylyn, and del Campo in 1938.

BOTTOM: Marylyn, age fourteen, playing cards with her mother at their San Remo Drive home.

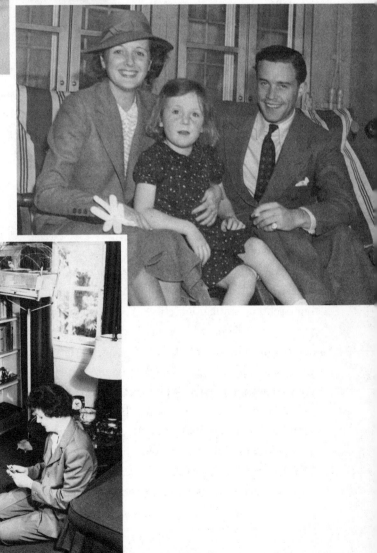

and obedience, she needed to have the final say on everything. There were no debates in the Astor home. Like Fritzi Haller, Mary Astor was not a woman with whom you wanted to argue. When Mary Astor was angry, her temper up, the last thing you wanted was to be a target. Consequently, Marylyn learned never to disagree with or question her mother's decisions, and perceived her mother not as a care-giver but as a disapproving and critical authoritarian. By being critical Astor believed she was merely correcting inappropriate behavior. Unfortunately, Marylyn didn't interpret it that way. What Marylyn saw was a mother who believed there was something wrong with her daughter, who was a constant disappointment to her mother.

This was the furthest thing from the truth. Marylyn and her brother were perhaps the only human beings Mary Astor ever loved unconditionally. Unfortunately, Astor was incapable of showing how she felt because, in the home in which she had been raised, Mary Astor learned never to express her true emotions lest it bring down her father's wrath.

• • •

When Marylyn was finally ready for school, each school was carefully selected by her mother. Then, at age eleven, her mother enrolled Marylyn at a boarding school, where she would remain until her high school graduation. This was during the war, and Astor was rarely home, so boarding school seemed the best option. With her son off at military school, as Astor saw it, Marylyn and her brother would be raised in a disciplined, structured environment where they could freely interact with children their own age.

Unfortunately, that was not how Marylyn saw it. In a single moment she abruptly lost her childhood home and, with her baby brother in military school, a brother she dearly missed. Although Marylyn quickly adjusted to boarding school, after her once-a-month weekend visits home were over and it was time to return to school, she hated to go back. Marylyn knew she wouldn't see her mother again for weeks, and that was extremely painful.

Boarding school meant another loss as well. Once she was off to school, Marylyn's father was pretty much out of the picture, and Marylyn saw him less and less. Prior to boarding school her father had abided by the custody agreement, regularly visiting his daughter on Thursdays and Sundays and having her with him in his apartment during her summers. Unfortunately, since her father was always busy with patients, father and daughter could never become close, and Marylyn spent her childhood summers basically alone, drawing and listening to Deanna Durbin records. When Thorpe couldn't find a sitter, Marylyn practically lived in her father's medical office, keeping out of everyone's way and not making any trouble so as to avoid her father's ire.

In addition—and this was very hard on the little girl—Franklyn Thorpe was not an overly affectionate or particularly playful father. As she grew older it was Marylyn who did the hugging and kissing, not her father. Suffering migraines, Franklyn Thorpe was a perfectionist who lost patience easily, and as a child Marylyn found these sudden outbursts quite frightening. It wasn't until years later, when Thorpe became his daughter's family physician, that the two finally had the close father-daughter relationship that had eluded Marylyn growing up.

• • •

If Mary Astor was adamant about one thing it was protecting her daughter's childhood from the film business. Consequently, Marylyn learned to see the tinsel in Tinsel Town for what it was, and never became a subscriber to the "cult of celebrity," something for which she is extremely grateful. Meeting everyone from Tyrone Power to Humphrey Bogart, instead of the iconic representations that the world saw, Marylyn saw people just like her mother: actors doing a job. On the nannies' days off, if Astor couldn't find a sitter, she brought her daughter to the set. These studio visits taught Marylyn

ABOVE: Marylyn in the early '50s with her father and grandfather, Sam Thorpe.

LEFT: Marylyn with her mother on location in Big Bear for *Brigham Young*.

BELOW: Marylyn, age seventeen, in her mother's portable dressing room during the filming of 1949's *Little Women*.

that there was nothing glamorous about making movies, that it was instead a tedious process where actors were required to sit around all day waiting to be called to the set. In fact, she thought the whole thing pretty boring.

Yet, during the summer vacation prior to her senior year, as a lark, Marylyn was given a bit part in *Little Women*, in which her mother plays Marmee. Marylyn appears in the scene where Elizabeth Taylor is admonished by the teacher. Filing past Taylor on the way to the coatroom, Marylyn had a single line of dialogue: "That'll teach her not to cut up didoes." Terrified, she repeatedly flubbed her line, requiring several takes to get it right.

Fluffed lines or no, it was obvious Marylyn had talent, and when she performed in college her mother was always supportive, giving her daughter helpful suggestions on how to improve her performances. Eventually Marylyn went on casting calls, and was interviewed for the part of Annie Oakley in the popular TV series of the same name. But Marylyn was considered too pretty, and she didn't have her mother's capacity or discipline for learning lines. Also, Marylyn absolutely hated rehearsals, and loathed the idea of spending her days inside a dark studio. Astor's daughter neither had the drive nor the interest to become an actress. Instead Marylyn would eventually drop out of college, marry at eighteen, and raise four children as a hands-on-mother, which, years earlier, had been the life Mary Astor had so yearned for.

Nevertheless, this acting stint helped Marylyn appreciate her mother's professionalism and discipline. Still living at home, Marylyn often watched her mother learn lines by taking ten matches and using them to count how many times it took to memorize a scene. Then, prior to shooting *The Great Lie*, in which Astor had to appear playing sections of a Tchaikovsky Piano Concerto, Marylyn's mother sat at the Steinway in their living room for what to a child seemed like months, practicing. In later years this was the thing that Marylyn came to truly admire most about her mother—her iron-willed determination and inability to accept anything less than the best from herself.

Marylyn's wedding day on her eighteenth birthday. With her are her new husband and mother.

In the 1960s Marylyn had one last opportunity to observe her mother on a movie set. It was in one of Astor's last films. Marylyn's mother stood up and, in front of cast and crew, gave a ten-minute speech flawlessly on the very first take. Everyone on the set watched in awe, as this was "one-take Mary" at her absolute best. Consequently, when Marylyn's mother finished, the entire crew, extras and visitors alike, gave her a standing ovation. It was on days like this that Marylyn was extremely proud to be Mary Astor's daughter.

• • •

When Marylyn's mother traveled east in 1953 to restart her career, Marylyn, her husband, and little baby girl moved into her mother's Encino home, where she and her husband became surrogate parents to Marylyn's thirteen-year-old brother.

This separation from her family was not something Astor was happy about. "Since I had to pull myself out of a financial debacle and 'hit the road' and earn a living, my children have no active part in my life." Mary Astor's role as an active mother had come to an abrupt end.

Once a child becomes an adult, some parents and children become friends; others don't. Marylyn and her mother were the latter. Mary Astor had fought hard to raise a secure, well-adjusted daughter. Unfortunately she wasn't able to enjoy her accomplishment, because as Marylyn moved into adolescence Mary Astor couldn't permit Marylyn to be herself; an ebullient, joyful, talkative girl who had no trepidation in showing her emotions. It conflicted too much with Astor's coping method of keeping a tight rein on her emotions. So Marylyn hid her true self from her mother to avoid receiving a disapproving look or cutting remark. Marylyn saw this as disapproval rather than one of her mother's shortcomings, "and it hurt—hurt a lot."

Later, as an adult, Marylyn resented not feeling free to openly express her feelings because her mother needed to have things her way. All Marylyn ever wanted was for her mother to accept her for who she was and enjoy a daughter who dearly loved her. She wanted a mother who would let her express herself the way she wanted instead of needing to become someone else simply to eliminate possible friction.

These resentments were never resolved, because of Astor's inability to change and Marylyn's inability to confront her mother about it. This inevitably created a gulf between mother and daughter, because they had temperaments that simply didn't mix, preventing them from achieving the closeness both craved.

In the years that followed, while her mother was acting and writing, Marylyn was busy raising four children and the two had only sporadic contact. When her mother began writing full-time, they saw even less of each other. As Marylyn's own children grew into adults, she and her mother weren't particularly close. When her mother moved to the Motion Picture Country House, Marylyn and her husband were living in Big Bear City, CA—a three-hour drive from LA—and the two rarely saw each other. Sadly, considering how hard Mary Astor had fought to have her daughter, at this point theirs had become a non-relationship.

• • •

The last time Marylyn saw her mother it was in the hospital at the MPCH. Marylyn and her husband had made the three-hour drive down from Big Bear City. Mother and daughter hadn't seen each other for quite a while, and seeing her mother so ill and sitting on a hospital bed, Marylyn felt a sudden swell of emotion, and told her mother that she had really missed her.

Her mother's reply was quintessential Mary Astor: "Don't get too sentimental."

Even close to death, Marylyn's mother remained the tough woman she had been her entire adult life. In fact, it could very well have been Fritzi Haller speaking.

Four months later, at night, Marylyn's brother phoned, and all he said was, "Mom's gone."

• • •

In 1959 Mary Astor wrote of her daughter, "We are as close as two generations can be. We have an unspoken sense of each other's attitude toward life and work. We consent, each to the other, the fact that we are as we are, accepted and made room for, appreciated in each other's life."

Over fifty years later Marylyn would thoughtfully reflect on those words. "She wrote well about how we felt about each other. Because of our given 'humanities' perhaps we both expected more from each other than we could give. Warts and all I still wouldn't have changed her for anyone else. She was the only mother I had. She was the best mother I had."

POSTSCRIPT

In Howard Teichmann's 1972 book on George Kaufman, Teichmann not only wrote that Thorpe had sold the diary to the *New York Daily News* but also that it was locked in the "Managing Editor's Confidential File," in a vault three levels under East Forty-Second Street, where Mr. Teichmann had been granted permission to view it. Thirteen years later, on September 27, 1987, the *Daily News* informed its readers that an employee had entered that vault with a locksmith to open the aforementioned "Confidential File." He found not the diary but the same photostats Joseph Anderson had handed out on August 10, 1936. With them were a group of letters between Thorpe and the paper's editors regarding the newspaper's publication of Thorpe's sterilized biography, *I Married an Actress.*

Mary Astor's son believed that his mother had the diary in her possession and, shortly before her death, had given it to friend, while others in the family felt that it might be among the personal papers Astor had donated to the Boston University Archive.

Contrary to rumor, and to what some creative writers would have readers believe, what happened to the diary is exactly as Mary Astor described in her 1959 autobiography. In July 1952, after Marylyn had reached her twenty-first birthday, the ledger books containing the diary as well as two photostatic copies were removed from a bank vault where they had lay hidden for nearly sixteen years. Then, as Mary Astor requested, and as Franklyn Thorpe agreed, the two ledger books and photostatic copies were burned in secret, lest reporters make themselves a nuisance.

The story was eventually reported in almost every newspaper in the country, including the *New York Times* and *Time Magazine.*

On this occasion, though, the infamous diary's demise didn't make headlines. Instead, most newspapers consigned it to a single-column, three-inch story buried deep within the paper.

However, the *New York Daily News* did a bit more. Milking the story for one last bit of sensationalism, the newspaper's page-four article announced, "Film Folks Can Sleep Now; Astor Diary Destroyed." No two ways about it; that diary made great copy right up until it went up in flames.

ACKNOWLEDGEMENTS

The genesis of this book occurred a number of years ago, when I was assembling a massive conceptual piece consisting of a series of newspaper collage works dealing with the American film industry from the '20s through the '90s. One collage per decade, it would alternate coverage of a film release with a Hollywood scandal. For the 1930s I had chosen the Mary Astor custody battle. The material intrigued me. The story of a woman who, for the sake of her little baby, took on the national media as well as the Hollywood establishment to do what she believed was best for her child. As I read and reread this material I began to understand how tremendously difficult it had been for Astor to go to court, but go to court she did, and I saw this as something heroic.

The idea of utilizing the Astor material to write a book was first sparked when I read the Mary Astor chapter in Kenneth Anger's hugely successful book, *Hollywood Babylon*. It was Anger's intention to scandalize, and he succeeded quite well at this; the piece on Astor was filled with so many falsehoods, often substituting the salacious for the truth, that I felt the record needed to be set straight. Unfortunately this idea languished for a number of years, until I read a short piece in *New York Magazine* on the trial using Anger's book as the principal source. In short, *Hollywood Babylon* and its many falsehoods had, and would continue to be, source material for any writer wanting to discuss the Mary Astor–Franklyn Thorpe custody trial. This proved to be the motivation I needed to finally write a book that would "set the record straight."

In writing this book there can be no doubt that the person to whom I am most indebted is Marylyn Thorpe Roh—the little girl at the heart of the custody hearing and now a woman in her 80s. When I initially contacted Marylyn she told me flat out that she preferred that I not write the book. Like her mother, Marylyn will—politely of course—tell you exactly what she thinks. Her reasons were personal and have been touched upon in the text. Nevertheless, because I was committed to the project, Marylyn, despite her personal reservations, let me know that she would help me in any way she could. Consequently, because of her, both Mary Astor and Franklyn Thorpe became living breathing human beings, rather than the iconic representations the media often makes of the famous. Over the course of the five months that it took to write the principle sections of this book Marylyn—via e-mail—answered each and every question I put to her, and the material I received from her eventually totaled over twenty-six thousand words. It should be noted that during this period her brother, Tono, died, and despite her immense grief she continued to answer my questions in depth and with great acuity. At eighty-two she has a mind as sharp as a twenty-year-old, and I greatly benefited from this. In short, Marylyn proved herself to be a very great lady, and one of the perks of writing this book is that she and I have become close personal friends. In the process, and in innumerable ways, she has enriched my life as well as my wife's, and I will be indebted to her in ways that go far beyond the writing of this book.

Next to Marylyn, the person to whom I am most grateful is her daughter and Mary Astor's granddaughter, Gabrielle Roh. In the midst of teaching, taking care of a score of grandchildren, and earning another college degree—while also dealing with a plethora of personal dilemmas—Gabrielle took the time to dig through the Astor-Thorpe material of the Roh family picture and document collection to make available to me the many photographs and documents used in this book. During Mary Astor's later years the two grew close, and so Gabrielle has made great strides at preserving this material for future use by film historians. For these efforts I want to laud as well as thank her.

Also helpful was Andrew Yang, who like his Aunt Gabrielle

feels compelled to do his best to make sure that the memory of his great-grandmother is not dimmed. Throughout his life Mary Astor's talent and iron-willed determination to do her best at whatever she attempted have been an inspiration for him. So, in addition to his unstinting support, Andrew made his picture file on Mary Astor available to me. He was also kind enough to share with me some Mary Astor-Roh family lore and, in doing so, like his grandmother and aunt before him, helped me to see Mary Astor in an infinitely more complex light. In fact, it was Andrew who suggested the title of this book.

I also want to express my thanks to Andrew's sister Alyssa Yang for her encouragement and the positive input that she provided from the moment she first read the unedited manuscript. Great thanks also to her mother, Frances, Mary Astor's first grandchild, for her help as well.

I am most especially indebted to writer and film historian Scott O'Brien, not only for his excellent and definitive biography of Ruth Chatterton, but also for his editorial suggestions and help in writing about Roland Rich Woolley. Scott not only provided me with research material but gently pushed me to see that, in order to understand the man, I needed first to understand what it meant to be a Mormon. I want to add that his wonderful biography of Ruth Chatterton literally brings the woman to life, and helped me to both understand this remarkable and generous hearted person— O'Brien's book makes you feel you know the woman personally— and allowed me to write about her with a great degree of insight.

I also want to thank Ken Bass for his advice regarding the legal aspects of the book. I was fortunate enough to edit one of his books, and he is not only a wonderful writer but also an able and skilled attorney. This book greatly benefited from his input.

Also, many thanks to agent Kristine Dahl and writer Charles McGrath. Also Sandy Birnhardt, who told me the book could work; my agent Rita Rosenkrantz, who helped me make it work better; Alexa Foreman for fact-checking the manuscript as well for as her astute editorial suggestions; and Sarah Masterson Hally and Sarah

Jacobson at Diversion Books. And finally Tiberiu Stanescu, who is entirely responsible for the Purple Diaries and Mary Astor Websites. Without his unstinting help I would have been completely adrift regarding the web. He is without question the most generous and good hearted man I have ever known. I consider it both an honor and privilege to be his friend.

I want to thank the libraries at Columbia University, New York University, and Barnard College as well as the New York Public Library Research Division at the main facility as well as the collections of the Lincoln Center branch and the library's annex. The NYPL staff not only made available to me the vast clipping collection at Lincoln Center but also the clipping morgue of the old *New York Sun* now held at the main facility. I should also like to note that without the interlibrary loan service of the NYPL this book could never have been written. I think a great many writers would probably say the same, and I am happy to have joined that very long list.

Finally, thanks to my editor, Randall Klein, who forced me to see the book I actually wrote and not the one I thought I wrote.

Joseph Egan

JOSEPH EGAN is something of a renaissance figure. Soon after earning a degree in film and theatre, he wrote for and edited a weekly entertainment newspaper. In addition, he is the editor of a privately printed anthology, has edited several college literary magazines, worked as a freelance editor, and is a professional researcher. Mr. Egan has also worked in motion picture promotion, has had several film scripts optioned, and served as a judge at an international independent film festival. As a conceptual artist, he has presented installations in New York City as well as in the Midwest.

Joseph Egan is also a close personal friend of Marylyn Thorpe Roh, the child at the center of this famous custody case. He is an expert on a wide range of subjects, including the motion picture *Heaven's Gate*, producer David O. Selznick, inventor Nikola Tesla, and of course, Mary Astor. Mr. Egan and his wife live on the side of a mountain in Dutchess County, New York, where their daily visitors are restricted to white-tailed deer, wild turkeys, chipmunks, rabbits, raccoons, and a rather reclusive family of possums.

APPENDICES

IMAGE CREDITS

All photographs, other than those noted below, are from the author's collection. Much thanks to the following:

Every effort has been made to trace the copyright holders of the photographs included in this book; if any have been inadvertently overlooked, the author will be pleased to make the necessary changes.

NOTES

Since newspapers and wire services had stenographers in the courtroom, the tabloids printed up various portions of the testimony verbatim. Therefore, utilizing trial coverage from all the LA and NY newspapers as well as the wire services, I was able to painstakingly reconstruct major portions of the trial transcript. When referring to this reconstruction the abbreviation "Trans" is used.

FREQUENTLY USED ABBREVIATIONS
American Film-AF
Baby Diary-BD
Brooklyn Eagle-BE
Columbia Oral History-CULOHRO.
Life Magazine-LM
Life On Film-LOF
London Daily Express-LDE
Los Angeles Examiner-LAE
Los Angeles Evening Herald Express-LAHE
Los Angeles Times-LAT
Mary Astor Autobiographical Writings-MAAW
Marylyn Thorpe-Roh-MTR
My Story-MS
New York American-NYA
New York Daily News-NYDN
New York Evening Journal-NYEJ
New York Mirror-NYM
New York Post-NYP
New York Sun-NYS
New York Times-NYT
New York World-Telegram-NYWT
Newark Star Ledger-NSL
Reading Times-RT
San Francisco Call-Bulletin-SCB

CHAPTER 1

I wish I-**NYM 8-11-36:15** / Feeling lowish-**NYM 8-11-36:3** / Like what-**NYM 8-11-36:3** / Should I wait-**NYM 8-11-36:3** / I practically went-**NYM 8-11-36:12** / That scene with-**Teichmann: 168** / straighten-**LAHE 8-5-36:1** / man-to-man-**LAHE 8-5-36:1** / Does Mary know-**NYDN 8-17-36** / fight to protect-**LAHE 8-5-36:1** / I'm sorry, and-**LAHE 8-5-36:1** / Mid-Victorian fool-**LAHE 8-5-36:1**

CHAPTER 2

Madonna-Child-**LOF: 9** / You're so goddamned-**LOF: 17** / moo-vies-**LOF: 21** / was a walking-**LOF: 11** / cultivated and awed-**MS: 72** / too self-conscious-**MS: 73** / Much like a-**MS: 75** / Most important-**LOF: 20** / He gave me-**MB: 24** / I could make-**LOF: 46** / You can never-**MS: 76** / tender, verbal, witty-**Youtube.com** / You don't have-**LOF: 46** / Not just now-**LOF: 46** / We couldn't afford-**MS: 87** / You haven't changed-**MS: 88** / preposterously beautiful-**Parish: 2** / all my hopes-**MS: 91** / Lucile, I want-**MB: 91** / I don't feel-**LOF: 54** / You are going-**MS: 91** / You keep your-**MS: 91**

CHAPTER 3

cocktails-**LOF: 55** / I had experienced-**MS: 105** / curl-up in his-**MS: 116** / We often slept-**MS: 120** / rainbows around it-**LOF: 73** / couple-**MS: 132** / grief under tight-**MS: 143** / His soft soothing-**NYDN 8-9-36:4** / She was in-**NYND 8-19-36** / her physician as-**LAE 8-13-36:1** / I'll get that-**NYDN 8-9-36:4** / There he was-**NYDN 8-9-36:4** / a magnificent friendship-**NYEJ 8-13-36:1** / You're the only-**NYDN 8-14-36:3** / I looked in-**NYDN 8-16-36** / now that I-**LAHE 8-10-36:1** / patients that won't-**NYM 8-11-36:3** / a bump on-**NYM 8-11-36:3** / while beautifully educated-**NYM 8-11-36:3** / To My Pal-**NYDN 8-14-36:3** / pseudo intellectual-**NYM 8-12-36** / he is a-**NYM 8-11-36:9** / the little bit-**NYM 8-11-36:3**

CHAPTER 4

I'm dying to see-**CULOHRO** / like George but-**MS: 160** / smartest gal in-**Bach: 127** / I met George and-**NYM 8-11-36:3** / they just disappeared-**CULOHRO** / Kaufman was a man-**Teichmann: 158** / Kaufman was only-**Marx G: 204** / male nymphomaniac-**Meredith: 559** / We were *both* virgins-**Teichmann: 45** / could no longer-**Meredith: 146** / set the styles-**Teichmann: 50** / thrilling and beautiful-**NYM 8-11-36:3** / It was just-**NYM 8-11-36:3** / sensible-**NYM 8-11-36:3** / she was only-**Meredith: 7** / eyes to play-**NYM 8-11-36:3** / in a comfortable-**NYM 8-11-36:3** / I don't like-**NYM 8-12-36** /a series of-**MS: 161** / He's very happy-**NYM 8-11-36:3** / I'm fond of Franklyn-**NYM 8-11-36:3** / I like to-**NYM 8-11-**

36:3 / I may as-**NYM 8-13-36:3** / I will not-**NYM 8-13-36** / Only ten days-**NYDN 8-11-36:3** / our 21-**NYM 8-11-36:3** / lovely-**NYM 8-11-36:3** / glorious ecstasy in-**NYM 8-11-36:3** / back into low-**NYM 8-11-36:3** / It's a wonder-**LAT 8-11-36:1** / big-**NYDN 8-17-36** / It's a remarkable-**NYDN 8-17-36** / The only real-**NYM 8-11-36:3**

CHAPTER 5

George dragged into-**NYM 8-11-36:3** / Kaufman is a man-**NYM 8-11-36:3** / very wretched with-**NYM 8-11-36:3** / Is it that-**NYDN 8-17-36** / that made you-**NYEJ 8-13-36:3** / Why do you-**LAE 8-14-36:1** / Was it to-**NYM 8-11-36:3** / How do you-**NYDN 8-5-36:3** / Why didn't Kaufman-**LAE 8-13-36** / I practically went-**NYM 8-11-36:3** / Because I went-**LAE 8-13-36** / and told him-**LAE 8-13-36:1** / and he was-**NYDN 8-5-36:3** / How *dare* you-**LAHE 8-5-36:1** / What did you-**NYM 8-11-36:3** / What do you-**NYA 8-6-36** / By what right-**NYEJ 8-5-36:1** / Do you think-**NYDN 8-5-36:3** / It's none of-**NYEJ 8-13-36:1** / You're a big-**LAHE 8-5-36:1** / If I was-**LAHE 8-5-36:1** / I wouldn't have-**NYEJ 8-5-36:1** / I talked to-**LAHE 8-5-36:1** / a man-**LAE 8-13-36** / who would hide-**NYM 8-14-36** / I can't-**NYM 8-11-36:3** / Why would you-**NYM 8-4-36:3** / Now that this-**NYWT 8-4-36:1** / You've known about-**NYA 8-4-36:1** / and since we-**NYA 8-4-36:1** / I don't care-**NYA 8-4-36:1** / I need you-**NYM 8-11-36:3** / I want to have-**NYM 8-11-36:3** / It will all blow-**Teichmann: 169** / It is a thoroughly-**NYM 8-11-36:3** / safety valve-**NYDN 8-6-36:3** / I wanted to-**NSL 1-7-59:3** / exactly what his-**NYDN 8-18-36** / astounded reading through-**NYDN 8-16-36** / sucker-**NYDN 8-17-36** / I felt the-**NYDN 8-17-36** / My wife was-**NYDN 8-18-36** / anyone else who-**NYDN 8-17-36** / terribly attractive-**MS: 171** / was suddenly transformed-**MS: 163** / a horrible thing-**NYEJ 8-3-36:1** / You can't do-**NYEJ 8-4-36:1** / do anything-**NYEJ 8-4-36:1** / You should understand-**NYEJ 8-4-36:1** / Ethel you're going-**NYEJ 8-14-36:1** / thought it better-**NYT 4-12-36:10**

CHAPTER 6

too busy moaning-**CULOHRO** / He would take-**NYEJ 7-31-36:1** / I prepared myself-**MS: 170** / I want her-**NYEJ 7-31-36:1** / You've already caused-**LAE 7-31-36:1** / I'll do exactly-**NYEJ 7-31-36:1** / You're being so-**NYEJ 7-31-36:1** / Don't interfere or-**LAE 7-31-36:1** / I'm getting tired-**LAE 7-31-36** / You're the selfish-**LAHE 7-31-36:1** / That's not true-**NYDN 7-31-36:3** / She's my child-**NYM 8-13-36** / I won't stand-**NYWT 7-31-36:1** / I never did-**NYWT 7-31-36:3** / there was going-**NYWT 7-30-36:1** / publicly scandalize her-**NYDN 7-14-36:3** / be set aside-**NYDN 7-15-36:3** / her continuous gross-**NYDN 7-28-36:3** / the motion picture-**MS: 167**

CHAPTER 7

steel trap-**MS: 165** / Willful overbearing, domineering-**NYP 7-14-36** / Thorpe was thoroughly-**NYDN 7-19-36** / I regret Mary's attitude-**NYDN 7-15-36:3** / It seems to-**LAHE 7-15-36** / alleges that the-**LAE 7-28-36** / February 6-35-**LAE 7-28-36** / clamoring for the diary-**MS: 167**

CHAPTER 8

was not a-**AF 4-76** / made actors sweat-**AF 4-76** / got into step-**LOF: 118** / I've struggled along-**NYM 8-12-36** / treadmill of trash-**MS: 111** / You don't have-**LOF: 117** / If he trusted actors-**Loy: 197** / he could use-**LOF: 119** / she played Fran-**Madsen: 148** / the character was-**LOF: 119** / I loved Ruth-**MS: 166** / I spent many-**MS: 166** / a genial, sympathetic-**MS: 165** / she was going-**MS: 169** / was going to-**Herman: 156** / what the hell-**Herman: 156**

CHAPTER 9

Yes, but I-**LAHE 7-28-36** / a luxuriously furnished-**LAHE 7-28-36** / There is absolutely-**LAHE 7-28-36** / different issues were-**LAT 7-29-36:1** / The person that-**LOF: 126** / Do you have-**MS: 166** / beau-**O'Brien: xvi** / Woolley said she-**MS: 166**

CHAPTER 10

I had hoped-**NYP 7-29-36** / it was all-**LOF: 125** / under a great-**LOF: 125** / walking a very-**AF 4-77** / Beverly Hills Matron-**LAHE 7-29-36** / for the best interests-**NYM 7-29-36** / tight lipped and-**LAHE 7-29-36** / an unfit and-**NYS 7-28-36** / She told me-**Trans** / steel blue eyes-**NYP 7-29-36** / goggle-eyed and gasping-**NYP 7-29-36** / It is perfectly-**LAHE 7-29-36:1** / when the time-**LAT 7-30-36:1**

CHAPTER 11

Movies Fight Astor-**NYDN 7-29-36:1** / And what did-**Trans**

CHAPTER 12

Do you know-**Trans** / gay lothario-**LAE 7-30-36**

CHAPTER 13

Carried on a-**LAHE 7-30-36** / February 8, 1935-**LAHE 7-30-36** / thoughts and ideas-**LAE 7-31-36:5** / any and all-**LAE 7-31-36:5** / turkey fork-**LAHE 7-31-36** / state of collapse-**NYS 7-31-36** / compelled to give-**NYS 7-31-36** / You know it-**NYA 7-31-36** / throw a series-**LAHE 7-31-36:3** / I got my lawyers-**NYEJ 7-21-36** / pupil-**NYM 7-31-36** / Norma denied everything-**NYM 7-31-36**

CHAPTER 14

Titian hair-**NYM** 7-29-36 / handsome brunette-**NYEJ** 7-31:1 / gay Lothario-**LAE** 7-30-36 / two certain diaries-**Tran** / innuendo-**LOF: 125** / the pretty former nursemaid-**NYEJ** 8-1-36

CHAPTER 15

numbed by the-**MS: 169** / Shortly after the-**Trans** / her testimony climaxed a day of sensations-**NYEJ** 7-31-36:1 / filled the room with electric intensity-**NYP** 7-31-36 / startling dramatic appearance-**LAHE** 7-31-36:8 / composed-**LAT** 7-31-36:1 / demure and lovely-**LAHE** 7-31-36:8 / Although she appeared-**NYWT** 7-31-36:1 / her demeanor spoke-**LAHE** 7-31-36:8 / Her low deep-**LAE** 7-31-36 / strong-**LAT** 7-31-36 / vibrant-**LAHE** 7-31-36 / throaty voice-**LAT** 7-31-36 / There is no-**LAT** 7-31-36:1

CHAPTER 16

former nightclub dancer-**NYA** 8-1-26 / a full transcript-**NYEJ** 7-31-36 / throw a series-**LAHE** 7-31-36:8 / against all persons-**LAHE** 7-31-36:8 / The charges against-**NYT** 8-1-36 / The only relations-**NYT** 8-1-36 / There is likely-**NYDN** 8-1-36 / My client Norma-**NYM** 8-1-36 / Dr. Thorpe saved-**NYEJ** 8-1-36 / Our friendship might-**NYEJ** 8-1-36 / vivacious blond-**LAHE** 7-29-36:1 / Dignified Dr. Franklyn-**NYM** 7-31-36 / willfully abandoned-**NYT** 8-1-36 / We can prove-**NYT** 8-1-36 / outstanding leading men-**NYDN** 8-2-36:3 / after dark-**NYEJ** 8-1-36 / is one of-**LAE** 8-2-36:1 / world know all-**NYM** 8-3-36 / I cannot make-**NYDN** 8-2-36:3 / deliberately and fraudulently-**NYT** 8-2-36 / If Miss Astor-**NYT** 8-2-36 / Hollywood and Thorpe-**NYA** 8-2-36 / Astor Sensations Scare-**NYDN** 8-2-36:1 / At least six-**NYEJ** 8-1-36 / There is—everybody-**NYM** 8-3-36

CHAPTER 17

Miss Taylor did-**LAE** 8-2-36 / tried to maintain-**MS: 163** / Daddy-**LAT** 8-2-36:1 / We can never-**NYDN** 8-2-36:3 / Come see the-**LAHE** 8-1-36:1 / Daddy-**LAT** 8-2-36:1 / What lovely surroundings-**LAHE** 8-1-36:1 / Do you like-**LAE** 8-2-36:26 / Do you love-**NYS** 8-1-36 / The attorneys declare-**LAE** 8-2-36:26 / I've got the-**LAT** 8-2-36:1

CHAPTER 18

platinum blonde-**LAHE** 7-31-36 / Hollywood-**NYEJ** 7-31-36 / and Broadway-**LAHE** 7-31-36 / beauty-**NYM** 8-1-36 / getting ready to-**NYM** 8-3-36 / Don't believe what-**Teichmann: 172** / a hunk of-**Goldstein: 254** / Are you George-**LAT** 8-3-36 / What is this-**LAHE** 8-4-36:1 / It was

NYDN 8-5-36:3 / You know, I-**LAHE 8-5-36:1** / Our temperaments were-**NYDN 8-5-36:3** / Remember that old-**LAHE 8-5-36:1**

CHAPTER 23

He is perfect-**NYDN 8-5-36:3** / the superman-**NYDN 8-6-36:3** / Although Miss Astor-**NYDN 8-6-36:3** / famous carving-knife-**NYWT 8-4-36** / beauteous Brunette French-**Time 8-17-36:42** / Sure, I got-**NYWT 8-4-36** / Norma needed-**LAE 8-5-36** / Tommy knew I-**NYWT 8-4-36** / She's a darling-**NYP 8-4-36** / world famous men-**NYA 8-6-36** / You can go-**LAE 8-6-36** / stated that he-**LAE 8-6-36** / I wanted some-**NYP 8-4-36** / Mary Astor was-**LAHE 8-6-36:1** / the most panic-**NYEJ 8-6-35** / fits me perfectly-**NYDN 8-6-36:5** / Every time I-**NYWT 8-7-36:1** / quick dash back-**NYM 8-7-36:2** / would seem as-**NYM 8-7-36:2** / Kaufman was often-**NYM 8-7-36** / Everyone on Broadway-**NYM 8-7-36** / I'd frequently seen-**NYM 8-6-36:3** / If there is-**NYM 8-6-36:3** / Dr. Thorpe introduced-**NYM 8-6-36:3** / If they weren't-**NYEJ 8-7-36** / She was pretty-**NYWT 8-7-36:1** / She is showing-**NYWT 8-7-36:1**

CHAPTER 24

Well-known Hollywood-**NYEJ 8-2-36** / Franklyn Thorpe married-**NYEJ 8-6-36:2** / Then, early in-**NYEJ 8-6-36:2** / February 22, 1920-**NYM 8-8-36** / He proposed to-**NYEJ 8-6-36:1** / Franklyn told the-**NYEJ 8-6-36:1** / a widow with-**NYEJ 8-6-36:1** / because Thorpe's family-**NYA 8-6-36** / Thorpe eloped with-**NYEJ-8-8-36** / The bill was-**NYEJ 8-7-36** / Deceased, Mrs. May-**NYEJ 8-8-36** / husband's address, 2074-**NYDN 8-9-36** / late Thursday Thorpe-**NYM 8-7-36:3** / The tale that-**LAHE 8-7-36:1** / Before he married-**NYEJ 8-7-36** / That's all I can-**NYA 8-7-36** / I'm not saying-**NYEJ 8-7-36** / anything in her-**NYEJ 8-8-36** / wedding reception-**LAHE 8-7-36** / I don't know-**LAHE 8-7-36** / pretty wild parties-**NYEJ 8-8-36** / I will testify-**LAE 8-8-36:13** / Mary is proceeding-**LAE 8-8-36** / We didn't want-**NYA 8-8-36** / If the text-**NYM 8-8-36** / The tragedy of-**NYM 8-8-36:6** / it was said-**NYA 8-8-36** / the quaking Casanovas-**NYM 8-8-36:3** / Marylyn will not-**NYM 8-9-36** / My decision-**NYS 8-7-36**

CHAPTER 25

all nerves hid-**NYWT 8-14-36:1** / Is Kaufman going-**NYEJ 8-10-36** / I'm going to-**NYA 8-9-23** / I made my-**AF 4-76** / It's good, you'll-**LOF: 124** / It was fine-**AF 4-76** / an assembly of-**MS: 167** / Everyone was whispering-**MS: 167** / create a vicious-**MS: 167** / give the industry-**MS: 167** / would be wiser-**MS: 167** / drop the case-**MS: 167** / They had heard-**LOF: 126** /

I could only-**MS: 168** / I was not-**LOF: 126** / I'm sorry, gentlemen-**MS: 167** / A woman fighting-**MS: 170**

CHAPTER 26

I do not-**NYDN 8-10-36** / I will say-**NYDN 8-10-36** / with the cross-examination-**NYA 8-10-35** / Well, he'd better-**LAE 8-10-36** / I'll seek a-**NYEJ 8-10-36** / A certain person-**MS: 167** / contained a box-**MS: 168** / I was becoming-**MS: 133** / because I knew-**MS: 134** / Why wait? Let's-**MS: 134** / up the importance-**MS: 167** / asked her to-**NYEJ 8-10-36**

CHAPTER 27

Mr. Thalberg is-**NYWT 8-10-36:1** / I know no-**NYS 8-10-36:1** / There are eighteen-**NYM 8-10-36:3** / Thorpe's amorous-**NYM 8-10-36:3** / Have you properly-**Trans** / completely rattle proof-**LOF: 126**

CHAPTER 28

I'm just here-**LAT 8-11-36:1** / I admire Mary-**Time 8-17-36:42** / Did anyone else-**Trans** / Franklyn is simply-**BD** / It will be-**LAE 8-11-36:1** / I went out-**NYT 8-11-36** / And we were-**LAE 8-11-36** / I dare say she-**NYA 8-11-36** / Miss Astor was-**NYS 8-11-36** / Miss Astor is-**LAE 8-8-36** / every afternoon-**MS: 169**

CHAPTER 29

achieve the reputation-**LOF: 126** / An over emotional-**LOF: 125** / now in the-**NYM 8-12-36:1** / possible criminal prosecution-**NYDN 8-12-36:3** / several hundred fan-**NYS 8-12-36:1** / I wish the-**NYM 8-13-36:3** / Dr. Thorpe is-**NYM 8-11-36** / I give you-**Trans** / pertinent passages-**NYM 8-13-36:3** / Don't feel so-**NYEJ 8-12-36:1** / I am about-**Trans**

CHAPTER 30

I'm so furious-**LAE 8-12-36** / being offered for-**LAE 8-12-36:1** / I want no money-**LAE 8-12-36:1** / There is tremendous-**NYT 8-12-36** / moral victory-**LAE 8-12-36:1** / I warn you gentlemen-**Trans** / Look at what-**NYM 8-12-36:1**

CHAPTER 31

This thing just-**LAT 8-13-36:1** / I'll be a-**LAE 8-13-36:1** / let a harvest-**RT 8-19-36:6** / she shouldn't be-**Photoplay 1-38:22** / shunt the child-**LAHE 8-13-36:1** / marvelous-**LAT 8-13-36:1** / We have made-**NYDN 8-13-36:1** / a neutral custodian-**NYA 8-13-36:1** / No-**NYDN 8-13-36:1** / The essentials have-**NYA 8-13-36** / I think we-**NYA 8-13-36:1** / No, I am-**NYM 8-14-36:3** / I am going-**Trans** / The settlement fully-**NYHT**

8-13-36 / And contrary to-**NYS 8-13-36:1** / I am only-**LAT 8-13-36:1** / As a result-**LAE 8-13-36:1**

CHAPTER 32

Depend on it-**NYP 8-13-36** / Thorpe is my-**NYEJ 8-14-36:1** / sent him several-**NYP 8-13-36** / at least a-**LAT 8-13-36** / No; you've had-**NYEJ 8-14-36:1** / I'm too tired-**NYA 8-14-36:1** / last minute meeting-**NYDN 8-14-36:3** / But I have-**LAT 8-14-36:1** / I am happier-**NYDN 8-14-36:3** / Everybody's happy—well-**NYA 8-14-36:1** / While I admit-**NYDN 8-14-36:3** / Do you mean-**NYA 8-14-36:1** / What about Kaufman-**NYDN 8-14-36:3** / The proceeding has-**Trans** / clear the names-**NYDN 8-14-36:3** / These women have-**NYA 8-14-36:1** / testimony that was-**NYDN 8-14-36:3** / Dixieland accent-**LAE 8-14-36:1** / He hasn't asked-**LAE 8-14-36:1** / Please. Not now-**NYDN 8-14-36:3** / I'm tired, awfully-**LAE 8-14-36:1** / What are your-**NYM 8-14-36** / A month ago-**NYA 8-14-36:1** / Thirty days ago-**NYEJ 8-15-36** / We agreed not-**NYT 8-14-36** / We demand that-**LAT 8-14-36:1** / to see what-**NYM 8-14-36:3** / There was an-**NYM 8-14-36:3** / For the best-**NYA 8-14-36:1** / raw deal-**NYM 8-14-36:1** / I capitulated because-**NYM 8-14-36:3** / Am I happy-**NYA 8-14-36** / I will of-**NYA 8-14-36** / I'm no prophet-**NYT 8-14-36** / I have definite-**NYDN 8-11-36:1** / It was grossly-**LAE 8-14-36:1** / that Anderson is-**LAHE 8-14-36:1**

CHAPTER 33

top to bottom-**NYT 8-15-36** / behind every door-**NYM 8-15-36:3** / I'll put this-**LAT 8-15-36:1** / Our first move-**NYEJ 8-14-36:1** / My patience is-**LAHE 8-15-36:1** / I believe that-**NYEJ 8-15-36:1** / The reference that-**LAHE 8-15-36:1** / I Married an-**NYDN 7-14-36** / a distinguished document-**NYDN 8-18-36** / I decided to-**LAHE 8-15-36:1, NYM, NYDN, NYT, NYHT, NYA 8-16-36** / As long as-**NYA 8-16-36** / I tell you-**NYDN 8-28-36** / I have nothing-**LAT 8-28-36:1** / How am I doing-**BE 8-27-36** / What I said-**NYA 8-28-36** / How are you-**NYM 8-28-36** / I said all-**LAHE 8-27-36** / I still have-**LAHE 8-27-36** / Would you like-**NYDN 8-28-36** / Drive on. Just-**Teichmann: 175** / Why didn't Mr.-**NYA 8-28-36** / Were you with-**NYDN 8-28-36** / We have only-**NYM 8-28-36** / Mr. Kaufman and-**NYT 8-29-36**

CHAPTER 34

We are making-**NYWT 9-1-36** / Anything with Astor-**NYDN 8-15-36** / The character I-**MS: 170** / Great work, Mary-**NYWT 9-17-36** / kindness-**NYWT 9-17-36** / In view of-**NYP 9-24-36** / On the screen-**NYDN 9-24-36** / Mary Astor gives-**NYM 9-24-36** / Why don't you-**Time 9-28-36** /

For a long-**MS: 170** / At the time-**NYDN 9-1-57:42** / But the effect-**MS: 170** / I have always-**NYDN 9-18-57:42**

CHAPTER 35

the Tattling Nurse-**TIME 8-17-36:42** / Brat-**MTR** / famously-**MTR** / had known-**MTR** / own master-**O'Brien: 396** /the best sea-**NYT 2-2-41** / a remarkable work-**N Yorker 2-1-41:53** / heel clicking nobleman-**LAE 8-12-36:1**

CHAPTER 36

even with cue-**LOF: 143** / It's a good thing-**MS: 74** / I was on-**LOF: 144** / When a building-**Teichmann: 212** / Ah, the old-**MTR** / I've gotta get-**MTR**

CHAPTER 37

For the sake-**MS: 171** / The sword of-**MS: 170** / The only truth-**MS: 171** / The rest of-**LOF: 127** / I sharpened my-**MS: 171** / went on innumerable-**MS: 218** / spot-announcement records-**MS: 218** / large quantities of-**MS: 250** / But alcohol she-**MS: 18** / blind drunk-**MS: 259** / through-**MS: 266** / I was never bored-**LOF: 204** / short period of-**LOA: 214** / I'd seen my-**LOF: 213** / It was a-**LOF: 214** / was beginning to-**LOF: 215** / Writing and walking-**MA Letter 7-7-64** / There's this cameo-**LOF: 215** / There comes-**LOF: 215** / I seem to-**MA Letter 10-2-64** / There are five-**LOF: 194** / So, people won't-**LM 2-80:112** / As one gets-**MA Letter 8-21-63** / favorite topic of-**LOF: 217** / organ recitals-**MTR**

CHAPTER 38

daughter in the-**NYM 8-24-36** / never had enough-**MS-186** / no undue pampering-**BE 9-17-33:15** / *Desert Fury* was-**MTR** / That'll teach her-**MTR** / one-take Mary-**MTR** / Since I had-**MAAW June 1955** / And it Hurt-**MTR** / Don't get too-**MTR** / Mom's gone-**MTR** / We are as-**MS: 326** / She wrote well-**MTR**

CHAPTER 39

the Managing Editor's-**Teichmann: X** / Confidential File-**NYDN 9-27-87:4** / Film Folks Can-**NYDN 7-10-52:4**

BIBLIOGRAPHY

FULL LENGTH WORKS

Abbe, James. *Stars Of The Twenties*. Viking Press. (1975)

Adamson, Joe. *Groucho, Harpo, Chico And…* Simon & Schuster. (1973)

Agee, James. *Agee On Film: Reviews And Comments*. Beacon Press. (1968)

Alicoate, Jack. *1952 Film Daily Year Book*. Film Daily. (1952)

Allyson, June. *June Allyson*. G.P. Putnam's Sons. (1982)

Anger, Kenneth. *Hollywood Babylon*. Bell Publishing. (1975)

———. *Hollywood Babylon 2*. E.P. Dutton. (1984)

Anobile, Richard J. *The Maltese Falcon*. Universe Books. (1974)

———, ed. *Why A Duck?* Darien House. (1971)

Arce, Hector. *Groucho*. Putnam. (1979)

Arrington, Leonard J. *Adventures Of A Church Historian*. University Of Illinois. (1998)

Astor, Mary. *A Life On Film*. Delacorte Press. (1971)

———. *A Place Called Saturday*. Delacorte. (1968)

———. *My Story*. Doubleday. (1959)

———. *The Image Of Kate*. Doubleday. (1963)

Bach, Steven. *Dazzler: The Life and Times Of Moss Hart*. Da Capo Press. (2002)

Baker, Fred, Ross Firestone. *Movie People*. Lancer Books. (1973)

Balio, Tino. *United Artists*. University Of Wisconsin Press. Dell. (1973)

Barrymore, Elaine, S. Dody. *All My Sins Remembered*. Popular Library. (1964)

Bayer, William. *The Great Movies*. Ridge Press. (1973)

Bazter, John. *The Cinema Of James Ford*. A.S. Barnes. (1971)

Behlmer, Rudy. *Memo From David O. Selznick*. Viking. (1972)

———. *Inside Warner Brothers: 1935-1951*. Simon & Schuster. (1985)

———. *Memo From Darryl F. Zanuck*. Grove Press. (1993)

Belafonte, Dennis. *The Films Of Tyrone Power*. Citadel. (1979)

Berg, Scott. *Goldwyn: A Biography*. Alfred A. Knopf. (1989)

Bergan, Ronald. *The United Artists Story*. Crown. (1986)

Block, Geoffrey Holden. *Richard Rogers*. Yale University Press. (2003)

Bodeen, De Witt. *Ladies Of the Footlights*. Pasadena Playhouse Ass. (1937)

Bogdanovich, Peter. *John Ford*. University Of California Press. (1968)

Brown, Jared. *A Prince of the Theatre*. Back Stage Books. (2006)

Boleslavsky, Richard. *Acting: The First Six Lessons*. Theatre Arts. (1975)

Brown, Peter Harry, Pamela Brown. *The MGM Girls*. St. Martins. (1983)

Brownlow, Kevin, John Kobal. Hollywood *The Pioneers*. Alfred Knopf. (1979)

Brownlow, Kevin. *The Parade's Gone By*. Alfred Knopf. (1968)

Cagney, James. *Cagney By Cagney*. Doubleday. (1976)

Cameron, Ian, Elisabeth Cameron. *Dames*. Praeger. (1959)

Capra, Frank. *The Name Above the Title*. MacMillan. (1971)

Chaplin, Charles. *My Autobiography*. Simon & Schuster. (1964)

Crist, Judith. *The Private Eye, the Cowboy, and the Very Naked Girl: Movies from Cleo to Clyde*. Paper Back Library. (1970)

Crowther, Bosley. *Hollywood Rajah: Life Of Louis B. Mayer*. Henry Holt. (1960)

———. *The Lion's Share*. Dutton. (1957)

Demille, Cecilia. *Cecil B.DeMille*, Running Press. (2014)

Dickens, Homer. *The Films Of James Cagney*. Citadel. (1974)

Dunne, John Gregory. *The Studio*. Farrar, Straus & Giroux. (1968)

Eames, Douglas. *The Paramount Story*. Crown. (1985)

Eames, John Douglas. *The MGM Story*. Crown. (1977)

Edwards, Anne. *Judy Garland*. Simon & Schuster. (1974)

Eels, George. *Ginger, Loretta And Irene Who?* G.P. Putnam's Sons. (1976)

Egan, Joseph, ed. *Held Over*. Privately Printed. (1992)

Eliot, Marc. *Jimmy Stewart: A Biography*. Three Rivers Press. (2006)

Epstein, Daniel Mark. *Sister Aimee*. Harcourt Brace Lovanovich. (1993)

Essoe, Gabe. *The Films Of Clark Gable*. Citadel. (1969)

Faber, Stephen, Marc Green. *Hollywood Dynasties*. Delilah. (1984)

Fairbanks, Douglas Jr. *The Fairbanks Album*. New York Graphic Society. (1975)

Finch, Christopher. *Rainbow: Life Of Judy Garland*. Ballantine Books. (1975)

Ford, Dan. *Pappy: The Life Of John Ford*. Prentice Hall. (1979)

Fordin, Hugh. *World Of Entertainment*. Doubleday. (1975)

Fowler, Gene. *Good Night Sweet Prince*. Mercury House. (1989)

Frank, Gerold. *Judy*. Harper And Row. (1975)

Franklin, Joe. *Classics Of the Silent Screen*. Citadel. (1959)

Funke, Lewis, John Booth, ed. *Actors Talk About Acting*. Discus Books. (1961)

Garceau, Jean, Inez Cooke. *Dear Mr. Gable*. Little, Brown and Company. (1961)

Gershuny, T. *Soon To Be a Major Motion Picture*. Holt, Rinehart And Winston. (1980)

Giannetti, Louis. *Understanding Movies*. Prentice Hall. (2002)

Giles, Sarah. *Fred Astaire: His Friends Talk*. Doubleday. (1988)

Glasner, John, ed. *Twenty Best Film Plays*. Crown. (1943)

Goldsmith, Barbara. *Little Gloria...Happy At Last*. Alfred A. Knopf. (1980)

Goldstein, Malcolm. *George S. Kaufman*. Oxford University Press. (1979)

Goodrich, Marcus. *Delilah*. Time-Life. (1941, 1965)

Green, Abel. *Show Biz: From Vaude To Video*. Henry Holt And Company. (1951)

Green, Stanley. *Encyclopedia Of the Musical Film*. Oxford University Press. (1981)

Griffith, Richard, Arthur Mayer. *Movies*. Firestone-Simon & Schuster. (1957)

Hagan, Uta. *Respect For Acting*. Macmillan. (1971)

Halliwell, Leslie. *Mountain Of Dreams*. Stonehill Publishing. (1976)

Harris, Warren J, *Gable And Lombard*. Simon & Schuster. (1974)

Hart, Moss. *Act One*. Random House. (1959)

Haskell, Molly. *From Rape To Reverence*. Holt, Rinehart And Winston. (1974)

Haver, Ronald. *David O. Selznick's Hollywood*. Alfred A. Knopf. (1980)

Hawks, Howard. *Hawks On Hawks*. Faber & Faber. (1996)

Herman, Jan. *A Talent for Trouble: The Life of Hollywood's Most Acclaimed Director, William Wyler*. G. P. Putnam's Sons. (1995)

Herndon, Booton. *Mary Pickford And Douglas Fairbanks*. W. W. Norton. (1977)

Heston, Charlton. *Charlton Heston's Hollywood*. GT Publishing. (1998)

———. *The Actor's Life*. R. P. Dutton. (1976, 1978)

———. *In the Arena: An Autobiography*. Simon & Schuster. (1995)

Higham, Charles. *Marlene*. W. W. Norton. (1977)

———. *Sisters*. Coward McCann. (1984)

Hirschhorn, Clive. *The Universal Story*. Crown. (1983)

———. *The Warner Brothers Story*. Crown. (1979)

Howard Hawks: Interviews. University Press of Mississippi. (2006)

Huss, Ray, Norman Silverstein. *The Film Experience*. Delta. (1968)

Huston, John. *An Open Book*. Alfred A. Knopf. (1980)

Hyland, William. *Richard Rodgers*. Yale University Press. (1998)

Jewell, Richard, Vernon Harbin. *The RKO Story*. Arlington House. (1982)

Kael, Pauline. *Kiss Kiss Bang Bang*. Bantam. (1969)

Kaminsky, Stuart. *John Huston: Maker Of Magic*. Houghton Mifflin. (1978)

Kanin, Garson. *Moviola*. Simon & Schuster. (1979)

Kaufman, George, Morrie Ryskind. *Screenplay: A Night at the Opera*. Viking. (1972)

Kerr, Walter. *The Silent Clowns*. Alfred Knopf. (1975)

Kimball, Robert, Alfred Simon. *The Gershwins*. Atheneum. (1973)

Knappman, Edward W. *Great American Trials*. New England Publishing. (1994)

Knight, Arthur. *The Liveliest Art*. Mentor. (1957)

Kobler, John. *Damned In Paradise: The Life Of John Barrymore*. Atheneum. (1977)

Lambert, Gavin. *Norma Shearer*. Alfred Knopf. (1990)

Lamparski, Richard. *Whatever Became Of...? Second Series*. Crown. (1968)

Lasky, Jesse L. *Whatever Happened To Hollywood*. Funk & Wagnalls. (1973)

Lasky, Betty. *RKO, the Biggest Little Major Of Them All*. Prentice Hall. (1984)

Leff, Leonard J. *Hitchcock and Selznick*. Weidenfeld & Nicolson. (1987)

Leff, Leonard J., Jerold L Simmons. *Dame In The Kimono*. Grove Weidenfeld. (1990)

Leider, Emily W. *Myrna Loy*. University Of California. (2011)

Leish, Kenneth. *Cinema*. Newsweek Books. (1974)

Lindgren, Ernest. *The Art Of the Film*. Collier. (1979)

Loos, Anita. *A Girl Like I*. Viking Press. (1966)

———. *Kiss Hollywood Good-bye*. Viking. (1974)

Loy, Myrna. *Myrna Loy: Being and Becoming*. Alfred A. Knopf. (1987)

MacCann, Richard Dyer. *Film: A Montage Of Theories*. E. P. Dutton. (1966)

Madsen, Axel. *John Huston: A Biography*. Doubleday. (1978)

———. *William Wyler: Authorized Biography*. Thomas Y. Cromwell. (1973)

———. *Billy Wilder*. Indiana University Press. (1969)

Maltin, Leonard, ed. *Hollywood Kids*. Popular Library. (1978)

———. *Behind the Camera*. New American Library. (1971)

Mank, Gregory, Don Stanke. *The Hollywood Beauties*. Rainbow Books. (1979)

Manville, Anita. *The Lives And Wives Of Tommy Manville*. W.H. Allen. (1972)

Marx, Groucho, Anobile, R. *The Marx Brother's Handbook*. Darien House. (1973)

Marx, Samuel. *Thalberg And Mayor*. Samuel French. (1988)

Masi, Gerald. *Howard Hawks, Storyteller*. Oxford University Press. (1984)

McBride, Joseph. *Hawks On Hawks*. University Of California. (1982)

———, ed. *Focus On Howard Hawks*. Prentice-Hall. (1972)

McCarthy, Todd. *Howard Hawks*. Grove Press. (2000)

Meredith, Scott. *George Kaufman and His Friends*. Doubleday. (1974)

Michael, Paul. *Humphrey Bogart: The Man and His Films*. Bobbs-Merrill. (1965)

Miller, Edwin. *Seventeen Interviews: Film Stars and Superstars*. Macmillan. (1970)

Montague, Iver. *Film World*. Pelican. (1964)

Moore, Colleen. *Silent Star: Talks About Hollywood*. Doubleday. (1968)

New York Times. *New York Times Directory Of the Film*. Arno Press. (1971)

Niven, David. *Bring On the Empty Horses*. Dell. (1975)

———. *The Moon's a Balloon: An Autobiography*. G. P. Putnam's Sons. (1972)

O'Brien, Scott. *Ann Harding: Cinema's Gallant Lady*. BearManor Media. (2010)

———. *Ruth Chatterton, Actress, Aviator, Author*. BearManor Media. (2013)

O'Leary, Liam. *The Silent Cinema*. Dutton. (1968)

Osborne, Robert. *Academy Awards Illustrated*. Marvin Miller Enterprises. (1965)

Parish, James Robert. *Hollywood Character Actors*. Rainbow Books. (1979)

———. *MGM Stock Company*. Bonanza Books. (1972)

Peary, Danny. *Guide For the Film Fanatic*. Fireside. (1986)

———, ed. *Close-Ups: The Movie Star Book*. Workman Publishing. (1978)

Penny Stallings. *Flesh And Fantasy*. St. Martin's Press. (1978)

Peters, Margot. *The House Of Barrymore*. Knopf. (November 21, 1990)

Parsh, Robert Seaton, George Oppenheimer. *A Day At the Races*. Viking. (1972)

Pratley, Gerald. *The Cinema Of John Huston*. A.S. Barnes. (1977)

———. *The Cinema Of Otto Preminger*. Castle Books. (1971)

Preminger, Otto. *Preminger*. Doubleday. (April 1977)

Quirk, Lawrence J. *The Films Of Ronald Colman*. Citadel. (1977)

Robinson, David. *Chaplin: His Life and Art*. McGraw-Hill. (1985)

Rogers, Richard. *Musical Stages: An Autobiography*. Da Cap Press. (April 16, 2002)

Sarris, Andrew. *Confessions Of a Cultist*. Simon & Schuster. (1970)

———. *The American Cinema*. E.P. Dutton. (1968)

Sarris, Andrew. *The John Ford Movie Mystery*. Indiana University Press. (1975)

Schatz, Thomas. *The Genius Of the System*. Pantheon. (1988)

Scherle, Victor, William Turner Levy. *The Films Of Frank Capra*. Citadel. (1977)

Scherman, David, ed. *Life Goes To The Movies*. Time-Life Books. (1976)

Scheuer, Steven H. *Movies On TV*. Bantam (1984)

Schickel, Richard. *D. W. Griffith: An American Life*. Simon & Schuster. (1984)

———. *The Men Made The Movies*. Atheneum. (1975)

Secrest, Meryle. *Somewhere For Me*. Applause Theatre & Cinema Books. (2002)

Shipman, David. *The Great Movie Stars*. Hill And Wang. (1972)

Simon, John. *Reverse Angle*. Clarkson N. Potter. (1982)

Sinclair, Andrew. *John Ford*. Dial Press. (1979)

Sinclair, Upton. *William Fox*. Upton Sinclair. (1933)

Skinner, Kiron. *Read On: A Life In Letters*. Free Press. (2004)

Spring, Calra, Madeline Goss. *Yoga For Today*. Holt Rinehart And Winston. (1959)

Springer, John. *All Talking, All Singing, All Dancing*. Citadel. (1966)

St. Johns, Adela Rogers. *Love Laughter And Tears*. Doubleday. (1978)

Steen, Max. *Hollywood Speaks: An Oral History.* G. P. Putnam's Sons. (1974)

Stephenson, Ralph. *The Cinema As Art.* Penguin. (1965)

Sturges, Preston. *Preston Sturges: His Life And Work.* Simon & Schuster. (1990)

Talbot, Daniel. *Film: An Anthology.* University of California Press. (1967)

Teichmann, Howard. *George Kaufman: An Intimate Portrait.* Atheneum Press. (1972)

Thomas, Bob. *King Cohn: The Life and Times Of Harry Cohn.* Bantam Books. (1967)

———. *Thalberg: Life and Legend.* Doubleday. (1969)

Thomas, Lawrence. *The MGM Years.* Columbia House. (1971)

Thomas, Tony. *The Films Of the Forties.* Citadel Press. (1975)

Thomson, David. *Showman: The Life Of David O. Selznick.* Alfred A. Knopf. (1992)

Tibbetts, John, James Welsh. *The Cinema Of D. Fairbanks, Sr.* A.S. Barnes. (1977)

Tornabebe, Lyn. *Long Live The King.* G.P. Putnam's Sons. (1976)

Tranberg, Charles. *Fredric Mach: A Consummate Actor.* BearManor Media. (2013)

Trent, Paul. *The Fabulous Movie Years: The 1930s.* Barre-Crown Publishing. (1975)

Tyler, Parker. *Magic and Myth of the Movies.* Simon & Schuster. (1947)

———. *Sex In Films.* Citadel. (1974)

———. *The Hollywood Hallucination.* Simon & Schuster. (1970)

Vance, Malcolm F. *The Movie Quiz Book.* Paperback Library. (1970)

Vieira, Mark. *Irving Thalberg: Boy Wonder.* University Of California Press. (2010)

Vizzard, Jack. *See No Evil.* Simon & Schuster. (1970)

Walker, Alexander. *Sex In the Movies.* Pelican. (1969)

Wellman, William. *A Short Time For Insanity.* Hawthorn Books. (1974)

Wellman, William, Jr. *Wild Bill Wellman: Hollywood Rebel.* Pantheon. (2015)

Wollen, Peter. *Signs And Meaning In the Cinema.* Indiana University Press. (1969)

Wood, Robin. *Howard Hawks.* Wayne State University Press. (2006)

Zolotow, Maurice. *Billy Wilder In Hollywood.* G.P. Putnam's Sons. (1977)

UNPUBLISHED

Actors' Equity Withdrawal Card, Unsigned. November 11, 1959.

American Federation of TV and Radio Artists Withdrawal Card. November 1, 1965.

Announcement Card. Clara Spring Studio. Season 1961-1962.

Astor, Mary. Autobiographical Writings. June 1955.

————. Autobiographical Writings. December 25, 1955.

————. Autobiographical Writings. November 21, 1957.

————. Baby Diary. 1932-1935.

————. Christmas Card. Undated.

————. Diary Excerpts. 1932-1935.

————. Draft of Telegram to Barrymore Regarding Mrs. Carrington. Undated.

————. Henrietta Log. May 7–June 22, 1932.

————. Letter Regarding Groucho Marx Show. Undated.

————. Letter Regarding Costume Purchase. November 1, 1962.

————. Letter Regarding "The Defenders" Appearance. November 16, 1962.

————. Letter To Book Agent Gloria Safier Re: Autobiography. June 19, 1957.

————. Letter To Book Agent Gloria Safier Re: Commercial Work. Undated.

————. Note To Book Editor Gloria Safier Re: Press. January 22, 1958.

————. Letter To Book Agent Gloria Safier Re: Agent Fees. September 2, 1959.

————. Letter To Book Agent Gloria Safier. June 9, 1960.

————. Letter To Book Agent Gloria Safier Regarding Campaign. July 9,1960.

————. Letter To Book Agent Gloria Safier Re: Film Of My Story. April 20, 1961.

————. Letter To Book Agent Gloria Safier. April 20, 1961.

————. Letter To Book Agent Gloria Safier. November 9, 1961.

————. Letter To Book Agent Gloria Safier. December 19, 1961.

————. Letter To Book Agent Gloria Safier Re: Writing. January 1, 1962.

————. Letter To Book Agent Gloria Safier Re: The O'Conners. July 4, 1963.

————. Letter To Book Editor Gloria Safier Re: Aging. August 21, 1963.

————. Letter To Book Editor Gloria Safier Re: Movie Location. July 7, 1964.

————. Letter To Book Agent Gloria Safier Re: Race Riots. July 26, 1964.

————. Letter To Book Agent Gloria Safier Re: Mexican House. May 22, 1960s.

————. Letter To Book Agent Gloria Safier Re: Discussing Christmas. January 1, 1965.

————. Letter To Book Agent Gloria Safier Re: Book Revision. October 17, 1966.

———. Telegram; Re: Trip To Norway. July 17, 1924.

———. Telegram; Re: Theatrical Plans. July 10, 1924.

———. Telegram; Re: Astor Playing Peter Pan. July 25, 1924.

———. Telegram; Re: Asking When Astor arriving New York. October 7, 1924.

———. Telegram; Re: Arrival in Hollywood From London In May. March 7, 1925.

———. Telegram; Re: Arriving In New York May 5. April 16, 1925.

———. Telegram; Re: Missing Astor. May 29, 1925.

———. Telegram; Re: Joke Engagement. May 31, 1925.

———. Telegram; Re: Plans To Make Moby Dick. June 2, 1925.

———. Telegram; Re: Offers Astor Part *Moby Dick* and *Don Juan*. June 6, 1925.

———. Telegram; Re: Astor Set For *Don Juan*. June 15, 1925.

———. Telegram; Re: Reaction To New Langhanke House. June 17, 1925.

———. Telegram; Re: Reactions to Photos Sent Him. June 30, 1925.

———. Telegram; Re: Lubitsch Will Not Direct *Don Juan*. July 13, 1925.

———. Telegram; Re: Working On Moby Dick. July 19, 1925.

———. Telegram; Re: Astor's Performance in *Don Q*. July 22, 1925.

———. Telegram; Re: Astor Playing Lady Anne In *Richard III*. July 30, 1925.

———. Telegram; Re: Possible *Don Juan* Shooting Schedule. July 20, 1925.

———. Telegram; Re: Clearing Up *Don Juan* Contract Signing. August 4, 1925.

———. Telegram; Re: Seeing Astor Again. August 6, 1925.

———. Telegram; Re: *Don Juan* Interpretation. August 19, 1925.

———. Telegram; Re: Lubitsch Might Still Direct *Don Juan*. September 2, 1925.

———. Telegram; Re: Astor's Costumes For *Don Juan*. September 10, 1925.

CBS. Contract For Playhouse 90. November 4, 1958.

Chief Dull Knife, Christmas Poem. Undated.

———. Letter to Marylyn Roh. January 19, 1967.

Claiborne, Ross. Note to Safier Re: Royalties. Nov 13, 1968.

Interlocutory Judgment Of Divorce. August 31, 1953.

Editing Notes For *My Story*. Undated.

Kapiolani Maternity & Gynecological Hospital. Bill For Care. June 21, 1932.

Matsonia: Manifest Of Alien Passengers. May 6, 1938.

MGM. Autograph Consent Form. November 8, 1946.

———. Permission Letter to Mary Astor. June 6, 1944.

Money Order to Son, Anthony del Camp. February 13, 1971.

NBC. Today Show File Reference for Mary Astor Appearance. June 2, 1976.

Note To Astor Re: Possible Magazines For Publication Of Story. Undated.

News Syndicate-Photo Release Authorization. May 16, 1944.

Parker V. James Granger, Inc. 1935. Decision On Hawks Plane Crash Lawsuit. L A Nos. 15204 to 15211, Inclusive. Cal. Sup. Ct. November 29-35.

Passport. Mary Astor. Issued October 2, 1963.

Purchase Agreement For Cemetery Plot. November 9, 1961.

Residual Rental Agreement-Thousand Oaks, Tennyson Street Apartment. May 3, 1972.

Safier, Gloria. Letter To Astor Concerning 1964 Presidential Election. July 29, 1964.

————. Letter To Astor Regarding Book Club Monies. November 14, 1968.

Stoddard, Carole. Memorandum Re: Book Club Royalties. November 11, 1968.

Thorpe, Franklyn. "Alice's Birthday." Undated Poem.

————. "Record For File In Connection With Custody Trial." Payment Memorandum regarding Final Payment to Joseph Anderson. July 19, 1937.

————. Telegram To Amanda Wright. June 15, 1932.

————. Telegram To Secretary Re: Marylyn's Birth. Dated June 15, 1932.

————. Thoughts On Sister Alice Thorpe's Death. October 5, 1916.

PERIODICALS

"All Those Memories Going." *Life*. 5-22-70: P41.

Crews, Watson. "Dr. Thorpe's Unhappy Year." *American Weekly*. 5-16-48: P4.

Daniel H. Silberberg. *The New Yorker*. 5-22-84: P134.

Driscoll, Marjorie. "Mary Astor's Baby." Uncited Clipping-*King Features*. 1938.

"End Of a Diary." *Time*. 7-28-52.

"Hollywood Goes White Over Mary's Purple Ink." *Newsweek*. 8-22-36: P17.

Jacobson, L. "Mary Astor's Scandalous Diary." *Hollywood Studio Mag*. 11-88: P15.

Jahr, Cliff. "Hollywood Scandals." Undated Clipping.

John Barrymore. *Vanity Fair*. 10-92: P310.

Lake, Veronica, Niven Busch. "I Veronica Lake." *Life*. P77.

"Life Calls On Hollywood Kids." *Life*. 1-10-44: P98.

"Mary Astor Blushes When Her Filthy Diary Leaks." *New York Magazine*. 4-9-12: P44.

"Okay, Print It Mary Astor." *American Film*. 4-76.

Palmer, Gretta. "A Girl's Best Friend Is Her Opposite." Photoplay. 1-38: P22.

"Scandals." *People Magazine*. 2-9-87.

Schulberg, Budd. "How Are Things In Panicsville?" *Life*. 12-20-63: P79.

"Terry Hunt's Job." *Life*. 7-15-40: P55.

"That's All There Is…" *Life Magazine*. 6-29-59: P116.

"The Girls Mix It Up." *Life*. 2-28-55: P48.

"The New Pictures." *Time*. 9-28-36.

"Thorpe vs. Astor." *Time*. 8-17-36: P42.

"Thorpe vs. Astor 2." *Time*. 8-24-36.

Watters, Jim. "Whatever Became Of Mary Astor." "Life. 2-80: P112.

NEWSPAPERS

"10 Men Named In Astor Diary." *NY Mirror*. 8-7-36: P1.

"100,000 To Hush Diary." *NY Mirror*. 8-10-36: P1.

"1-2-3 In Mary Astor's Charm List." *London Daily Express*. 8-8-36: P1.

"1st Pages From Astor Diary." *NY Daily News*. 8-11-36: P1.

"2 Previous Marriages Of Dr. Thorpe Revealed." *NY American*. 8-7-36: P5.

"3-sided Battle of Wits Over Astor Diary." *LA Evening Herald Express*. 8-12-36: P1.

"A Lonely Bride Is Mary Astor." *NY Sun*. 2-19-37.

"A Memo For Dear Diary: Married." *NY American*. 2-19-37.

"Accord Gives Child To Mary Astor." *NY American*. 8-12-36: P1.

"Accord In Astor Case." *NY Evening Journal*. 8-11-36: P1.

"Actress Diary To Be Offered In Court Case." *Evening Independent*. 7-28-36.

"Actress Fights." *LA Examiner*. 7-14-36: P1.

"Actress May Pay Visit To Los Angeles." *LA Evening Herald Express*. 7-31-36: P3.

"Actress Tells Love For Child." *NY Sun*. 7-31-36: P3.

"Acts Condoned Says Miss Astor." *NY Times*. 8-4-36: P1, 5.

"Actual From Astor Diary Relates Tryst." *LA Times*. 8-12-36: P2.

"Admirer Travels Far To Attend Astor Trial." *LA Times*. 8-14-36: P2.

"Another Thorpe Bride Revealed." *NY Evening Journal*. 8-7-36: P4.

"Are You In The Diary Is Newest Hollywood Game." *LA Examiner*. 8-12-36: P3.

"Asbestos Heir Home To Quench Astor Fires." *NY Mirror*. 8-4-36: P1, 2.

"Asking No Quarter." *NY American*. 8-2-36: P6.

"Astor Affair O.K. To Wife Of Kaufman." *NY Daily News*. 8-5-36.

"Astor Armistice Splits Custody, Buries Diary." *Herald Tribune*. 8-13-36.

"Astor Attorneys Sift Thorpe Past." *LA Examiner*. 8-4-36: P1.

"Astor Baby To Have Say In Visit With Judge." *NY Evening Journal*. 8-1-36: P5.

"Astor Battle Ends As Judge Approves Pact." *NY Sun*. 8-13-36.

"Astor Battle Ends As Judge Demands Diary." *NY Sun*. 8-13-36: P1.

"Astor Beaux Sigh Special." *NY Mirror*. 8-9-36: P3.

"Astor Case A B'way Worry." *Variety*. 8-12-36: P1.

"Astor Case Cost Him 7 Lbs., Kaufman Admits." *NY Post*. 8-15-36: P1.

"Astor Case Girl Hiding In Hills." *Daily Mirror*. 7-31-36: P3.

"Astor Case In Whisper Stage." *NY Sun*. 8-8-36: P1.

"Astor Case Lid Rumored." *LA Times*. 8-7-36: P3.

"Astor Case Peace Move Fails." *NY Sun*. 8-5-36: P16.

"Astor Case Reopening To Be Sought." *LA Times*. 8-14-36: P1.

"Astor Case Settled." *NY Daily News*. 8-13-36: P1.

"Astor Case Settled: Diary Fate Mystery." *LA Times*. 8-13-36: P1.

"Astor Child Is Judge's Concern." *NY Sun*. 8-7-36: P13.

"Astor Diary Battle Ends." *NY Mirror*. 8-13-36: P1.

"Astor Diary Buried." *NY Sun*. 9-8-36.

"Astor Diary Ecstasy." *NY Daily News*. 8-3-36: P1.

"Astor Diary Holds Key To Fight." *NY Evening Journal*. 7-29-36: P1.

"Astor Diary Is Seen As Bar In Settlement." *NY Sun*. 8-12-36: P1.

"Astor Diary Lists Stars By Charm." *London Daily Express*. 8-7-36: P1.

"Astor Diary Made Public." *LA Times*. 8-11-36: P1.

"Astor Diary May Go Unpublished." *LA Examiner*. 8-8-36: P3.

"Astor Diary Names 5 Actors." *NY Evening Journal*. 8-3-36: P1.

"Astor Diary: Husband's Bid To Frighten." *London Daily Express*. 8-12-36: P9.

"Astor Fight Reopened." *NY Evening Journal*. 8-14-36: P1.

"Astor Judge Speaks The Last Word." *London Daily Express*. 8-15-36: P9.

"Astor Lawyer Draws Rebuke." *LA Examiner*. 8-15-36: P3.

"Astor Love Story Fells One Beauty." *NY Mirror*. 8-1-36: P3.

"Astor Nurse Saw Woman Visit Thorpe." *NY World Telegram*. 7-30-36: P1.

"Astor Penned 'Misstep Diary' for Child, Ex Declares." *NY Daily News*. 7-28-36: P3.

"Astor Says Thorpe Condoned Affair." *NY American*. 8-4-36.

"Astor Sensations Scare Film Moguls." *Sunday NY Daily News*. 8-2-36: P1.

"Astor Settlement Signed." *LA Examiner*. 8-13-36: P1.

"Astor Suit Ends, Mother to Have Child 9 Months." *Herald Tribune*. 8-14-36.

"Astor Suit May Hit 12 More." *LA Examiner*. 8-6-36: P3.

"Astor Suit Pays Dividends." *NY Sun*. 8-15-36: P3.

"Astor Suit Terms-Mary Wins Daughter." *NY Mirror*. 8-12-36: P1.

"Astor Terms." *London Daily Express*. 8-13-36: P1.

"Astor Tilts Love's Diary." *NY Mirror*. 7-29-36.

"Astor Trial Halts; Settlement Near." *NY Times*. 8-12-36: P1.

"Astor Trial Sensations Frighten Moguls Of Filmdom." *NY Daily News*. 8-2-36: P3.

Astor, Mary. "Actress Finds Gift In Faith." *Spokane Daily Chronicle*. 4-4-60: P11.

———. "Am Battling For My Rights." *LA Examiner*. 8-6-36: P3.

———. "Bogie Was For Real." *NY Times*. 4-23-67: P21.

———. "Mary Astor Has First Day." *NY Evening Journal*. 8-17-36.

———. "Court Rules Out The Astor Diary." *Chicago Tribune*. 1-23-59: P2.

"Astor's Baby To Judge Row." *NY Daily News*. 8-1-36: P1.

"Astor's Big 10." *NY Mirror*. 8-11-36: P3.

"Astor's Diary Names Lover." *NY Daily News*. 7-30-36: P1.

"Astor's Ex's Love Life Bares." *NY Evening Journal*. 7-30-36: P1.

"Astor-Thorpe Suit Reported Nearly Settled." *Herald Tribune*. 8-12-36: P3.

Atkinson, Brooks. *Play Review*. 2-1-40.

"Attempt For Peace In Astor Case Fails." *LA Examiner*. 8-2-36: P2.

"Attends Film Preview." *NY Sun*. 9-17-36.

"Attorney Dies In Auto Crash." *Los Angeles Times*. 4-4-41.

Baer, Arthur. "Dear Diary." *LA Examiner*. 8-17-36: P1.

Bancroft, G. "Mary Astor Diary Lures Hollywood To Trial." *NY Evening Journal*. 7-29-36: P4.

"Bare Astor Mate's Loves." *NY Evening Journal*. 7-30-36: P1.

"Bare Love Diary Of Mary Astor." *NY Daily News*. 7-28-36: P1.

"Bare Mary Astor Diary Kaufman Affair." *LA Evening Herald Express*. 8-10-36: P1.

"Bare New Astor Diary Secrets." *NY Daily News*. 8-12-36: P1.

Barnes Eleanor. "Astor To Rear Child." *World Telegram*. 8-14-36.

———. "Too Bad Mary Astor Learned To Write." *World Telegram*. 8-10-36: P4.

———. "Pals Frolic While Mary Fights Suit." *Pittsburg Press*. 8-11-36.

Barron, Mark. "New York: Today And Yesterday." *Sandusky Register*. 9-10-31: P4.

"Barrymore Call Fixed." *LA Times*. 7-30-36: P2.

"Barrymore Next In Astor Diary." *NY Daily News*. 8-4-36: P1.

"Barrymore Next." *NY Mirror*. 8-9-36: P3.

"Barrymore Seriously Ill." *NY Daily News*. 8-5-36.

"Barrymore Suit Opens." *LA Times*. 8-6-36: P2.

"Barrymore's Ex-Man Friday Says He Shooed Away Elaine." *New York Post*. 6-2-36.

"Battle Over Astor Diary Delays Settlement Of Case." *LA Examiner*. 8-12-36: P1.

"Beauty In Astor Suit Collapses." *NY American*. 8-1-36: P1.

Belser, Lee. "Astor Says Autobiography Finished." *Corsicana Daily Sun*. 2-13-58. P18.

"Best Wishes." *NY Daily News*. Undated Clipping: P1.

"Betting On Next Kaufman Play." *LA Examiner*. 8-12-36: P3.

"Blonde In Astor Battle Fights Back At Charge." *NY Daily News*. 8-1-36: P3.

"Bon Repos: The Fortress Days Are Gone." *Herald Statesman*. 5-4-62: P20.

"Both Fronts Claim Points." *LA Examiner*. 8-9-36: P20.

"Both Glad Suit To End." *LA Times*. 8-14-36: P2.

"Broadway Knows Kaufman As Money, Not Love Maker." *World Telegram*. 8-11-36: P1.

"Broadway Rues Kaufman Slip." *NY Mirror*. 8-7-36.

Bromley, D. "Women Only Seem Addicted To Diaries." *World Telegram*. 8-6-36: P1.

Burton, Tony. "Diary Mystery Rivals Maltese Falcon." *NY Daily News*. 9-27-87.

———. "She Was Star Of Scandal." *NY Daily News*. 9-27-87: P4.

Cameron, Douglas. "When Hollywood Was Really Wild." *NY Daily News*. 9-18-57: P3.

Cameron, Kate. "Dodsworth." *NY Daily News*. 9-24-36.

"Candid Camera Depicts Emotions." *LA Times*. 7-31-36: P1.

"Cast In Real Life Drama." *LA Evening Herald Express*. 7-29-36: P2.

"Casual Friend, Cerf Asserts." *World Telegram*. 8-11-36: P17.

"Center Court Fight." *LA Evening Herald Express*. 8-11-36.

"Chief Points In Ruling Settling Astor Case." *NY Evening Journal*. 8-15-36: P4.

"Child Fight Explained By Actress' Lawyer." *LA Times*. 8-14-36: P2.

"Child In Legal Battle Placed Under Guard." *LA Times*. 8-15-36: P3.

Churchill, Allen. "Was He The Greatest Hamlet?" *NY Times*. 11-14-82: P6.

"Coerced Into Divorce, Mary Astor Charges." *NY Herald Tribune*. 7-14-36.

"Coerced Into Giving Divorce." *LA Examiner*. 7-14-36: P1.

"Come On Is Kissless Greeting of Kaufman To Wife." *Brooklyn Eagle*. 8-27-36.

"Compromise In Custody Fight May Blow Up." *LA Evening Herald Express*. 8-12-36: P1.

"Contrite Mary Hangs Up Pen Forever." *NY Mirror*. 8-13-36: P3.

Coons, Robbin. "Hollywood Sights And Sounds." *Niagara Falls Gazette*. 12-21-33: P17.

"Court Burns Astor Diary." *NY Times*. 7-19-52.

"Court Counsel Confer Over Mary Astor Case." *LA Evening Herald Express.* 7-28-36: P1.

"Court Decree Ends Mary Astor's Suit." *NY Times.* 8-14-36: P1.8.

"Court In Mystery Move Halts Astor's Story." *LA Evening Herald Express.* 8-11-36: P1.

"Court Rebukes Rival Lawyers In Astor Case." *NY Sun.* 8-11-36.

"Court Spurs Kaufman Hunt." *NY Evening Journal.* 8-15-36: P1.

"Court To Admit Diary In Case." *LA Examiner.* 8-4-36: P3.

"Court To Seize Astor Diary." *NY Evening Journal.* 8-12-36: P1.

"Court Trap Set For Mary Astor." *NY Mirror.* 8-6-36: P3.

"Custody Pact Signatures." *LA Times.* 8-14-36: P2.

Dakin, Roger. "Astor Battle Is Closed Forever." *NY Daily News.* 8-14-36: P3.

———. "Astor Case Imperiled." *NY Daily News.* 8-14-36: P3.

———. "Astor Child To Judge Parents." *NY Daily News.* 8-1-36: P3.

———. "Astor Diary Rates 10 Top Movie Lovers." *NY Daily News.* 8-7-36: P3.

———. "Astor Ex-Mate Brings Love Diary To Court." *NY Daily News.* 8-4-36: P3.

———. "Love Diary Bares 'Ecstasy' With Kaufman." *NY Daily News.* 8-3-36: P3.

———. "Trial Deadlocked Over Who Gets Diary." *NY Daily News.* 8-12-36: P3.

———. "Diary Bares Mary's First Love Lesson." *NY Daily News.* 8-6-36: P3.

———. "Hint Settlement Of Astor Suit." *NY Daily News.* 8-9-36: P3.

———. "John Barrymore To Be Called." *NY Daily News.* 8-4-36: P3.

———. "Judge Orders Clean-Up Speed In Trial." *NY Daily News.* 8-12-36: P3.

———. "Kaufman Vanishes; Astor Diary Is Bared." *NY Daily News.* 8-11-36: P3.

———. "Kaufman Vanishes As Mary Testifies II." *NY Daily News.* 8-11-36: P3.

———. "Kaufman Vanishes As Mary Testifies." *NY Daily News.* 8-11-36: P3.

———. "Lured To Alter By Mary's Love Making." 8-5-36. *NY Daily News.* P3.

———. "Mary Recovers Baby. Court Holds Diary." *NY Daily News.* 8-13-36: P3.

———. "Misstep Diary Issue Settled." *NY Daily News.* 8-13-36: P3.

———. "Mystery Woman To Tattle On Thorpe." *NY Daily News.* 8-10-36.

———. "Six Actors Face Astor Diary Grill." *NY Daily News.* 8-2-36: P3.

————. "Threatens Jail." *NY Daily News.* 8-15-36: P8.

————. "Mary Had 3 Other No. 1 Men." *NY Daily News.* 8-8-36: P3.

Daniel H. Silberberg Obituary. *New York Times.* May 9, 1984.

"Dear George Nets Kaufman In Astor Suit." *NY Mirror.* 8-3-36.

Deaths. "Woolley, Roland Rich." *LA Times.* 5-12-79.

"Decision Allotting Child's Time, Excoriates Parents." *NY Daily News.* 8-14-36.

"Defense Gets New Data In Astor Battle." *NY Post.* 8-11-36: P1.

"Deputies Dent To Run Down Playwright." *World Telegram.* 8-10-36: P1.

"Diary 'Accuses' Mary Astor." *NY Daily News.* 7-28-36.

"Diary Adherents Going Strong." *LA Examiner.* 8-20-36: P6.

"Diary Bares Dream Of Holding Kaufman." *NY Evening Journal.* 8-11-36: P1.

"Diary Of Actress Read In Suit." *NY Sun.* 7-28-36: P6.

"Diary Perils Astor Case Armistice." *LA Times.* 8-12-36: P1.

"Diary Read In Court." *NY Daily News.* 8-4-36: P1.

"Diary To Reveal More Charmers." *NY Evening Journal.* 8-11-36: P1.

"Divided Christmas For Her Decreed In Settlement." *NY American.* 12-16-36.

"Doctor's Marital History." *LA Examiner.* 8-6-36: P3.

Doherty, R. "Wife Returns Without Kiss For Kaufman." *NY Daily News.* 8-28-36: P3.

"Dr. Thorpe Ends Rumors In Fight." *NY Evening Journal.* 8-15-36: P1.

"Dr. Franklyn Thorpe Obit." *Variety.* 3-9-77: P87.

"Dr. Thorpe Accuses Star In Affidavit." *LA Evening Herald Express.* 7-30-36: P9.

"Dr. Thorpe Admits Prior Wedding." *NY American.* 8-7-36: P5.

"Dr. Thorpe Denies Ties." *LA Times.* 8-6-36: P2.

"Dr. Thorpe's Move Blocked." *NY Sun.* 8-7-36.

"Dramatist Called To Testify." *NY Evening Journal.* 8-3-36: P1.

"Elusive News Of Son Irks One Of Goodrich's Ex-Wives." *Pittsburg Post Gazette.* 9-12-46.

"Evelyn Laye: I Know Nothing Of Astor Case." *London Daily Express.* 8-6-36: P1.

"Ex-Husband Accuses Mary Astor Of Fraud." *NY Times.* 8-2-36: P2.

"Ex-Mate 'Cruel' To Child Mary Astor Says." *NY Evening Journal.* 7-31-36: P1.

"Extra: Thorpe Yields Baby To Film Star In Pact." *NY Evening Journal.* 8-11-36: P1.

"Extracts From Mary Astor's Diary." *London Daily Express.* 8-11-36: P2.

"Fear Thorpe Will Publish Other Names." *World Telegram.* 8-7-36: P2.

Feller, J. "Secrets In Mary Astor's Face." *NY Daily News.* 8-16-36.

"Fight Looms In Mary Astor's Child Case." *LA Evening Herald Express.* 7-20-36: PB1.

"Fight Opened By Mary Astor." *World Telegram.* 7-28-36: P1.

"Filial Love Undimmed." *LA Examiner.* 8-17-36: P3.

"Film Chiefs Band To End Astor Case." *LA Times.* 8-10-36: P1.

"Film Colony Wonders Who Else Will Be Named." *NY American.* 8-2-36: P1.

"Film Folk Shy At Keeping Diaries." *LA Evening Herald Express.* 8-13-36: P1.1.

"Film Greats Ban Diaries." *LA Examiner.* 8-17-36: P3.

"Film Heads To Give Mary 'A Long Rest.'" *NY Daily News.* 8-17-36.

"Film Producers In Bid To Stop Astor Case." *London Daily Express.* 8-5-36: P3.

"Film Star Dares 'Ruin' For Child." *NY Daily News,* 7-14-36: P1.

"Film Star Will Get Baby Nine Months." *NY Evening Journal.* 8-12-36: P1.

"Film Star's Child May Decide Suit." *NY Sun.* 8-1-36: P9.

"Filmdom Dreads Untold Secrets Of Mary's Diary." *NY Daily News.* 8-16-36: P3.

"Final Chapter Near In Chaplin Divorce." *Reading Eagle.* 8-21-28.

"Final Settlement Follows Quarrel." *LA Evening Herald Express.* 8-13-36: P1.

"Find Kaufman, Astor Judge Orders." *LA Evening Herald Express.* 8-14-36: P1.

"First Astor Romance Was Blighted In Test Chapter 5." *NY Mirror.* 8-12-36.

"Five Astor Witnesses Hunted." *NY Evening Journal.* 8-5-36: P1.

Flint, Peter. "Mary Astor, 81, Is Dead." *NY Times.* 9-26-87.

"Florida Marriage Is Astor Target." *NY Mirror.* 8-5-36.

"Friends Shielded By Astor On Stand." *LA Times,* 8-11-36: P1.

"Friendships Explained." *LA Times.* 8-12-36: P2.

"Gay Thorpe Nights Aired." *LA Times.* 7-30-36: P1.

"George Enters Mary Astor Case." *NY Post.* 7-30-36: P1.

"George Kaufman Hid Behind Mary Astor's Skirt." *NY Evening Journal.* 8-13-36: P3.

"George Kaufman Located In NY." *LA Evening Herald Express.* 8-15-36: P1.

"George S. Kaufman Silent On Astor Case." *NY Herald Tribune.* 8-16-36: P6.

"George: No.1 Kaufman Met By His Wife." *LA Evening Herald Express.* 8-27-36: P1.

Gibson, Stephen. "Attorney's Pioneer Traits." *Desert News.* 11-13-71 P4.

"Girl Wed To Thorpe In '17." *LA Examiner.* 8-6-36: P3.

"Girl's Kin Tells Of Thorpe's Love." *NY Evening Journal.* 8-7-36: P1.

Gwynn. "Hot From Hollywood." *Reading Eagle.* 11-18-33: P9.

———. "Hot From Hollywood." *Reading Eagle.* 11-2-33: P21.

"Happiness Plan Drawn By Mary Chapter 8." *NY Mirror.* 8-15-36.

Harrison, P. "Astor Diaries Scare Filmdom." *World Telegram.* 8-7-36: P1.

"Hawks Taught Mary To Love Literature Chapter 6." *NY Mirror.* 8-13-36.

"Hawks Unit On Retakes When Air Crash." *Variety.* 1-8-30.

Heavy, Hubbard. "Mary Astor Trying To Rear Her Daughter." *Chicago Tribune.* 6-12-41.

"Hint Movie Czars Settle Astor Suit." *Sunday NY Daily News.* 8-9-36: P1.

"Hollywood Actress Charges Physician Sterilized Her." *Pittsburg Press.* 12-23-47.

"Hollywood Diarist and Insurance Man Elope." *NY Sun.* 2-18-37: P1.

"Hollywood Fears Effect." *World Telegram.* 8-6-36: PA6.

"Hollywood Rocked By Kaufman's Role." *LA Examiner.* 8-4-36: P1.

"Hollywood S-S-Shushes Astor Case." *World Telegram.* 8-7-36: P1.

"Hollywood Stirred By New Rift." *NY Evening Journal.* 8-14-36: P1.

"Hunt Five Astor Witnesses." *NY Evening Journal.* 8-5-36: P1.

"Hunt For Kaufman Ordered By Judge." *NY Times.* 8-15-36: P1.3.

"Hurley, Joseph. Barrymore's Hamlet Aimed For the Sublime." *NY Times.* 9-5-93: P5.

"Husband Hypnotized Me. Mary Astor Tells Court." *San Francisco Call-Bulletin.* 8-4-36.

"Husband Is Guardian Of Mary Astor's Daughter." *NY Sun.* April 18-35.

"Hypnotic Control By Mate Told…" *NY Evening Journal.* 8-3-36: P1.

"I Am Forced To Fight Asserts Physician Dr. Thorpe." *NY American.* 8-7-36: P5.

"I Can't Say: Kaufman." *LA Examiner.* 8-10-36: P3.

"I Keep No Diary, Says Kaufman." *LA Times.* 8-16-36: P1.

"I Know About It Says Wife Of Kaufman." *NY Evening Journal.* 8-5-36: P1.

"Illegally Wed Says Mary Astor Suit." *LA Evening Herald Express.* 7-15-36: PA5.

"In Ordeal On Stand." *LA Evening Herald Express.* 8-4-36.

"Interview Show Bills Actress Mary Astor." *Register-Guard.* 11-10-60.

"Irate Judge Pledges Jail For Kaufman." *NY Daily News.* 8-13-36.

"Jail Faced By Kaufman." *LA Times.* 8-12-36: P2.

Johaneson, Bland. "Mary Astor Plays Romantic Lead." *NY Mirror.* 9-24-36.

"John Barrymore Named By Husband." *London Daily Express.* 8-4-36: P3.

Jordan, R. "Cinema Home Fires Aglow–Diaries." *NY Evening Journal.* 8-13-36: P3.

"Judge Calls All Witnesses In Astor Case." *NY Sun.* 8-12-36.

"Judge Child Fail To Dent Astor Enmity." *NY Mirror.* 8-2-36: P3.

"Judge Closes Astor Case." *NY Post.* 8-14-36: P1.

"Judge Confers With Lawyers in Astor Suit." *NY Post.* 8-12-36: P1.

"Judge Demands Astor Secrets." *NY Mirror.* 8-6-36: P1.

"Judge Fails In Plea For Astor Peace." *NY Daily News.* 8-2-36: P3.

"Judge Imposes Terms. Astor Warriors Sulk." *NY Mirror.* 8-14-36: P3.

"Judge Raps Astor Case Attorneys." *LA Times.* 8-15-36: P1.

"Judge Says He Has 'High Hopes' For Compromise." *NY Evening Journal.* 8-12-36: P1.

"Judge Stunned By Astor Diary." *Daily Mirror.* 8-14-36: P1.

"Judge Tests Astor Child's Filial Love." *LA Times.* 8-2-36: P1.

"Judge Tests Child's Love." *London Daily Express.* 8-8-36: P1.

"Judge To See Astor Child At Home Of Screen Star." *World Telegram.* 8-1-36: P4.

"Just Casual Friend Says Bennett Cerf." *NY American.* 8-11-36.

"Just Patient: Actress Denies Undue Thorpe Friendship." *LA Examiner.* 7-31-36: P6.

"Kaufman Called As Astor Witness." *NY American.* 8-3-36: P1.

"Kaufman Called In Astor Case." *NY Sun.* 8-3-36: P7.

"Kaufman Called In Mary Astor Litigation." *Herald Tribune.* 8-3-36.

"Kaufman Forgiven." *NY Sun.* 3-12-37.

"Kaufman Here Not Bitter." *NY American.* 8-16-36.

"Kaufman Here." *NY Mirror.* 8-16-36: P1.

"Kaufman Here: Sad For Wife." *Daily Mirror.* 8-16-36.

"Kaufman Here. No. 1 Man Talks." *NY Daily News.* 8-16-36: P1.

"Kaufman Inveigled Mary, Says Thorpe." *NY Mirror.* 8-14-36: P3.

"Kaufman Is Ordered Arrested." *NY Sun.* 8-14-36: P1.

"Kaufman Linked In Astor Suit." *NY Sun.* 8-4-36: P1.1.

"Kaufman Out Of Hiding." *World Telegram.* 8-15-36: P1.

"Kaufman Parries Astor Case Queries." *NY Times.* 8-16-36: P2.

"Kaufman Reunion Kissless." *NY Mirror.* 8-28-36: P1.

"Kaufman Role In Real Life Drama Stirs Filmdom." *NY American.* 8-5-36.

"Kaufman Scared, Dr. Thorpe Says." *LA Examiner.* 8-6-36: P3.

"Kaufman Subpoenaed As Mystery George." *NY Post.* 8-3-36: P1.

"Kaufman Tells Own Story In NY Home." *NY Evening Journal.* 8-15-36: P1.

"Kaufman To 'Explain' Tryst." *NY Evening Journal.* 8-4-36: P1.

"Kaufman To Flee Coast." *NY Evening Journal.* 8-10-36: P1.

Abrams, Norma. "Kaufman Turns Up In NY." *NY Daily News.* 8-16-36: P3.

"Kaufman Warrant Dropped On Coast." *NY American.* 4-1-37.

"Kaufman, Safe From Subpoena In NY, Talks." *LA Examiner.* 8-16-36: P1.

"Kaufman's Own Story." *NY Evening Journal.* 8-15-36: P1.

"Kaufman's Wife In Icy Greeting." *LA Examiner*. 8-28-36: P3.

"Kaufman's Wife Mute." *LA Times*. 8-28-36: P1.

"Kaufman's Wife Says She Knew All About Astor." *NY Mirror*. 8-5-36: P3.

"Kaufman's Words Are All Platonic." *NY Daily News*. 8-17-36.

"Kenneth Hawks Obit." *Variety*. 1-8-30.

"Kin Of Thorpe's 1st 'Wife' Ready To Aid Mary." *NY Evening Journal*. 8-8-36: P3.

"Lawyers Of Both Sides Believe Fight Near End." *LA Times*. 8-12-36: P2.

"Lawyers Row Perils Astor Pact." *NY Evening Journal*. 8-14-36: P1.

"Legendary Actress Dies." *Lyons Daily News*. 9-25-87.

"Letter To Editor: Reply To Van Loon H. Weinberger." *NY Times*. 8-26-36: P20.

"Lillian Angered By Astor Truce." *NY Mirror*. 8-12-36.

"Little Marylyn Is My Life, Says Actress Mary Astor." *NY American*. 8-7-36: P5.

"Loves Of Mary Astor Told." *NY Evening Journal*. 7-30-36: P1.

"Man To Man Talk Bared By Doctor." *LA Evening Herald Express*. 8-5-36: P1.

"Marylyn Astor Greets Judge In Custody Quiz." *LA Evening Herald Express*. 8-1-36: P1.

"Marion Spitzer Obit." *NY Times*. 7-22-83.

"Marcus Goodrich Obit." *NY Times*. 10-22-91.

"Mary Admits Kaufman Is Her George." *NY Mirror*. 8-4-36: P3.

"Mary Admits Kaufman Love." *NY Mirror*. 8-4-36.

"Mary Alice Woolley: Obit." *Desert News*. 8-18-03.

"Mary Astor Admired Kaufman 10 Years Ago." *LA Examiner*. 8-15-36: P3.

"Mary Astor Alleges Hypnotism." *London Daily Express*. 8-4-36: P1.

"Mary Astor And New Husband." Undated and Uncited Clipping. 1937.

"Mary Astor And Thorpe Meet With Daughter." *Herald Tribune*. 8-2-36: P2.

"Mary Astor Asks Court To Set Aside Divorce." *Herald Tribune*. 7-15-36.

"Mary Astor Brands Thorpe 'Cruel.'" *NY Evening Journal*. 7-31-36: P1.

"Mary Astor Calls Ex-Mate A Bigamist." *NY Daily News*. 7-15-36: P3.

"Mary Astor Case Closed, Ex-Mate Decides." *NY Evening Journal*. 8-15-36: P1.

"Mary Astor Case Goes On." *NY Times*. 8-10-36: P3.

"Mary Astor Dies." *Variety*. 9-30-87.

"Mary Astor Divorced By Physician Husband." *NY Times*. 4-13-35: P10.

"Mary Astor Faces Court." *NY American*. 7-29-36: P3.

"Mary Astor Faces Questions On Diary." NY *World Telegram*. 8-3-36: P1.

"Mary Astor Feared Thorpe." *NY Sun*. 8-3-36.

"Mary Astor Fights For Diary." *NY Evening Journal*. 8-12-36: P1.

"Mary Astor Files For Daughter's Custody." *LA Times*. 7-14-36: P1.

"Mary Astor Finds Fame In Contest Chapter 2." *NY Mirror.* 8-8-36.

"Mary Astor Given Injunction." *LA Evening Herald Express.* 7-23-36: PB1.

"Mary Astor Gives Her Ex-Spouse Tit For Tat." *Sunday NY Daily News.* 7-19-36: P4.

"Mary Astor Goes Home, Lonesome On Honeymoon." *NY Post.* 2-19-37.

"Mary Astor Is Sued." *NY Times.* 4-9-35: P24.

"Mary Astor NY Friend Identified." *LA Examiner.* 8-11-36: P2.

"Mary Astor On Stand: Sobs Halt Testimony." *LA Times.* 7-31-36: P1.

"Mary Astor On Witness Stand." *NY Daily News.* 7-31-36: P1.

"Mary Astor Ordered To Rest." *NY American.* 8-17-36.

"Mary Astor Picks Up Pen: Stars Shiver." *NY Daily News.* 9-1-36.

"Mary Astor Prepares For Fight On Diary." *LA Evening Herald Express.* 8-8-36: P2.

"Mary Astor Quickly Won Movie Plaudits Chapter 3." *NY Mirror.* 8-9-36.

"Mary Astor Reveals Truth London." *Daily Express.* 8-14-36: P1.4.

"Mary Astor Says She's Wed." *Herald Tribune.* 2-19-37.

"Mary Astor Says They're Wed." *LA Times.* 2-19-37: P1.

"Mary Astor Sees Thorpe At Home." *NY Sun.* 8-1-36.

"Mary Astor Sobs On Stand." *NY Daily News.* 7-31-36: P1.

"Mary Astor Sobs Over Baby's Woes." *NY Post.* 7-31-36: P1.

"Mary Astor Starts Writing Book." *World Telegram,* 9-1-36.

"Mary Astor Sues Former Husband." *NY Sun.* 7-14-36.

"Mary Astor Takes Child." *NY Mirror.* 10-2-36.

"Mary Astor Tells Her Own Story Of Court Ordeal." *LA Examiner.* 8-19-36: P1.

"Mary Astor Tells Secrets In Court Fight." *LA Examiner.* 8-4-36: P1.

"Mary Astor Ties Up Ex's $60,000 Assets." *NY Daily News.* 7-24-36.

"Mary Astor To Accuse Ex-Mate." *NY Evening Journal.* 7-28-36: P1.

"Mary Astor To Face Love Quiz." *NY Daily News.* 7-30-36: P1.

"Mary Astor To Share Child." *London Daily Express.* 8-12-36: P1.

"Mary Astor To Take Stand In Custody Case." *LA Evening Herald Express.* 7-29-36: P1.

"Mary Astor To Take Stand In Own Defense." *NY Times.* 7-30-36: P2.3.

"Mary Astor Tryst Told." *NY Evening Journal.* 8-3-36: P3.

"Mary Astor Tutored For Stage As Child Chapter 1." *NY Mirror.* 8-7-36.

"Mary Astor Unafraid Of Diary Secrets." *NY American.* 8-5-36: P3.

"Mary Astor Weds Mexican But Returns Home Alone." *Evening Journal.* 2-19-37: P1.

"Mary Astor Weds Mexican In Yuma." *NY Times.* 2-19-37.

"Mary Astor Weeps At Cheers Of Movie Fans." *NY World Telegram.* 2-17-36.

"Mary Astor Weeps, Says Husband Was Cruel." *London Daily Express*. 8-1-36: P1.

"Mary Astor Writes Of Elopement." *NY Daily News*. 2-20-37.

"Mary Astor Ex-Mate Call Holiday Truce." *NY Daily News*. 12-23-36.

"Mary Astor." *St. Louis Post-Dispatch Mag*. April 12-35: P1.

"Mary Astor." Uncited Clipping. January 1937.

"Mary Astor's Career Safe. Hays Won't Act." *NY American*. 8-16-36.

"Mary Astor's Daughter To Wed." *Herald Tribune*. 6-13-50.

"Mary Astor's Diary Aired In Guardianship Contest." *NY Post*. 7-28-36: P1.

"Mary Astor's Diary Bared By Ex-Mate." *NY Evening Journal*. 7-28-36: P1.

"Mary Astor's Diary Gives Kaufman Saga." *NY Evening Journal*. 8-3-36: P3.

"Mary Astor's Diary Goes Into Los Angeles Tomb." *Herald Tribune*. 9-9-36.

"Mary Astor's Diary Secrets Bared In Suit." *LA Examiner*. 7-28-36: P9.

"Mary Astor's Diary." *NY Mirror*. 8-11-36: P3.

"Mary Astor's Ex Put On The Rack In Suit." *NY Post*. 7-29-36: P1.

"Mary Astor's George." *London Daily Express*. 8-17-36: P1.

"Mary Astor's Husband Files Suit For Divorce." *NY Herald Tribune*. 4-9-35.

"Mary Astor's Husband Wants Freedom." *NY Daily News*. 4-9-35.

"Mary Astor's Life Story Begins Today." *LA Examiner*. 8-17-36: P1.

"Mary Astor's Life Story Will Start Tomorrow." *LA Examiner*. 8-16-36: P1.

"Mary Astor's Love Diary Bares Ecstasy." *NY Daily News*. 8-9-36: P3.

"Mary Astor's Own Story." *NY Evening Journal*. 8-3-36: P1.

"Mary Astor's Third." *NY Daily News*. 2-21-37: P46.

"Mary Astor's Writings Quoted In Case." *LA Times*. 7-29-36: P1.

"Mary Gets Baby, Diary To Court." *NY Daily News*. 8-13-36: P1.

"Mary Gets Baby, End Diary Fight." *NY Daily News*. 8-13-36: P1.

"Mary Gets News Of Other Wife." *NY Daily News*. 8-7-36: P1.

"Mary Had A Diary." *NY Mirror*. 8-14-36.

"Mary Learns Diary Lesson, Hangs Up Pen." *NY Daily News*. 8-13-36.

"Mary On Stand Admits Trysts." *NY Daily News*. 8-4-36: P1.

"Mary Tricked." *NY Mirror*. 8-15-36: P1.

"Mary, Thorpe Give Views On Raising Child." *NY Daily News*. 8-14-36.

"Marylyn Has Happy Reunion." *LA Times*. 8-17-36: P1.

"Marylyn's Custody Divided In Truce." *LA Examiner*. 8-14-36: P3.

"Mary's Big 10 All Identified." *NY Mirror*. 8-11-36: P1.

"Mary's Heart-Ache Healed By Thorpe Chapter 7." *NY Mirror*. 8-14-36.

"Mary's Lawyer Probes Thorpe's Florida Loves." *NY Mirror*, 8-5-36: P3.

"Mary's Loves: Kaufman Tops Astor List." *NY Mirror*. 8-7-36: P3.

Marsh, Fred. "Story Of A Fighting Ship." *NY Times*. 2-2-41.

"Mate Condoned Tryst Says Miss Astor." *World Telegram*. 8-4-36: P1.

"Mate Drops Plan To Gag Mary Astor." *NY Mirror*. 8-30-36: P3.

"Mate Knew Of Other Man, Says Astor." *LA Times*. 8-4-36: P1.

"May Settle Astor Suits." *NY Mirror*. 7-29-36: P3.

"Meet Miss Thorpe." *NY Daily News Sunday Mag*. 6-28-36.

"Menjou Lauds Mary Astor." *NY Evening Journal*. 8-7-36: P4.

"Merely His Patient Says Miss Taylor." *NY American*. 7-31-36: P3.

"Miss Astor Charges Severity With Child." *NY Times*. 7-31-36: P16.

"Miss Astor Says Husband Knew Of Kaufman." *Herald Tribune*. 8-4-36: P3.

"Miss Astor's Charge Is Denied." *NY Sun*. 8-6-36: P7.

"Misstep Diary Issue Settled." *NY Daily News*. 8-13-36: P1.

"Mommy's Auto Toots Bring Joy To Marylyn." *LA Times*, 8-13-36: P2.

"More Astor Diary Secrets." *NY Daily News*. 8-12-36: P1.

"More Diary Revelations." *NY Mirror*. 8-12-36.

"More Entries From Astor Diary Loom." *LA Examiner*. 8-2-36: P1.

"More Love Secrets Of Mary Astor Revealed." *LA Examiner*. 8-11-36: P1.

"More Secrets Of Astor Diary." *NY Daily News*. 8-6-36: P1.

Morrison, D. "Tragedy Had Big Role." *NY Evening Journal*. 8-13-36: P3.

"Mother Backs Mary In Court." *LA Examiner*. 8-13-36: P2.

"Mother Love Verses Father's." *LA Examiner*. 8-6-36: P3.

"Mother Of Thorpe Mum On Son's Past." *NY Evening Journal*. 8-7-36: P1.

"Motherhood Changes Mary Astor's Outlook Chapter 9." *NY Mirror*. 8-16-36.

"Movie Moguls Fight Expose In Astor Suit." *NY Daily News*. 7-29-36: P3.

"Movies Fight Astor Expose." *NY Daily News*. 7-29-36: P1.

"Mrs. G. S. Kaufman Returns." *NY Times*. 8-28-36: P20.

"Mrs. Kaufman Denies Rift." *NY Times*. 8-29-36: P6.

"Mrs. Kaufman Forgives Mate." *NY Mirror*. 8-5-36: P1.

"Mrs. Kaufman Greets Husband At Pier." *World Telegram*. 8-27-36: P1.

"Mrs. Kaufman Home, Greeted By Handshake." *NY American*. 8-28-36: P3.

"Mrs. Kaufman Makes Light of Flirtation." *LA Times*. 8-5-36: P3.

"Mrs. Kaufman's Chin Is Up Special." *NY Post*. 8-6-36.

Muir, Florabel. "Film Folks Can Sleep Now." *NY Daily News*. 7-19-52: P4.

"N.J. Wedding Of Thorpe Revealed." *NY Evening Journal*. 8-6-36: P1.

"Name 3 Women In Astor Trial." *NY Daily News*. 7-29-36: P1.

"Names Barrymore And Cerf." *NY Sun*. 8-10-36.

"New Move To Settle Dispute Hunted." *LA Evening Herald Express*. 8-11-36: P1.

"New Secret Is Bared As Mary Drops Quill." *NY Mirror*. 8-13-36.

"No. 1 Lover Stages Act II." *Daily Mirror*. 8-17-36.

"No Kiss To Diary Hero." *NY Mirror*. 8-28-36: P3.

"No Oscar, It Isn't Lockjaw." *NY Post*. 8-12-35: P1.

"Norma Denies Tryst In Home Of Thorpe." *NY Evening Journal*. 7-31-36: P3.

"Norma Taylor At Manville's." *World Telegram*. 8-4-36: P1.

"Norma Taylor Finds Refuge With Manville." *LA Examiner*. 8-5-36: P4.

"Norma Taylor Hides Following Interview." *LA Evening Herald Express*. 7-31-36: P8.

"Norma Taylor Lawyer Probes Testimony." *LA Examiner*. 8-2-36: P2.

"Norma Taylor Shuns Press At Manville's." *NY Daily News*. 8-5-36.

"Norma Warns On Slurs In Astor Case." *NY Evening Journal*. 8-1-36: P5.

"Norma Worn By Astor Case." *NY Post*. 8-4-36: P1.

"Not Worried About Husband." *LA Times*. 8-17-36: P20.

"Noted Writer In Astor Quiz." *LA Examiner*. 8-3-36: P5.

"Nurse Describes Thorpe Parties." *LA Examiner*. 7-30-36: P3.

"Nurse Tells Hollywood Scandal." *NY Sun*. 7-30-36: P6.

"Odd Court At Home Of Actress." *LA Evening Herald Express*. 8-1-36: P1.

"On Solo Honeymoon." *NY Mirror*. 2-20-37: P3.

"Orders Arrest Of Kaufman In Astor Case." *NY World Telegram*. 8-10-36: P1.

"Other Wife Of Thorpe Is Held Ruse Of Widow Special." *NY Daily News*. 8-9-36: P3.

"Pages Of Mary Astor's Diary." *NY Mirror*. 8-11 36: P1.

"Parents Aided Mary In Custody Battle Chapter 10." *NY Mirror*. 8-17-36.

"Parents' Suit For Support Now Forgotten." *LA Examiner*. 8-8-36: P3.

Parsons, Louella. Column. *Milwaukee Sentinel*. 5-5-36: P21.

Parton, Lemuel. "Who's News Today." *NY Sun*. 7-16-36.

"Peace Reigns Over Kaufman Marriage." *NY American*. 8-29-36: P3.

"Perjury Hint Brings Check On Witnesses." *World Telegram*. 8-11-36: P1.

"Persons Named In Astor Case Threaten Suit." *NY Post*. 8-13-36: P1.

"Play Based On Diary?" *NY American*. 8-12-36.

"Playwright Greets His Wife At NY." *LA Examiner*. 8-28-66: P1.

"Playwright Hunted As New Trial Banned." *LA Evening Herald Express*. 8-14-36: P1.

"Playwright Reveals He Kept No Diary." *LA Evening Herald Express*. 8-15-36: P1.

"Playwright Silent On Astor Case." *NY Evening Journal*. 8-17-36: P3.

"Playwright To Testify." *LA Times*. 8-8-36: P1.

"Pleas To Drop Case Rejected By Mary Astor." *World Telegram*. 8-5-36: P1.

"Previous Wedding Denied By Thorpe." *NY Times*. 8-6-36: P2.

"Prim Movie Roles Irked Mary Astor Chapter 4." *NY Mirror*. 8-10-36.

"Probe Thorpe Florida Loves." *Daily Mirror*. 8-5-36: P1.

"Probers Fail To Find Thorpe's Marriage." *NY Evening Journal*. 8-8-36: P3.

"Prosecutor Enters Astor Case." *World Telegram*. 8-11-36: P1.

"Quits Mary Astor." *NY Sun.* 4-9-36.

"Receives Divorce From Mary Astor." *NY Sun.* 4-12-35.

"Report Truce In Astor Fight For Daughter." *World Telegram.* 8-12-36: P1.

"Reveal Charm Rating In Mary Astor Diary." *LA Evening Herald Express.* 8-6-36: P1.

Reynolds, R. "When Dear Diary Becomes Tattler." *NY Daily News.* 8-9-36: P5.

"Rift Imperils Astor Truce." *NY Daily News.* 8-14-36: P1.

"Risked All For Baby Declares Mary Astor." *LA Examiner.* 8-14-36: P3.

Rochlen A. "Direct From Heart: I Begged For Baby." *LA Examiner.* 8-19-36: P1.

Roe, Dorothy. "Actress Reveals Disillusionment Part 7." *LA Examiner.* 8-23-36: P2.

———. "Astor Accord Nearly Upset." *NY American.* 8-14-36: P1.

———. "Astor Grilled About Kaufman—He Vanishes." *NY American.* 8-11-36: P1.

———. "Astor Suit End Splits Custody, Impounds Diary." *NY Mirror.* 8-13-36: P3.

———. "Custodian For Mary Astor's Diary." *NY American.* 8-13-36: P1.

———. "Diary Balks Astor Settlement." *NY American.* 8-12-36.

———. "Fate Dealt Hard With Mary Astor Part 3." *LA Examiner.* 8-19-36: P6.

———. "Film Folk In Fear Seek Astor Truce." *NY American.* 8-9-36: PL3.

———. "I'm Betting On Mary Astor." *King Features.* 1937: P5.

———. "Life Seems Worth Living Part 6." *LA Examiner.* 8-22-36: P1.

———. "Love Happiness Still Mirage Part 8." *LA Examiner.* 8-24-36: P2.

———. "Mary Astor Bars Peace At Any Price." *NY American.* 8-10-36.

———. "Mary Astor Grilled On Kaufman." *NY American.* 8-11-36: P1.

———. "Mary Astor I Was Serious, Intense Part 2." *LA Examiner.* 8-18-36: P1.

———. "Mary Astor Story Part 4." *LA Examiner.* 8-20-36: P6.

———. "Mary Astor's Diary Feared By Hollywood." *NY American.* 8-9-36.

———. "Mary Astor's Diary Subpoenaed." *NY American.* 8-12-36.

———. "Mary Astor's Life An Amazing Story Pt 1." *LA Examiner.* 8-17-36: P5.

———. "Thorpe To Bare Mary Astor's Diary Secrets." *NY American.* 8-8-36: P3.

———. "Mary Astor's Story Pt 5." *LA Examiner.* 8-21-36: P9.

"Romance Strikes Reef." *NY Post.* 4-8-35.

"Ruin Dared By Mary Astor In Fight For Child." *NY Daily News.* 7-14-36: P3.

Ryon, Ruth. "Hot Property." *LA Times.* 7-25-04.

"Says Astor Diary Action Broke Him." *NY Sun*. 3-11-37.

"Says Mary Astor Abandoned Child." *NY Times*. 8-1-36: P1.

"Scandal Hit The Star Public Says So What." Sunday *NY Mirror Magazine*. 8-30-36.

"Screen Lover No. 1 Named." *London Daily Express*. 8-4-36: P1.

"Seeks Tampa Evidence To Aid Mary Astor." *NY Times*. 8-5-36: P1.

Seely, Nancy. "Famous Custody Battles." *NY Post*. 9-7-64.

"Should Girl Keep Love Diary?" *LA Evening Herald Express*. 8-12-36: P1.

"Should Mary Astor's Diary Be Returned?" *LA Examiner*. 8-15-36: P3.

Skolsky, Sidney. "Tintypes." *NY Post*. 9-30-36.

"Snapshots Shown In Astor Battle." *LA Examiner*. 8-10-36. P3.

"Sought On Warrant In Custody Battle." *NY Evening Journal*. 8-11-36: P1.

Spencer, S. "Mary Astor's Writing Reveals Impulsive Action." *NY Daily News*. 8-13-36.

Spitzer, A. "Her Rise From Star To Mother." *Brooklyn Eagle Mag*. 9-17-33: P1.5.

"Stage Set For Astor Showdown." *LA Evening Herald Express*. 8-7-36: P1.

"Star Discovered By D.W. Griffith." *LA Examiner*. 8-13-36: P2.

"Star Faces Battering Queries." *LA Examiner*. 8-11-36: P1.

"Star Looks Tired." *LA Examiner*. 8-11-36: P2.

"Star Makes Hot Reply To Mate's Sizzling Charges." *LA Examiner*. 7-31-36: P5.

"Star Parries Warrant Issued For Playwright." *LA Evening Herald Express*. 8-10-36: P1.

"Star Tells Of Her Fear Of Mate." *LA Evening Herald Express*. 8-3-36: P1.

"Star Wants Truth To Be Told." *LA Evening Herald Express*. 8-4-36: P1.

"Star Wins Week-end Custody Battle." *LA Evening Herald Express*. 8-13-36: P1.

"Star's Counsel Irks Anderson." *LA Examiner*. 8-14-36: P1.

"Star's Diary To Be Read." *London Daily Express*. 8-3-36: P1.

"Stars Live In Dread Of Diary's Secrets." *NY Daily News*. 8-16-36: P1.

"Star's Secret: First Photo Of A Page From Love Book." *LA Examiner*. 8-12-36: P2.

"Story Sobbed By Mary Astor." *World Telegram*. 7-31-36: P1.

"Strain Of Ordeal Shown By Actress In Contest." *LA Times*. 8-11-36: P5.

"Strangers." *LA Examiner*. 8-14-36: P3.

"Studio Head Denies Rift With Astor." *LA Examiner*. 8-22-36: P14.

"Subpoenas Kaufman In Astor Hearing." *NY Times*. 8-3-36: P11.

"Sued, Mary Astor Gives Up Child." *NY Daily News*. 4-9-35.

"Tampa Hunts Proof Of Thorpe Nuptials." *NY Evening Journal*. 8-8-36: P3.

"Fell Like A Ton Of Bricks." *LA Evening Herald Express*. 8-10-36: P1.

"Tells Meeting Playwright On Trip In East." *LA Times.* 8-11-36: P1.

"Terms For Ending Astor Case Drawn." *NY Times.* 8-13-36: P7.

"Terms Of Astor Case Settlement." *NY Mirror.* 8-13-36.

"Terms Of Astor Settlement." *NY Daily News.* 8-14-36: P1.

"Text Of Astor Victory Claim." *NY Evening Journal.* 8-15-36: P4.

"Text Of Court Decision." *LA Times.* 8-14-36: P2.

"Text Of Testimony By Screen Star." *NY Evening Journal.* 8-3-36: P1.

"Thalberg Makes Move For Peace." *LA Examiner.* 8-9-36: P20.

"The Mother Should Have The Child." Editorial. *NY Daily News.* 7-15-36.

"They Figure In Suit." *LA Examiner.* 8-12-36: P3.

"They're Man And Wife Now." *NY Mirror.* 2-1937: P1.

"This Diary May Not Be Scarlet But It's All Red." *LA Examiner.* 8-16-36: P1.

Thomas, B. "Tells How Film Brass Tried To Gag Her." *Newark Star-Ledger.* 1-7-59: P3.

Thompson, George C. "Judge Orders Arrest." *London Daily Express.* 8-11-36: P1.

"Thorpe And Tiny Daughter Hold Playful Reunion." *LA Examiner.* 8-17-36: P3.

"Thorpe Attorney Will Move To Reopen Case." *LA Examiner.* 8-14-36.

"Thorpe Baby In Gay Mood." *LA Times.* 8-17-36: P1.

"Thorpe Bares 3 New Astor Loves." *NY Daily News.* 8-8-36: P1.

"Thorpe Denies Bigamy Charge." *World Telegram.* 8-6-36: P2.

"Thorpe Denies Links To Mary Astor Nurse." *World Telegram.* 7-29-36: P1.

"Thorpe Explains Child's Return To Mary Astor." *LA Examiner.* 7-29-36.

"Thorpe Hoped Daughter Would Benefit Mary Astor." *Herald Tribune.* 7-29-36: P3.

"Thorpe Love Letters." *NY Mirror.* 8-8-36: P7.

"Thorpe Names J. Barrymore." *NY Mirror.* 8-4-36: P1.

"Thorpe Now Admits Previous Marriage." *NY Times.* 8-7-36: P1, 7.

"Thorpe Outlines Child's Future." *LA Examiner.* 8-16-36: P1, 7.

"Thorpe Recommended Star To NY Doctor." *LA Examiner.* 8-12-36: P3.

"Thorpe Sees Child Today." *NY Mirror.* 8-17-36: P3.

"Thorpe Shook Child, Says Mary Astor." *LA Examiner.* 7-31-36: P1.

"Thorpe Spurns Own Price For Astor Secrets." *NY Mirror.* 8-8-36: P3.

"Thorpe Tells History Of Astor Romance Dr. Thorpe." *NY Evening Journal.* 8-13-36: P1.

"Thorpe Tells Of 'Scare' He Gave Kaufman." *NY American.* 8-6-36: P3.

"Thorpe Tells Philosophy For Child." *LA Evening Herald Express.* 8-15-36: P4.

"Thorpe Visits Child, Takes Her For Drive." *NY Evening Journal.* 8-17-36: P3.

Thorpe, Dr. "I'm Best Fitted To Guide My Child's Life." *LA Examiner*. 8-6-36: P3.

Thorpe, Franklyn. "Third Party Gave Me Love Diary." *LA Examiner*. 8-13-36: P1.

————. "I Married An Actress-Chapter I." *NY Daily News*. 8-14-36.

————. "I Married An Actress-Chapter II." *NY Daily News*. 8-15-36.

————. "I Married An Actress-Chapter III." *NY Daily News*. 8-16-36.

————. "I Married An Actress-Chapter IV." *NY Daily News*. 8-17-36.

————. "I Married An Actress-Chapter V." *NY Daily News*. 8-18-36.

————. "I Married An Actress-Chapter VI." *NY Daily News*. 8-19-36: P47.

"Thorpe's Love Letters To Dead Wife Quoted." *NY American*. 8-8-36: P3.

"Thorpe's Name Irks Writer." *LA Examiner*. 8-17-36: P3.

"Thorpe's Wedding Bared." *NY Evening Journal*. 8-6-36: P1.

"Threat Is Laid To Ex-Husband By Mary Astor." *NY Post*. 7-14-36: P1.

"Threats Fly In Astor Suit." *LA Examiner*. 8-6-36: P3.

"To Air Mary Astor's Life." *NY Sun*. 8-6-36.

"To Settle Astor Case." *NY Mirror*. 8-12-36: P1.

"Transcript Of Testimony On Smart Set Friendships." *LA Times*. 8-11-36: P5.

"Trial Revelations: Star Describes Thorpe Threats." *LA Examiner*. 8-4-36: P1.

"Truce Fails, Astor Fight On To Finish." *NY Mirror*. 8-10-36: P3.

"Two Husky Guards Patrol Mary's Home." *NY Daily News*. 8-16-36: P4.

Cummins, S. "Voice." *NY Daily News*. 8-6-36.

"Vote For Return Of Diary Grows." *LA Examiner*. 8-19-36: P6.

Walker, F. "Astor Case Settled," Extra. *NY Evening Journal*. 8-13-36: P1.

————. "Astor Suit Aims To Air After Dark Gayety." *NY Evening Journal*. 8-1-36: P4.

————. "Astor Trial Will Hear Barrymore." *NY Evening Journal*. 8-8-36: P3.

————. "Astor's Diary Gives Men Ratings." *NY Evening Journal*. 8-6-36: P8.

————. "Beauty's Diary Bares Affair With George." *NY Evening Journal*. 7-30-36: P1.

————. "Child Fears Dad, Says Mary Astor." *NY Evening Journal*. 7-31-36: P1.

————. "Diary Due As Astor Evidence." *NY Evening Journal*. 8-10-36: P1.

————. "Diary, Or Not To Diary? That Is Question." *NY Evening Journal*. 8-12-36: P3.

————. "Film Star Cynosure Of Eyes." *LA Evening Herald Express*. 8-10-36: P1.

————. "J. Barrymore Subpoenaed." *NY Evening Journal*. 8-3-36: P1.

————. "Kaufman Disappears To Dodge Warrant." *NY Evening Journal*. 8-11-36: P1.

————. "Mary Astor Plays Most Dramatic Role." *NY Evening Journal*. 8-11-36: P4.

————. "Mary Astor's No. 1." *NY Evening Journal*. 8-7-36: P4.

————. "Row Forces Renewal Of Battle." *NY Evening Journal*. 8-14-36: P1.

————. "Sharing Of Astor Child Like Solomon Edict." *NY Evening Journal*. 8-13-36: P3.

"Warrant Is Out For Kaufman In Astor Case." *NY Herald Tribune*. 8-11-36: P2.

"Warrant Out For Kaufman In Astor Case." *NY Sun*. 8-10-36: P1.

"Warrant Out For Kaufman." *NY Times*. 8-11-36: P1.

Watchman, The. "Mormon Leader Praises Warren." *LA Times*. 6-6-36.

Watson, T. "Mrs. Kaufman Vows Loyalty." *NY American*. 8-5-36: P1.

————. Wife Forgives Kaufman. *LA Examiner*. 8-5-36: P3.

"We Divide A Child." *LA Evening Herald Express*. 8-13-36: P1.

"We Lived A Lie For Our Child's Sake." *London Daily Express*. 8-14-36: P1.

Weinberger, Loon H. Letter To Ed: "Rights Of Authors." *NY Times*. 8-20-36: P22.

"Why Thorpe Wed Mary Astor." *NY Daily News*. 8-5-36: P1.

"Wife O.K.s George's Flirtation With Star." *LA Evening Herald Express*. 8-5-36: P1.

"Wife Of Astor's Friend Says What Harm." *London Daily Express*. 8-5-36: P1.

"Wild Ovation To Mary Astor." *NY Mirror*. 9-16-36.

"Will Hays Moves For Astor Truce." *LA Examiner*. 8-10-36: P3.

Williams, Lena. "Private Thoughts, Public Revelations." *NY Times*. 12-16-93. PC2.

Winchell, Walter. "Walter Winchell On Broadway." *NY Mirror*. 8-11-36.

Winchell, Walter. "Up And Down Broadway." *Reading Times*. 8-19-36: P6.

Winston, Archer. "Dodsworth Is Perfect." *NY Post*. 9-24-36.

"Witness Tells Girl's Visits To Thorpe." *LA Evening Herald Express*. 7-30-36: P2.

"Woman In Astor Case Denies Charges." *LA Evening Herald Express*. 7-28-36: P1.

"Writer Sought." *LA Evening Herald Express*. 8-10-36.

"Writer Vague On Real Life Love Story." *NY Evening Journal*. 8-10-36: P8.

"Young Suitor." *LA Examiner*. 8-10-36: P3.

INTERNET

Answers. "Norma Shearer." http://www.answers.com/topic/norma-taylor#ixzz2z59RHiKE

Classic Movie Club. "Mary Astor." http://www.classicmoviehub.com/bio/mary-astor/

Columbia University Libraries Oral History Research Office. "Notable New Yorkers (2006)." http://www.columbia.edu/cu/lweb/digital/collections/nny/ erfb/transcripts/cerfb_1_11_474.html

Famous Fix. "Mary Astor and Dr. Franklyn Thorpe Couple." http://www.famousfix.com/tag/mary-astor-and-dr-franklyn-thorpe/

Find A Grave. "Mendal D. Silberberg." http://www.findagrave.com/cgi-bin/fg.cgi?page=gr&GRid=91839985

Geni. "Hyrum Smith Woolley Autobiography." Last updated November 13, 2014. http://www.geni.com/people/Hyrum-Smith-Woolley/6000000001220246012

Gray, Meredith. "L.A. La Land, Fortune, And Forensics." Last modified on June 27, 2012. http://lalalandhistory.blogspot.com/2012_06_01_archive.html

Harlow, Jayden. "Strange Stories From The Hollywood Walk Of Fame." Entertainment Scene 360. Last updated April 10, 2009. http://www.entertainmentscene360.com/index.php/strange-stories-from-the-hollywood-walk-of-fame-31095/

Hubpages. "Hollywood Scandal Mary Astor Divorce." Last modified on June 25, 2012. http://scout901.hubpages.com/hub/Hollywood-Scandal-Mary-Astor-Divorce

IMDB. "George S. Kaufman." http://www.imdb.com/name/nm0442151/bio

IMDB. "John Eldredge." http://www.imdb.com/name/nm0253141/?ref_=nv_sr_1

IMDB. "Norma Taylor." http://www.imdb.com/name/nm0852970/?ref_=fn_al_nm_1

IMDB. "Paul Schofield." http://www.imdb.com/name/nm0774539/?ref_=fn_al_nm_2

Internet Broadway Database. "Mary Astor." http://www.ibdb.com/person.php?id=30290

LA Times. "Times Past. Mary Astor's Diary Ends Up In Court." August 12, 2006. http://articles.latimes.com/2006/aug/12/local/me-a2anniversary12

LA Times, the Daily Mirror: Los Angles History. "Movie Star Mystery Photo." January 17, 2009. http://latimesblogs.latimes.com/thedailymirror/2009/01/movie-star-my-2.html

Law Encyclopedia. "Mary Astor Divorce Trial: 1936 – 'he'd shake her so hard her teeth rattled' The Diary Written in Purple, Playwright Flees in a Laundry Basket." http://law.jrank.org/pages/2956/Mary-Astor-Divorce-Trial-1936.html

Law Encyclopedia. "Mary Astor Divorce Trial 1936 – Diary Written in Purple." http://law.jrank.org/pages/2954/.html (page discontinued)

Lexie. "Biggest scandals of Hollywood." Last updated on August 8, 2010. http://www.listal.com/list/hollywood-scandals

Neglected Books Editor. "Mary Astor, Author." Last updated on December 14, 2008. http://neglectedbooks.com/?p=241

NY Times: Movies And TV. http://www.nytimes.com/movies/person/164660/Paul-Schofield

Nitrate Diva, The. "The Greatest Film Performance That Never Was." Last updated on February 16, 2014. https://nitratediva.wordpress.com/tag/john-barrymore/

Oppenheimer, George. http://www.rnh.com/bio/69/Oppenheimer-George

Rodgers and Hammerstein. "George Oppenheimer." http://www.rnh.com/bio/69/Oppenheimer-George

Sinister Cinema. "I Demand Payment." http://www.sinistercinema.com/product.asp?specific=33498

Thornton, Michael. "Revealed For The First Time–The Other Woman In The Queen's Mother's Marriage." http://www.dailymail.co.uk/femail/article-1206431/Revealed-time--woman-Queen-Mothers-marriage.html.

Trivia Library. "Hollywood Celebrity Scandals Mary Astor's Diary Parts 1, 2, 3." http://www.trivia-library.com/b/hollywood-celebrity-scandals-mary-astor-diary-part-1.htm, part-2.htm, part-3.htm.

TV Week. "Sex! Thrilling Ecstasy! Stabbing! More Sex! Hollywood! Scandal! It's One of the Most Salacious Pieces We've Ever Written." http://www.tvweek.com/open-mic/2014/02/sex-thrilling-ecstasy-stabbing-more-sex-hollywood-scandal-its-one-of-the-most-salacious-piece-weve-e/

Waldorf Conference. "Mendal Siberberg." http://waldorfconference.com/silberberg.html

Yang, Andrew. "Purple Diaries." Last updated on August 7, 2009. http://yangabang.blogspot.com/2009/08/purple-diaries.html/

Youtube. "John Barrymore Screen Test For Hamlet (1933)." Uploaded on February 27, 2010. https://www.youtube.com/watch?v=x2jWx4IqgEM